Spanish

phrasebooks
and
Marta López

Spanish audio phrasebook
1st edition – September 2009

Published by
Lonely Planet Publications Pty Ltd ABN 36 005 607 983
90 Maribyrnong St, Footscray, Victoria 3011, Australia

Lonely Planet Offices
Australia Locked Bag 1, Footscray, Victoria 3011
USA 150 Linden St, Oakland CA 94607
UK 2nd floor, 186 City Rd, London, EC1V 2NT

Cover illustration
Life in Park Güell by Yukiyoshi Kamimura

ISBN 9781741799309

10 9 8 7 6 5 4 3 2

Printed through SNP Leefung Printers Limited
Printed in China

acknowledgments

Lonely Planet Language Products and editor Meg Worby would like to thank this cast of thousands for living *la vida loca* …

Publishing manager Jim 'Gaudí' Jenkin, whose great vision saw the series develop from the ground up

Project manager Fabrice 'Don Qixote' Rocher

Series designer Yukiyoshi 'Ibiza' Kamimura

Commissioning editors Karin 'Macarena' Vidstrup Monk and Karina 'Las Ketchup' Coates and acting senior editor Emma 'Carmen' Koch

New managing editor Annelies 'Flamenco' Mertens who offered grammar and general Spanish expertise and editor Ben 'Rumba' Handicott for leading the way

Editor Piers 'Matador' Kelly for a gallant effort in sourcing regional languages and cultural information and editor Francesca 'Spanish Fly' Coles for assistance with the index

Layout designer Sally 'Arriba!' Morgan for super speedy layout

Layout designers Sonya 'Carnaval' Brooke and Katie 'Catalan' Cason for putting in the finishing touches

Freelance designer Patrick '*Jamón Jamón*' Marris for the ace illustrations throughout

Special projects managing cartographer Paul Piaia and map editor Wayne Murphy

Design manager Nina 'Tapas' Sturgess for coordinating layout checks

Freelance proofer Adrienne 'Castanets' Costanzo

Peter and Marta Gibney for careful proofing of the Spanish

Special thanks to contracted author Marta López, who also produced the Sustainable Travel section for this new edition. Marta thanks Graciela Recogzy, David García Campelo and Andrew Tsirigotis.

make the most of this phrasebook ...

Anyone can speak another language! It's all about confidence. Don't worry if you can't remember your school language lessons or if you've never learnt a language before. Even if you learn the very basics (on the inside covers of this book), your travel experience will be the better for it. You have nothing to lose and everything to gain when the locals hear you making an effort. Spanish, as well as Latin American, is spoken in over many countries in Latin America. Spanish is also very widely spoken in parts of the Pacific (ie the Philippines), and Africa (ie Morocco).

finding things in this book

For easy navigation, this book is in sections. The Tools chapters are the ones you'll thumb through time and again. The Practical section covers basic travel situations like catching transport and finding a bed. The Social section gives you conversational phrases, pick-up lines, the ability to express opinions – so you can get to know people. Food has a section all of its own: gourmets and vegetarians are covered and local dishes feature. Safe Travel equips you with health and police phrases, just in case. Remember the colours of each section and you'll find everything easily; or use the comprehensive Index. Otherwise, check the two-way traveller's Dictionary for the word you need.

being understood

Throughout this book you'll see coloured phrases on the right hand side of each page. They're phonetic guides to help you pronounce the language. You don't even need to look at the language itself, but you'll get used to the way we've represented particular sounds. The pronunciation chapter in Tools will explain more, but you can feel confident that if you read the coloured phrase slowly, you'll be understood.

using the audio

You'll notice the numbered tags (eg 32A) beside a selection of phrases in this book. The number refers to the audio track, the letter indicates the order it will be read in the audio track – so 'a' is first, 'b' is second etc. Use the audio to help master your own pronunciation, or use it on the road by transferring the MP3 files to your portable media player and letting it do some of the talking for you..

CONTENTS

5

spanish

United States of America

Mexico

Cuba

Dominican Republic
Puerto Rico

Guatemala
El Salvador
Honduras
Nicaragua
Costa Rica
Panama
Ecuador
Colombia
Venezuela

Peru

Bolivia

Paraguay

Uruguay

Chile
Argentina

■■■ national language
■■■ widely understood
■■■ regional language

For more details, see the **introduction**.

See Enlargement
Spain

Equatorial
Guinea

France

Basque

Galician

Andorra

Madrid
SPAIN

Catalan

Alguer ○
Sardinia
(Italy)

INTRODUCTION
introducción

Spanish, or Castilian, as it's also called in Spain, is the most widely spoken of the Romance languages, the group of languages derived from Latin which includes French, Italian and Portuguese. Outside Spain, it's the language of most of Latin America and the West Indies and is also spoken in the Philippines and Guam, as well as in some areas of the African coast and in the US. Worldwide, there are more than 30 countries or territories where Spanish is spoken.

Spanish is derived from Vulgar Latin, which Roman soldiers and merchants brought to the Iberian Peninsula during the period of the Roman conquest (3rd to 1st century BC). By 19 BC Spain had become totally Romanised and Latin became the language of the peninsula in the four centuries that followed. Today's Castilian is spoken in the north, centre and south of Spain.

People are intensely proud of their language and generally expect visitors to know at least a little. English is less widely spoken in Spain than in many other European countries, especially outside the major cities.

This book gives you the practical words and phrases you need to get by, and the fun, spontaneous phrases that lead to a better experience of Spain and its people. Need more encouragement?

at a glance ...

language name: Spanish

name in language:
Español es·pa·*nyol*

language family: Romance

key country: Spain

approximate number of speakers:
over 390 million worldwide

close relatives: Latin American Spanish, Portuguese, Italian

donations to english: alligator, bonanza (lit: fair weather), canyon, guerilla, rodeo, ranch, stampede, tornado and many more familiar words ...

Remember, the contact you make through using Spanish will make your travels unique. Local knowledge, new relationships and a sense of satisfaction are on the tip of your tongue, so don't just stand there, say something!

> basque, catalan & galician

We also give you the basics of these languages because they are each considered official in Spain, even though Spanish, or Castilian, covers by far the largest territory.

Basque, a non-latin language, is spoken in parts of the north. Catalan is spoken in the east and Galician in the north-west. These last two are also Romance languages, so are closer in origin to Spanish.

If you're travelling widely in Spain, see the special section on these regional languages for some basic expressions, page 100.

> abbreviations used in this book

f	feminine
inf	informal
m	masculine
sg	singular
pl	plural
pol	polite

- Spanish pronunciation isn't hard, as many sounds are similar to sounds used in English.
- There are some easy rules to follow and once you learn them it's likely you'll be understood.
- The relationship between Spanish sounds and their spelling is straightforward and consistent.
- Like most languages, pronunciation can vary according to region. This book focuses on Castilian Spanish.

word stress

énfasis

- There is stress in Spanish, which means you emphasise one syllable over another. Rule of thumb: when a written word ends in *n*, *s* or a vowel, the stress falls on the second-last syllable. Otherwise, the final syllable is stressed.
- If you see an accent mark over a syllable, it cancels out these rules and you just stress that syllable instead.

vowel sounds

vocales

symbol	english equivalent	spanish example
a	alms	*agua*
e	red	*número*
ee	bee	*día*
o	go	*ojo*
oo	book	*gusto*
ai	aisle	*bailar*
ow	cow	*autobús*
oy	boy	*hoy*

pronunciation

consonant sounds

symbol	english equivalent	spanish example
b	big	*b*arco
ch	chilli	*ch*ica
d	din	*d*inero
f	fun	*f*iesta
g	go	*g*ato
k	kick	*c*abeza/*qu*eso
kh	loch	*j*ardín/*g*ente
l	loud	*l*ago
ly	million	*ll*amada
m	man	*m*añana
n	no	*n*uevo
ny	canyon	se*ñ*ora
p	pig	*p*adre
r	run, but stronger and rolled	*r*itmo/bu*rr*o
s	so	*s*emana
t	tin	*t*ienda
th	thin	Bar*c*elona/man*z*ana
v	soft 'b', somewhere between 'v' and 'b'	a*b*rir
w	win	g*u*ardia
y	yes	*v*iaje

There are some key things to remember about consonants in Spanish writing:

- the letter *c* is pronounced with a lisp, bar·the·*lo*·na (Barcelona), except when it comes before *a*, *o* and *u* or a consonant, when it's hard like *k* in 'king'.
- when ending a word, the letter *d* is also soft, like a th, or it's so slight it doesn't get pronounced at all.
- the Spanish letter *j* stands for a harsh and gutteral sound, so we use a kh symbol in our phonetic guides.
- try to roll your double *r*'s.
- the letter *q* is pronounced hard like a k.
- the letter *v* sounds more like a b, said with the lips pressed together.
- there are a few letters which don't appear in the English alphabet: *ch*, *ll* and *ñ*. You'll see these have their own entries in the spanish–english dictionary.

spanish alphabet

a	A	a	b	B	be	c	C	the
ch	CH	che	d	D	de	e	E	e
f	F	e·fe	g	G	khe	h	H	a·che
i	I	ee	j	J	kho·ta	k	K	ka
l	L	e·le	ll	LL	e·lye	m	M	e·me
n	N	e·ne	ñ	Ñ	e·nye	o	O	o
p	P	pe	q	Q	koo	r	R	e·re
s	S	e·se	t	T	te	u	U	oo
v	V	oo·ve	w	W	oo·ve do·vle	x	X	e·kees
y	Y	ee·grye·ga	z	Z	the·ta			

false friends

Beware of false friends – those words that sound like familiar English, but could land you in a bit of trouble if you use them unwittingly in Spanish. Here are some mistakes it's a little too easy to make:

el suburbio   el soo·*boor*·byo   **slum district**
   not 'suburb' which is *el barrio*, el *ba*·ryo

Estoy   es·*toy*   **I have a cold.**
constipado/a. m/f   kons·tee·*pa*·do/a
   not 'I'm constipated' which is *estoy estreñido/a* m/f
   es·*toy* es·tre·*nyee*·do/a

Estoy   es·*toy*   **I'm pregnant.**
embarazada.   em·ba·ra·*tha*·da
   not 'I'm embarassed' which is *estoy avergonzado/a* m/f
   es·*toy* a·ver·gon·*tha*·do/a

la injuria   la een·*khoo*·ree·a   **insult**
   not 'injury' which is *la herida*, la e·*ree*·da

largo/a m/f   *lar*·go/a   **long**
   not 'large' which is *grande*, *gran*·de

los parientes   los pa·ree·*yen*·tes   **relatives**
   not 'parents' which is *los padres*, los *pa*·dres

sensible   sen·*thee*·ble   **sensitive**
   not 'sensible' which is *prudente*, proo·*den*·te

This chapter is designed to help you make your own sentences. It's arranged alphabetically for ease of navigation. If you can't find the exact phrase you need in this book, remember, there are no rules, only particular ways to say things! A little grammar, a few gestures, a couple of well-chosen words and you'll generally get the message across.

a/an & some

I'd like a ticket and a postcard.

Quisiera un billete y   kee·*sye*·ra oon bee·*lye*·te ee
una postal.   *oo*·na pos·*tal*
(lit: I-would-like a ticket
and a postcard)

Spanish has two words for 'a/an': *un* and *una*. The gender of the noun determines which one you use. *Un* and *una* have plural forms, *unos* and *unas*, meaning 'some'.

masculine	*un* sg	*un huevo* oon *hwe*·vo	an egg
	unos pl	*unos huevos* oo·nos *hwe*·vos	some eggs
feminine	*una* sg	*una casa* oo·na *ka*·sa	a house
	unas pl	*unas casas* oo·nas *ka*·sas	some houses

adjectives see describing things

articles see a/an & some and the

be

Spanish has two words for the English verb 'be': *ser* and *estar*.

use SER to express	examples	
permanent characteristics of persons/things	*Liz es muy guapa.* leez es mooy gwa·pa	Liz is very beautiful.
occupations or nationality	*Ana es de España.* a·na es de e·spa·nya	Ana is from Spain.
the time and location of events	*Son las tres.* son las tres	It's 3 o'clock.
possession	*De quién es esta mochila?* de kyen es es·ta mo·chee·la	Whose backpack is this?
use ESTAR to express	examples	
temporary characteristics of persons/things	*La comida está fría.* la ko·mee·da es·ta free·ya	The food is cold.
the time & location of persons/things	*Estamos en Madrid.* es·ta·mos en ma·dree	We are in Madrid.
the mood of a person	*Estoy contento.* es·toy kon·ten·to	I'm happy.

I	am	an anarchist	yo	soy	anarquisto
you sg inf	are	from Spain	tú	eres	de España
you sg pol	are	an artist	Usted	es	artista
he/she	is	an artist	él/ella m/f	es	artista
we	are	single	nosotros/as m/f	somos	solteros/as
you pl inf	are	kind	vosotros/as m/f	sois	simpáticos/as
you pl pol	are	students	Ustedes	son	estudiantes
they	are	students	ellos/as m/f	son	estudiantes

I	am	well	yo	estoy	bien
you sg inf	are	angry	tú	estás	enojado
you sg pol	are	drunk	Usted	está	borracho
he/she	is	drunk	él/ella m/f	está	borracho
we	are	happy	nosotros/as m/f	estamos	felices
you pl inf	are	on holiday	vosotros/as m/f	estáis	de vacaciones
you pl pol	are	learning	Ustedes	están	estudiando
they	are	learning	ellos/as m/f	están	estudiando

describing things

I'm looking for a comfortable hotel.

Estoy buscando un
hotel cómodo.
(lit: I-am looking-for a
hotel comfortable)

es·toy boos·kan·do oon
o·tel ko·mo·do

When using an adjective to describe a noun, you need to use a
different ending depending on whether the noun is masculine or
feminine, and singular or plural. Most adjectives have four forms
which are easy to remember:

	singular	plural
masculine	fantástico	fantásticos
feminine	fantástica	fantásticas

un hotel fantástico	oon o·tel fan·tas·tee·ko	a fantastic hotel
una comida fantástica	oo·na ko·mee·da fan·tas·tee·ka	a fantastic meal
unos libros fantásticos	oo·nos lee·bros fan·tas·tee·kos	some fantastic books
unas tapas fantásticas	oo·nas ta·pas fan·tas·tee·kas	some fantastic tapas

Adjectives generally come after the noun in Spanish. However, 'adjectives' of quantity (such as 'much', 'a lot', 'little/few', 'too much') and adjectives expressing possession ('my' and 'your') always precede the noun.

muchos turistas	moo·chos too·rees·tas	many tourists
primera clase	pree·me·ra kla·se	first class
mi coche	mee ko·che	my car

gender

In Spanish, all nouns – words which denote a thing, person or idea – are either masculine or feminine.

The dictionary will tell you what gender a noun is, but here are some handy tips to help you determine gender:
- gender is masculine when talking about a man and feminine when talking about a woman
- words ending in -o are often masculine
- words ending in -a are often feminine
- words ending in -d, -z or -ión are usually feminine

See also **a/an & some**, **describing things**, **possession** and **the**.

TOOLS

have

I have two brothers.
Tengo dos hermanos.   ten·go dos er·ma·nos
(lit: I-have two brothers)

Possession can be indicated in various ways in Spanish. The easiest way is by using the verb *tener*, 'have'.

I	have	a ticket	yo	tengo	un billete
you sg inf	have	the key	tú	tienes	la llave
you sg pol	have	the key	Usted	tiene	la llave
he/she	has	aspirin	él/ella m/f	tiene	aspirinas
we	have	matches	nosotros/as m/f	tenemos	cerillas
you pl inf	have	tapas	vosotros/as m/f	tenéis	tapas
you pl pol	have	tapas	Ustedes	tienen	tapas
they	have	problems	ellos/as m/f	tienen	problemas

See also **my & your** and **somebody's**.

is & are see be

location see this & that

more than one

I'd like two tickets.
Quisiera dos billetes.   kee·sye·ra dos bee·lye·tes
(lit: I-would-like two tickets)

In general, if the word ends in a vowel, you add -s for a plural. If the noun ends in a consonant (or y), you add -es:

| bed | cama | ka·ma | beds | camas | ka·mas |
| woman | mujer | moo·kher | women | mujeres | moo·khe·res |

my & your

This is my daughter.
   Ésta es mi hija.
   (lit: this is my daughter)

es·ta es mee ee·kha

A common way of indicating possession is by using possessive adjectives before the noun they describe. As with any other adjective, they always agree with the noun in number (singular or plural) and gender (masculine or feminine).

	singular		plural	
	masculine	feminine	masculine	feminine
	gift	room	friends	glasses
my	mi regalo	mi habitación	mis amigos	mis gafas
your sg inf	tu regalo	tu habitación	tus amigos	tus gafas
your sg pol	su regalo	su habitación	sus amigos	sus gafas
his/her/its	su regalo	su habitación	sus amigos	sus gafas
our	nuestro regalo	nuestra habitación	nuestros amigos	nuestras gafas
your pl inf	vuestro regalo	vuestra habitación	vuestros amigos	vuestras gafas
your pl pol	su regalo	su habitación	sus amigos	sus gafas
their	su regalo	su habitación	sus amigos	sus gafas

See also **have** & **somebody's**.

negative

Just add the word *no* before the main verb of the sentence:

I'm not going to try the speciality.
No voy a probar   no voy a pro·*bar*
la especialidad.   la es·peth·ya·lee·*da*
(lit: not I-go to try
   the speciality)

planning ahead

As in English, you can talk about your plans or future events by using the verb *ir* (go) followed by the word *a* (to) and the infinitive of another verb, for example:

Tomorrow, I'm going to travel to Madrid.
Mañana, yo voy a viajar   ma·*nya*·na yo voy a vya·*jar*
a Madrid.   a ma·*dree*
(lit: tomorrow I go to travel
   to Madrid)

I	am going	to call	yo	voy	a llamar
you sg inf	are going	to sleep	tú	vas	a dormir
you sg pol	are going	to dance	Usted	va	a bailar
he/she	is going	to drink	él/ella m/f	va	a beber
we	are going	to sing	nosotros/as m/f	vamos	a cantar
you pl inf	are going	to eat	vosotros/as m/f	vais	a comer
you pl pol	are going	to write	Ustedes	van	a escribir
they	are going	to learn	ellos/as m/f	van	a aprender

plural see more than one

pointing something out

To point something out, the easiest phrases to use are *es* (it is), *esto es* (this is) or *eso es* (that is).

Es una guía de Sevilla.	es oo·na gee·a de se·vee·lya	It's a guide to Seville.
Esto es mi pasaporte.	es·to es mee pa·sa·por·te	This is my passport.
Eso es gazpacho.	e·so es gath·pa·cho	That is gazpacho.

See also **this & that**.

possession see **have**, **my & your** and **somebody's**

questions

Is this the right stop?

> *Es esta la parada?*   es es·ta la pa·ra·da
> (lit: is this the stop)

When asking a question, simply make a statement, but raise your intonation towards the end of the sentence, as you can do in English. The inverted question mark in written Spanish prompts you to do this.

question words		
Who?	*¿Quién?* sg *¿Quiénes?* pl	kyen kye·nes
Who is it?	*¿Quién es?*	kyen es
Who are those men?	*¿Quiénes son estos hombres?*	kye·nes son es·tos om·bres
What?	*¿Qué?*	ke
What are you saying?	*¿Qué está Usted diciendo?* pol	ke es·ta oo·ste dee·thyen·do

Which?	¿Cuál? sg ¿Cuáles? pl	kwal kwa·les
Which restaurant is the cheapest?	¿Cuál restaurante es el más barato?	kwal res·tow·ran·te es el mas ba·ra·to
Which local dishes do you recommend?	¿Cuáles platos típicos puedes recomendar?	kwa·les pla·tos tee·pee·kos pwe·des re·ko·men·dar
When?	¿Cuándo?	kwan·do
When does the next bus arrive?	¿Cuándo llega el próximo autobús?	kwan·do lye·ga el prok·see·mo ow·to·boos
Where?	¿Dónde?	don·de
Where can I buy tickets?	¿Dónde puedo comprar billetes?	don·de pwe·do kom·prar bee·lye·tes
How?	¿Cómo?	ko·mo
How do you say this in Spanish?	¿Cómo se dice ésto en español?	ko·mo se dee·the es·to en es·pa·nyol
How much?	¿Cuánto?	kwan·to
How much is it?	¿Cuánto cuesta?	kwan·to kwes·ta
How many?	¿Cuantos?	kwan·tos
For how many nights?	¿Por cuántas noches?	por kwan·tas no·ches
Why?	¿Por qué?	por ke
Why is the museum closed?	¿Por qué está cerrado el museo?	por ke es·ta the·ra·do el moo·se·o

some see a/an & some

somebody's

In Spanish, ownership is expressed through the word *de* (of).

That's my friend's backpack.

Esa es la mochila de   e·sa es la mo·*chee*·la de
mi amigo.   mee a·*mee*·go
(lit: that is the backpack of
my friend)

See also **have** and **my & your**.

this & that

There are three 'distance words' in Spanish, depending on whether something is close (this), away from you (that) or even further away in time or distance (that over there).

masculine	singular	plural
close	*éste* (this)	*éstos* (these)
away	*ése* (that)	*ésos* (those)
further away	*aquél* (that over there)	*aquéllos* (those over there)
feminine		
close	*ésta* (this)	*éstas* (these)
away	*ésa* (that)	*ésas* (those)
further away	*aquélla* (that over there)	*aquéllas* (those over there)

See also **pointing something out**.

the

The Spanish articles *el* and *la* both mean 'the'. Whether you use *el* or *la* depends on the gender of the thing, person or idea talked about, which in Spanish will always be either masculine or feminine. The gender is not really concerned with the sex of something, for example a fox is a masculine noun, even if it's female! There's no rule as to why, say, the sea is masculine but the beach is feminine.

When talking about plural things, people or ideas, you use *los* in stead of *el* and *las* instead of *la*.

	singular	plural
masculine	*el*	*los*
feminine	*la*	*las*

el coche	el *ko*·che	the car
los coches	los *ko*·ches	the cars
la tienda	la *tyen*·da	the shop
las tiendas	las *tyen*·das	the shops

See also **gender** and **a/an** & **some**.

word order

Sentences in Spanish have a basic word order of subject-verb-object, just as English does.

I study business.

Yo estudio comercio.   yo es·*too*·dyo ko·*mer*·thyo
(lit: I study business)

However, Spanish often omits a subject pronoun: *'Estudio comercio'* is enough.

yes/no questions

It's not impolite to answer questions with a simple *sí* (yes) or *no* (no) in Spanish. There's no way to say 'Yes it is/does', or 'No, it isn't/doesn't'.

See also **questions**.

you

When talking to people familiar to you or younger than you, it's usual to use the informal form of you, *tú*, too, rather than the polite form, *Usted*, oo·ste. The plural versions are we, *vosotros/vosotras*, vo·so·*tros*/vo·so·*tras* and (all of) you, *Ustedes*, oo·ste·des. Phrases in this book use the form of 'you' that is appropriate to the situation.

For more on polite language, see the box in **business**, page 77.

m (masculine) or f (feminine)?

In this book, masculine forms appear before the feminine forms. If you see a word ending in -*o/a*, it means the masculine form ends in -*o*, and the feminine form ends in -*a*, (that is, you replace the -*o* ending with the -*a* ending to make it feminine). The same goes for the endings -*os/as* (the plural endings). If you see an *(a)* between brackets on the end of a word, it means you have to add it in order to make that word feminine. In other cases we spell out the whole word.

There are two words for 'Spanish': *español* and *castellano*. *Español* is used in Spain, whereas *castellano* is more likely to be used by South Americans.

I speak a little Spanish.
Hablo un poco de español. ab·lo oon po·ko de es·pa·nyol

1A Do you speak English?
¿Habla inglés? ab·la een·gles

Does anyone speak English?
¿Hay alguien que hable inglés? ai al·gyen ke ab·le een·gles

1B Do you understand?
¿Me entiende? me en·tyen·de

1C I understand.
Entiendo. en·tyen·do

1C I don't understand.
No entiendo. no en·tyen·do

How do you pronounce this word?
¿Cómo se pronuncia ko·mo se pro·noon·thya
esta palabra? es·ta pa·lab·ra

How do you write '*ciudad*'?
¿Cómo se escribe ko·mo se es·kree·be
'ciudad'? thee·oo·da

What does ... mean?
¿Qué significa ...? ke seeg·nee·fee·ka ...

1D Could you repeat that?
¿Puede repetir? pwe·de re·pe·teer

listen for ...		
ko·mo	*¿Cómo?*	**Pardon?**
no	*No.*	**No.**
see	*Sí.*	**Yes.**

1E Could you please speak more slowly?

¿Puede hablar más despacio, por favor?

pwe·de ab·lar mas des·pa·thyo por fa·vor

1F Could you please write it down?

¿Puede escribirlo, por favor?

pwe·de es·kree·beer·lo por fa·vor

dirty latin

Over the last 500 years, the Spanish spoken in Latin America has developed differently to the Spanish spoken in Europe. Variations in pronunciation, vocabulary and even grammar can lead to confusion or embarrassment. Here are two examples that could get you into trouble.

Quiero coger el autobús.
I want to catch the bus.
(Latin America: I want to bonk the bus.)

Hay un gran bicho en el baño.
There's a huge bug in the bathroom.
(Latin America: There's a big prick in the bathroom.)

cardinal numbers

los números cardinales

	0	*cero*	*the*·ro
3A	1	*uno*	*oo*·no
3A	2	*dos*	dos
3A	3	*tres*	tres
3A	4	*cuatro*	*kwa*·tro
3A	5	*cinco*	*theen*·ko
3A	6	*seis*	seys
3A	7	*siete*	*sye*·te
3A	8	*ocho*	*o*·cho
3A	9	*nueve*	*nwe*·ve
3A	10	*diez*	dyeth
	11	*once*	*on*·the
	12	*doce*	*do*·the
	13	*trece*	*tre*·the
	14	*catorce*	ka·*tor*·the
	15	*quince*	*keen*·the
	16	*dieciséis*	dye·thee·*seys*
	17	*diecisiete*	dye·thee·*sye*·te
	18	*dieciocho*	dye·thee·*o*·cho
	19	*diecinueve*	dye·thee·*nwe*·ve
3B	20	*veinte*	*veyn*·te
	21	*veintiuno*	veyn·tee·*oo*·no
	22	*veintidós*	veyn·tee·*dos*
3B	30	*treinta*	*treyn*·ta
3B	40	*cuarenta*	kwa·*ren*·ta
3B	50	*cincuenta*	theen·*kwen*·ta
3B	60	*sesenta*	se·*sen*·ta
3B	70	*setenta*	se·*ten*·ta
3B	80	*ochenta*	o·*chen*·ta
3B	90	*noventa*	no·*ven*·ta
3B	100	*cien*	thyen

101	*ciento uno*	*thyen·to oo·no*
102	*ciento dos*	*thyen·to dos*
500	*quinientos*	*kee·nyen·tos*
3C 1,000	*mil*	mil
3D 1,000,000	*un millón*	oon mee·*lyon*

ordinal numbers

los números ordinales

1st	*primero/a* m/f	pree·*me*·ro/a
2nd	*segundo/a* m/f	se·*goon*·do/a
3rd	*tercero/a* m/f	ter·*the*·ro/a
4th	*cuarto/a* m/f	*kwar*·to/a
5th	*quinto/a* m/f	*keen*·to/a

fractions

las fracciones

a quarter	*un cuarto*	oon *kwar*·to
a third	*un tercio*	oon *ter*·thyo
a half	*un medio*	oon *me*·dyo
three-quarters	*tres cuartos*	tres *kwar*·tos
all	*todo*	*to*·do
none	*nada*	*na*·da

amounts

las cantidades

a little	*un poquito*	oon po·*kee*·to
many	*muchos/as* m/f	*moo*·chos/as
some	*algunos/as* m/f	al·*goo*·nos/as
more	*más*	mas
less	*menos*	*me*·nos

telling the time

dando la hora

4A What time is it?	*¿Qué hora es?*	ke o·ra es
4B It's (one) o'clock.	*Es (la una).*	es (la oo·na)
It's (ten) o'clock.	*Son (las diez).*	son (las dyeth)
Quarter past one.	*Es la una y cuarto.*	es la oo·na ee kwar·to
Twenty past one.	*Es la una y veinte.*	es la oo·na ee veyn·te
Half past one.	*Es la una y media.*	es la oo·na ee me·dya
Twenty to one.	*Es la una menos veinte.*	es la oo·na me·nos veyn·te
Quarter to one.	*Es la una menos cuarto.*	es la oo·na me·nos kwar·to
It's early.	*Es temprano.*	es tem·pra·no
It's late.	*Es tarde.*	es tar·de
am	*de la mañana*	de la ma·nya·na
pm	*de la tarde*	de la tar·de

days of the week

los días de la semana

5A Monday	*lunes*	loo·nes
5A Tuesday	*martes*	mar·tes
5A Wednesday	*miércoles*	myer·ko·les
5A Thursday	*jueves*	khwe·ves
5A Friday	*viernes*	vyer·nes
5A Saturday	*sábado*	sa·ba·do
5A Sunday	*domingo*	do·meen·go

the calendar

el calendario

> months

5B	January	enero	e·ne·ro
5B	February	febrero	fe·bre·ro
5B	March	marzo	mar·tho
5B	April	abril	a·breel
5B	May	mayo	ma·yo
5B	June	junio	khoo·nyo
5B	July	julio	khoo·lyo
5B	August	agosto	a·gos·to
5B	September	septiembre	sep·tyem·bre
5B	October	octubre	ok·too·bre
5B	November	noviembre	no·vyem·bre
5B	December	diciembre	dee·thyem·bre

> seasons

5C	summer	verano	ve·ra·no
5C	autumn	otoño	o·to·nyo
5C	winter	invierno	een·vyer·no
5C	spring	primavera	pree·ma·ve·ra

dates

las fechas

What date?
¿Qué día? ke dee·a

6A What date is it today?
¿Qué día es hoy? ke dee·a es oy

It's (18 October).
Es (el dieciocho de octubre). es (el dye·thee·o·cho de ok·too·bre)

present

now	ahora	a·o·ra
right now	ahora mismo	a·o·ra mees·mo
this ...		
afternoon	esta tarde	es·ta tar·de
month	este mes	es·te mes
morning	esta mañana	es·ta ma·nya·na
week	esta semana	es·ta se·ma·na
year	este año	es·te a·nyo
6C today	hoy	oy
tonight	esta noche	es·ta no·che

past

el pasado

... ago	hace ...	a·the ...
(three) days	(tres) días	(tres) dee·as
half an hour	media hora	me·dya o·ra
a while	un rato	un ra·to
(five) years	(cinco) años	(theen·ko) a·nyos
day before yesterday	anteayer	an·te·a·yer
last night	anoche	a·no·che
7A last month	el mes pasado	el mes pa·sa·do
7B last week	la semana pasada	la se·ma·na pa·sa·da
7C last year	el año pasado	el a·nyo pa·sa·do
since (May)	desde (mayo)	des·de (ma·yo)
6B yesterday	ayer	a·yer
yesterday ...	ayer por la ...	a·yer por la ...
afternoon	tarde	tar·de
evening	noche	no·che
morning	mañana	ma·nya·na

future

in ...	dentro de ...	den·tro de ...
(six) days	(seis) días	(seys) dee·as
an hour	una hora	oo·na o·ra
(five) minutes	(cinco) minutos	(theen·ko) mee·noo·tos
a month	un mes	oon mes

8A next month	el mes que viene	el mes ke vye·ne
8B next week	la semana que viene	la se·ma·na ke vye·ne
8C next year	el año que viene	el a·nyo ke vye·ne

6D tomorrow	mañana	ma·nya·na
day after tomorrow	pasado mañana	pa·sa·do ma·nya·na

tomorrow ...	mañana por la ...	ma·nya·na por la ...
afternoon	tarde	tar·de
evening	noche	no·che
morning	mañana	ma·nya·na

until (June)	hasta (junio)	as·ta (khoo·nyo)

during the day

4D afternoon	tarde f	tar·de
dawn	madrugada f	ma·droo·ga·da
day	día m	dee·a
4E evening	noche f	no·che
midday	mediodía m	me·dyo·dee·a
midnight	medianoche f	me·dya·no·che
4C morning	mañana f	ma·nya·na
night	noche f	no·che
sunrise	amanecer m	a·ma·ne·ther
sunset	puesta f del sol	pwes·ta del sol

42B Where's an ATM?
¿Dónde hay un cajero automático?
don·de ai oon ka·khe·ro ow·to·ma·tee·ko

Can I use my credit card to withdraw money?
¿Puedo usar mi tarjeta de crédito para sacar dinero?
pwe·do oo·sar mee tar·khe·ta de kre·dee·to pa·ra sa·kar dee·ne·ro

What's the exchange rate?
¿Cuál es el tipo de cambio?
kwal es el tee·po de kam·byo

What's the charge for that?
¿Cuánto hay que pagar por eso?
kwan·to ai ke pa·gar por e·so

How much is this?
¿Cuánto cuesta esto?
kwan·to kwes·ta es·to

The price is too high.
Cuesta demasiado.
kwes·ta de·ma·sya·do

Can you lower the price?
¿Podría bajar un poco el precio?
po·dree·a ba·khar oon po·ko el pre·thyo

I'd like to change ...	*Me gustaría cambiar ...*	me goos·ta·ree·a kam·byar ...
money	*dinero*	dee·ne·ro
a travellers cheque	*un cheque de viajero*	oon che·ke de vya·khe·ro

Do you accept ...?	¿Aceptan ...?	a·*thep*·tan ...
credit cards	tarjetas de crédito	tar·*khe*·tas de kre·dee·to
debit cards	tarjetas de débito	tar·*khe*·tas de de·bee·to
travellers cheques	cheques de viajero	*che*·kes de vya·*khe*·ro

Do I need to pay up front?

¿Necesito pagar por adelantado?

ne·the·*see*·to pa·*gar* por a·de·lan·*ta*·do

Could I have a receipt please?

¿Podría darme un recibo por favor?

po·*dree*·a *dar*·me oon re·*thee*·bo por fa·*vor*

I'd like my money back.

Quisiera que me devuelva el dinero.

kee·*sye*·ra ke me de·*vwel*·va el dee·*ne*·ro

getting around

desplazándose

What time does the ... leave?	¿A qué hora sale el ...?	a ke o·ra sa·le el ...
boat	barco	bar·ko
bus	autobús	ow·to·boos
plane	avión	a·vyon
train	tren	tren
tram	tranvía	tran·vee·a

12A What time's the first (bus)?
¿A qué hora es el primer (autobús)?
a ke o·ra es el pree·mer (ow·to·boos)

12B What time's the last (bus)?
¿A qué hora es el último (autobús)?
a ke o·ra es el ool·tee·mo (ow·to·boos)

12C What time's the next (bus)?
¿A qué hora es el próximo (autobús)?
a ke o·ra es el prok·see·mo (ow·to·boos)

I'd like a/an ... seat.	Quisiera un asiento ...	kee·sye·ra oon a·syen·to ...
aisle	de pasillo	de pa·see·lyo
(non)smoking	de (no) fumadores	de (no) foo·ma·do·res
window	junto a la ventana	khoon·to a la ven·ta·na

asking for an address

What's the/your address?
¿Cuál es la/su dirección? kwal es la/soo dee·rek·thyon

avenue	avenida f	a·ve·nee·da
lane	callejón m	ka·lye·khon
street	calle f	ka·lye

Is there (a) ...?	¿Hay ...?	ai ...
air-conditioning	aire acondicionado	ai·re a·kon·dee·thyo·na·do
blanket	una manta	oo·na man·ta
toilet	servicios	ser·vee·thyos
video	vídeo	vee·de·o

The ... is delayed/cancelled.
El ... está retrasado/ cancelado.
el ... es·ta re·tra·sa·do/ kan·the·la·do

14A Is this seat free?
¿Está libre este asiento?
es·ta lee·bre es·te a·syen·to

14B That's my seat.
Ése es mi asiento.
e·se es mee a·syen·to

Can you tell me when we get to ...?
¿Me podría decir cuándo lleguemos a ...?
me po·dree·a de·theer kwan·do lye·ge·mos a ...

I want to get off here!
¡Quiero bajarme aquí!
kye·ro ba·khar·me a·kee

buying tickets

comprando billetes

11A Where can I buy a ticket?
¿Dónde puedo comprar un billete?
don·de pwe·do kom·prar oon bee·lye·te

How much is it?
¿Cuánto cuesta?
kwan·to kwes·ta

11B Do I need to book a seat?
¿Tengo que reservar?
ten·go ke re·ser·var

It's full.
Está completo.   es·*ta* kom·*ple*·to

13A How long does the trip take?
¿Cuánto se tarda?   *kwan*·to se *tar*·da

13B Is it a direct route?
¿Es un viaje directo?   es oon *vya*·khe dee·*rek*·to

13C How long will it be delayed?
¿Cuánto tiempo se   *kwan*·to *tyem*·po se
retrasará?   re·tra·sa·*ra*

Can I get a stand-by ticket?
¿Puede ponerme en la   *pwe*·de po·*ner*·me en la
lista de espera?   *lees*·ta de es·*pe*·ra

A one-way ticket to (Barcelona).
Un billete sencillo   oon bee·*lye*·te sen·*thee*·lyo
a (Barcelona).   a (bar·the·*lo*·na)

11C I'd like to cancel my ticket.
Me gustaría cancelar   me goos·ta·*ree*·a kan·the·*lar*
mi billete, por favor.   mee bee·*lye*·te por fa·*vor*

11D I'd like to change my ticket.
Me gustaría cambiar   me goos·ta·*ree*·a kam·*byar*
mi billete, por favor.   mee bee·*lye*·te por fa·*vor*

Two … tickets, please.	*Dos billetes …, por favor.*	dos bee·*lye*·tes … por fa·*vor*
child's	*infantil*	een·fan·*teel*
return	*de ida y vuelta*	de *ee*·da ee *vwel*·ta
student's	*de estudiante*	de es·too·*dyan*·te
1st-class	*de primera clase*	de pree·*me*·ra *kla*·se
2nd-class	*de segunda clase*	de se·*goon*·da *kla*·se

luggage

el equipaje

16A My luggage has been damaged.
*Mis maletas han
sido dañadas.*
mees ma·*le*·tas an
see·do da·*nya*·das

16B My luggage has been lost.
*Mis maletas han
sido perdidas.*
mees ma·*le*·tas an
see·do per·*dee*·das

16C My luggage has been stolen.
*Mis maletas han
sido robadas.*
mees ma·*le*·tas an
see·do ro·*ba*·das

My luggage hasn't arrived.
*Mis maletas se han
perdido.*
mees ma·*le*·tas se an
per·*dee*·do

I'd like a luggage locker.
*Quisiera un casillero
de consigna.*
kee·*sye*·ra oon ka·see·*lye*·ro
de kon·*seeg*·na

Can I have some coins/tokens?
*¿Me podía dar
monedas/fichas?*
me po·*dee*·a dar
mo·*ne*·das/fee·chas

plane

el avión

When's the next flight to ...?
*¿Cuándo sale el próximo
vuelo para ...?*
kwan·do sa·le el prok·see·mo
vwe·lo pa·ra ...

What time do I have to check in?
*¿A qué hora tengo que
facturar mi equipaje?*
a ke o·ra ten·go ke
fak·too·rar mee e·kee·pa·khe

bus

el autobús

Which city/intercity bus goes to ...?
¿Qué autobús/autocar
va a ...?
ke ow·to·*boos*/ow·to·*kar*
va a ...

This/That one.
Éste/Ése.
es·te/e·se

Bus number ...
El autobús número ...
el ow·to·*boos* noo·me·ro ...

15A Please tell me when we get to ...
¿Puede avisarme
cuando lleguemos a ...?
pwe·de a·vee·*sar*·me
kwan·do lye·ge·mos a ...

train

el tren

15B What station is this?
¿Cuál es esta estación?
kwal es es·ta es·ta·*thyon*

15C What's the next station?
¿Cuál es la próxima
estación?
kwal es la *prok*·see·ma
es·ta·*thyon*

Does this train stop at (Madrid)?
¿Para el tren en (Madrid)?
pa·ra el tren en (ma·*dree*)

Do I need to change trains?
¿Tengo que cambiar
de tren?
ten·go ke kam·*byar*
de tren

Which carriage is ...?	¿Cuál es el coche ...?	kwal es el *ko*·che ...
1st class	de primera clase	de pree·*me*·ra *kla*·se
for (Madrid)	para (Madrid)	pa·ra (ma·*dree*)
for dining	comedor	ko·me·*dor*

boat

el barco

Are there life jackets?
¿Hay chalecos salvavidas?   ai cha·*le*·kos sal·va·*vee*·das

What's the sea like today?
¿Cómo está el mar hoy?   *ko*·mo es·*ta* el mar oy

I feel seasick.
Estoy mareado.   es·*toy* ma·re·a·do

taxi

el taxi

17A **I'd like a taxi.**
Quisiera un taxi.   kee·*sye*·ra oon *tak*·see

17B **I'd like a taxi at (9am).**
Quisiera un taxi a   kee·*sye*·ra oon *tak*·see a
(las nueve de la mañana).   (las *nwe*·ve de la ma·*nya*·na)

I'd like a taxi tomorrow.
Quisiera un taxi mañana.   kee·*sye*·ra oon *tak*·see ma·*nya*·na

17C **Is this taxi available?**
¿Está libre este taxi?   es·*ta* lee·bre es·te *tak*·see

17D **How much is it to ...?**
¿Cuánto cuesta ir a ...?   *kwan*·to *kwes*·ta eer a ...

18A **Please put the meter on.**
Por favor, ponga el   por fa·*vor* pon·ga el
taxímetro.   tak·*see*·me·tro

18B **Please take me to (this address).**
Por favor, lléveme   por fa·*vor* lye·ve·me
a (esta dirección).   a (es·ta dee·rek·*thyon*)

I'm really late.
Voy con mucho retraso.   voy kon *moo*·cho re·*tra*·so

How much is the final fare?
¿Cuánto es en total?   *kwan*·to es en to·*tal*

18C Please slow down.
Por favor vaya más.
despacio
por fa·*vor* va·ya mas
des·*pa*·thyo

18D Please wait here.
Por favor espere aquí.
por fa·*vor* es·*pe*·re a·*kee*

18E Please stop here.
Por favor pare aquí.
por fa·*vor* pa·re a·*kee*

car & motorbike hire

alquiler de coches & motos

Does that include insurance/mileage?
¿Incluye el seguro/
kilometraje?
een·*kloo*·ye el se·*goo*·ro/
kee·lo·me·*tra*·khe

I'd like to hire a 4WD.
Quisiera alquilar
un todoterreno.
kee·*sye*·ra al·*kee*·lar
oon to·do·te·*re*·no

19A I'd like to hire a car.
Quisiera alquilar un coche.
kee·*sye*·ra al·*kee*·lar oon *ko*·che

19B I'd like to hire a motorbike.
Quisiera alquilar.
una moto
kee·*sye*·ra al·*kee*·lar
oo·na *mo*·to

with air	*con aire*	kon *ai*·re
conditioning	*acondicionado*	a·kon·dee·thyo·*na*·do
with a driver	*con chófer*	kon *cho*·fer

How much for hourly hire?
¿Cuánto cuesta
el alquiler por hora?
kwan·to *kwes*·ta
el al·*kee*·ler por *o*·ra

19D How much for daily hire?
¿Cuánto cuesta
el alquiler por día?
kwan·to *kwes*·ta
el al·*kee*·ler por *dee*·a

19E How much for weekly hire?
¿Cuánto cuesta
el alquiler por semana?
kwan·to *kwes*·ta
el al·*kee*·ler por se·*ma*·na

on the road

20A Is this the road to ...?
¿Es el camino a ...?   es el ka·*mee*·no a ...

Where's a petrol station?
¿Dónde hay una   *don*·de ai *oo*·na
gasolinera?   ga·so·lee·*ne*·ra

What's the ... speed limit?	*¿Cuál es el límite de velocidad ...?*	kwal es el *lee*·mee·te de ve·lo·thee·*da* ...
city	*en la ciudad*	en la thyoo·*da*
country	*en el campo*	en el *kam*·po
here	*por aquí*	por a·*kee*

signs

Acceso	ak·*the*·so	Entrance
Aparcamiento	a·par·ka·*myen*·to	Parking
Ceda el Paso	*the*·da el *pa*·so	Give Way
Desvío	des·*vee*·o	Detour
Dirección Única	dee·rek·*thyon oo*·nee·ka	One Way
Frene	*fre*·ne	Slow Down
Peaje	pe·*a*·khe	Toll
Peligro	pe·*lee*·gro	Danger
Prohibido Aparcar	pro·ee·*bee*·do a·par·*kar*	No Parking
Prohibido el Paso	pro·ee·*bee*·do el *pa*·so	No Entry
Stop	es·*top*	Stop
Vía de Acceso	*vee*·a de ak·*the*·so	Exit Freeway

Please fill it up.
Por favor, lléneme el depósito.
por fa·*vor* *lye*·ne·me el de·po·*see*·to

I'd like (20) litres of ...
Quiero (veinte) litros de ...
kye·ro (*veyn*·te) *lee*·tros de ...

petrol (gas)	*gasolina*	ga·so·*lee*·na
diesel	*diesel*	*dye*·sel
leaded (regular)	*gasolina normal*	ga·so·*lee*·na nor·*mal*
unleaded	*gasolina sin plomo*	ga·so·*lee*·na seen *plo*·mo

Please check the ...	*Por favor, revise ...*	por fa·*vor* re·*vee*·se ...
oil	*el nivel del aceite*	el nee·*vel* del a·*they*·te
tyre pressure	*la presión de los neumáticos*	la pre·*syon* de los ne·oo·*ma*·tee·kos
water	*el nivel del agua*	*nee*·vel del a·gwa

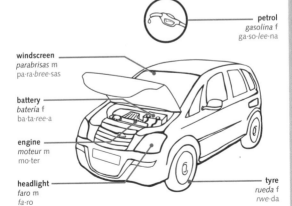

petrol
gasolina f
ga·so·*lee*·na

windscreen
parabrisas m
pa·ra·*bree*·sas

battery
batería f
ba·ta·*ree*·a

engine
moteur m
mo·ter

headlight
faro m
fa·ro

tyre
rueda f
rwe·da

de ke *mar*·ka es
¿De qué marca es?   **What make/model is it?**

(How long) Can I park here?
¿(Por cuánto tiempo)   (por *kwan*·to *tyem*·po)
Puedo aparcar aquí?   pwe·do a·par·*kar* a·*kee*

Where do I pay?
¿Dónde se paga?   *don*·de se *pa*·ga

problems

problemas

20B **I need a mechanic.**
Necesito un   ne·the·*see*·to oon
mecánico.   me·*ka*·nee·ko

The car has broken down (at ...).
El coche se ha averiado   el *ko*·che se a a·ve·*rya*·do
(en ...).   (en ...)

I had an accident.
He tenido un accidente.   e te·*nee*·do oon ak·thee·*den*·te

The motorbike won't start.
No arranca la moto.   no a·*ran*·ka la *mo*·to

20C **I have a flat tyre.**
Tengo un neumático   *ten*·go oon ne·oo·*ma*·tee·ko
desinflado.   de·seen·*fla*·do

I've lost my car keys.
He perdido las llaves   e per·*dee*·do las *lya*·ves
de mi coche.   de mee *ko*·che

I've locked my keys inside.
He cerrado con las llaves   e the·*ra*·do kon las *lya*·ves
dentro.   *den*·tro

20D I've run out of petrol.
Me he quedado sin gasolina.
me e ke·*da*·do seen ga·so·*lee*·na

Can you fix it (today)?
¿Puede arreglarlo (hoy)?
pwe·de a·re·*glar*·lo (oy)

How long will it take?
¿Cuánto tardará?
kwan·to tar·da·*ra*

bicycle

la bicicleta

19C I'd like to hire a a bicycle.
Quisiera alquilar una bicicleta.
kee·*sye*·ra al·kee·*lar* oo·na bee·thee·*kle*·ta

Where can I buy a (second-hand) bike?
¿Dónde se puede comprar una bicicleta (de segunda mano)?
don·de se pwe·de kom·*prar* oo·na bee·thee·*kle*·ta (de se·*goon*·da ma·no)

How much is it per ...?	*¿Cuánto cuesta por ...?*	*kwan*·to *kwes*·ta por ...
afternoon	*una tarde*	oo·na *tar*·de
day	*un día*	oon *dee*·a
hour	*una hora*	oo·na *o*·ra
morning	*una mañana*	oo·na ma·*nya*·na

I have a puncture.
Se me ha pinchado una rueda.
se me a peen·*cha*·do oo·na *rwe*·da

local transport

People usually walk around cities and municipalities, but if you want to catch a bus, you could ask:

Are you waiting for more people?

> ¿Está esperando a
> más gente?

> es·ta es·pe·ran·do a
> mas khen·te

Can you take us around the city please?

> ¿Nos puede llevar por
> la ciudad?

> nos pwe·de lye·var por
> la thyoo·da

For phrases on disabled access, see **disabled travellers**, page 85.

signs		
Aduana	a·dwa·na	Customs
Artículos Libres de Impuestos	ar·tee·koo·los lee·bres de eem·pwes·tos	Duty-Free Goods
Salida	sa·lee·da	Exit/Way Out
Control de Pasaporte	con·trol de pa·sa·por·te	Passport Control

passport control

control de pasaporte

listen for ...		
soo ... por fa·*vor*	*Su ... por favor.*	**Your ... please.**
pa·sa·*por*·te	*pasaporte*	**passport**
vee·*sa*·do	*visado*	**visa**
es·*ta*	*¿Está*	**Are you**
vya·*khan*·do ...	*viajando ...?*	**travelling ...?**
en oon *groo*·po	*en un grupo*	**in a group**
kon *oo*·na	*con una*	**with a family**
fa·*mee*·lya	*familia*	
so·lo	*solo*	**on your own**

10A I'm here on business.
Estoy aquí por negocios. es·*toy* a·*kee* por ne·*go*·thyos

10B I'm here on holiday.
Estoy aquí de vacaciones. es·*toy* a·*kee* de va·ka·*thyo*·nes

I'm here in transit.
Estoy aquí en tránsito. es·*toy* a·*kee* en *tran*·see·to

I'm here for ...	*Estoy aquí por ...*	es·*toy* a·*kee* por ...
days	*días*	*dee*·as
months	*meses*	*me*·ses
weeks	*semanas*	se·*ma*·nas

customs

10C I have nothing to declare.

No tengo nada que declarar.

no *ten*·go *na*·da ke de·kla·*rar*

10D I have something to declare.

Quisiera declarar algo.

kee·*sye*·ra de·kla·*rar* al·go

I didn't know I had to declare it.

No sabía que tenía que declararlo.

no sa·*bee*·a ke te·*nee*·a ke de·kla·*rar*·lo

filling in forms

Apellido(s)	surname(s) – many Spaniards use two surnames, their father's and their mother's
Domicilio	address (residence)
Exp. en	issued at
Fecha	date
Fecha di nacimiento	date of birth
Firma	signature
Lugar de nacimiento	place of birth
Nacionalidad	nationality
Nombre	given name
Pasaporte	passport
Profesión	occupation

finding accommodation

buscando alojamiento

Where's a bed & breakfast?
¿Dónde hay una pensión con desayuno?
don·de ai oo·na pen·syon kon de·sa·yoo·no

26A **Where's a guesthouse?**
¿Dónde hay una pensión?
don·de ai oo·na pen·syon

26B **Where's a hotel?**
¿Dónde hay un hotel?
don·de ai oon o·tel

26C **Where's a youth hostel?**
¿Dónde hay un albergue juvenil?
don·de ai oon al·ber·ge khoo·ve·neel

26D **Where's a camping ground?**
¿Dónde hay una zona de acampada?
don·de ai oo·na tho·na a·kam·pa·da

27A **Can you recommend somewhere cheap?**
¿Puede recomendar algún sitio barato?
pwe·de re·ko·men·dar al·goon see·tio ba·ra·to

27B **Can you recommend somewhere luxurious?**
¿Puede recomendar algún sitio de lujo?
pwe·de re·ko·men·dar al·goon see·tio de loo·kho

27C **Can you recommend somewhere nearby?**
¿Puede recomendar algún sitio cercano?
pwe·de re·ko·men·dar al·goon see·tio ther·ka·no

21B **What's the address?**
¿Cuál es la dirección?
kwal es la dee·rek·thyon

For more on how to get there, see **directions**, page 61.

local talk		
dive	*tugurio* m	too·goo·ryo
top spot	*lugar* m *guay*	loo·gar gwai

booking ahead & checking in

haciendo una reserva & registrándose

28A I'd like to book a room, please.
Quisiera reservar una habitación.
kee·*sye*·ra re·ser·*var oo*·na a·bee·ta·*thyon*

28B I have a reservation.
Tengo una reserva.
ten·go oo·na re·*ser*·va

My name's …
Me llamo …
me *lya*·mo …

For (three) nights/weeks.
Por (tres) noches/semanas.
por (tres) *no*·ches/se·*ma*·nas

From (July 2) to (July 6).
Desde (el dos de julio) hasta (el seis de julio).
des·de (el dos de *khoo*·lyo) *as*·ta (el seys de *khoo*·lyo)

Do I need to pay upfront?
¿Necesito pagar por adelantado?
ne·the·*see*·to *pa*·gar por a·de·lan·*ta*·do

How much is it per week?
¿Cuánto cuesta por semana?
kwan·to *kwes*·ta por se·*ma*·na

listen for …

lo *syen*·to es·*ta* kom·*ple*·to
Lo siento, está completo. **I'm sorry, we're full.**

por *kwan*·tas *no*·ches
¿Por cuántas noches? **For how many nights?**

soo pa·sa·*por*·te por fa·*vor*
Su pasaporte, por favor. **Your passport, please.**

28C How much is it per night?
¿Cuánto cuesta por noche?   *kwan·to kwes·ta por no·che*

28D How much is it per person?
¿Cuánto cuesta   *kwan·to kwes·ta*
por persona?   *por per·so·na*

Can I pay by ...?	*¿Puedo pagar con ...?*	*pwe·do pa·gar con ...*
credit card	*tarjeta de*	*tar·khe·ta de*
	crédito	*kre·dee·to*
travellers	*cheques de*	*che·kes de*
cheque	*viajero*	*vya·khe·ro*

For other methods of payment, see **money**, page 35.

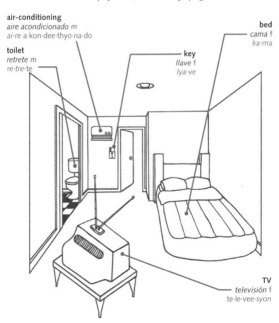

air-conditioning
aire acondicionado m
ai·re a·kon·dee·thyo·na·do

bed
cama f
ka·ma

toilet
retrete m
re·tre·te

key
llave f
lya·ve

TV
televisión f
te·le·vee·syon

29A Do you have a single room?

¿Tiene una habitación individual?

tye·ne oo·na a·bee·ta·thyon een·dee·vee·dwal

29B Do you have a doublee room?

¿Tiene una habitación doble?

tye·ne oo·na a·bee·ta·thyon do·ble

29C Do you have a twin room?

¿Tiene una habitación con dos camas?

tye·ne oo·na a·bee·ta·thyon kon dos ka·mas

with (a) ...	con ...	kon ...
without (a) ...	sin ...	seen ...
Can I see it?	¿Puedo verla?	pwe·do ver·la
It's fine. I'll take it.	Vale, la alquilo.	va·le la al·kee·lo

requests & queries

30A When's breakfast served?

¿Cuándo se sirve el desayuno?

kwan·do se seer·ve el de·sa·yoo·no

30B Where's breakfast served?

¿Dónde se sirve el desayuno?

don·de se seer·ve el de·sa·yoo·no

30C Please wake me at (seven).

Por favor, despiérteme a (las siete).

por fa·vor des·pyer·te·me a (las sye·te)

Can I get another ...?

¿Puede darme otro/a ...? m/f

pwe·de dar·me o·tro/a ...

Can I use the ...?	¿Puedo usar ...?	pwe·do oo·sar ...
kitchen	la cocina	la ko·thee·na
laundry	el lavadero	el la·va·de·ro
telephone	el teléfono	el te·le·fo·no

30D Is there a lift/elevator?
¿Hay ascensor?   ai as·then·*sor*

30E Is there a safe?
¿Hay una caja fuerte?   ai oo·na ka·kha *fwer*·te

Is there a message board?
¿Hay un tablón de anuncios?   ai ta·*blon* de a·*noon*·thyos

Is there a swimming pool?
¿Hay piscina?   ai pees·*thee*·na

Do you ... here?	*¿Aquí ...?*	a·*kee* ...
arrange tours	*organizan*	or·ga·*nee*·than
	recorridos	re·ko·*ree*·dos
change money	*cambian*	*kam*·byan
	dinero	dee·*ne*·ro

signs		
Centro Financiero	*then*·tro fee·nan·*thye*·ro	**Business Centre**
Recepción	re·thep·*thyon*	**Reception**
Salida de Emergencia	sa·*lee*·da de e·mer·*khen*·thya	**Emergency Exit**
Servicios	ser·*vee*·thyos	**Toilets**
Servicio de Lavandería	ser·*vee*·thyo de la·van·de·*ree*·a	**Laundry Service**

Can I leave a message for someone?
¿Puedo dejar un mensaje para alguien?   *pwe*·do de·*khar* oon men·*sa*·khe *pa*·ra al·gyen

Is there a message for me?
¿Tiene un mensaje para mí?   *tye*·ne oon men·*sa*·khe *pa*·ra mee

I'm locked out of my room.
Cerré la puerta y se me olvidaron las llaves dentro.   the·*re* la *pwer*·ta y se me ol·vee·*da*·ron las *lya*·ves *den*·tro

The (bathroom) door is locked.
La puerta (del baño) está cerrada.   la *pwer*·ta (del *ba*·nyo) es·*ta* the·*ra*·da

accommodation

55

complaints

quejas

It's too ...	Es demasiado ...	es de·ma·sya·do ...
cold	fría f	free·a
dark	oscura f	os·koo·ra
expensive	cara f	ka·ra
light	clara f	kla·ra
noisy	ruidosa f	rwee·do·sa
small	pequeña f	pe·ke·nya

31A The air-conditioning doesn't work.
No funciona el aire no foon·thyo·na el ai·re
acondicionado. a·kon· dee·thyo·na·do

31B The fan doesn't work.
No funciona el ventilador. no foon·thyo·na el ven·tee·la·dor

31C The toilet doesn't work.
No funciona el retrete. no foon·thyo·na el re·tre·te

The window doesn't work.
No funciona la ventana. no foon·thyo·na la ven·ta·na

This ... isn't clean.
Éste/Ésta ... no está es·te/es·ta ... no es·ta
limpio/a. m/f *leem·pyo/a*

a knock at the door

Who is it?	¿Quién es?	kyen es
Just a moment.	Un momento.	oon mo·men·to
Come in.	Adelante.	a·de·lan·te

Can you come back later, please?
¿Puede volver más *pwe·de vol·ver mas*
tarde, por favor? *tar·de por fa·vor*

checking out

32A What time is check out?
¿A qué hora hay que dejar   a ke o·ra ai ke de·khar
la habitación?   la a·bee·ta·thyon

How much extra to stay until (6 o'clock)?
¿Cuánto más cuesta   kwan·to mas kwes·ta
quedarse hasta (las seis)?   ke·dar·se as·ta (las seys)

Can I have a late check out?
¿Puedo dejar la   pwe·do de·khar la
habitación más tarde?   a·bee·ta·thyon mas tar·de

32B Can I leave my luggage here?
¿Puedo dejar las   pwe·do de·khar las
maletas aquí?   ma·le·tas a·kee

36D There's a mistake in the bill.
Hay un error en la cuenta.   ai oon e·ror en la kwen·ta

I'm leaving now.
Me voy ahora.   me voy a·o·ra

Can you call a taxi for me (for 11 o'clock)?
¿Me puede pedir un   me pwe·de pe·deer oon
taxi (para las once)?   tak·see (pa·ra las on·the)

32C Could I have my deposit, please?
¿Me puede dar mi   me pwe·de dar mee
depósito, por favor?   de·po·see·to por fa·vor

32D Could I have my passport, please?
¿Me puede dar mi   me pwe·de dar mee
pasaporte, por favor?   pa·sa·por·te por fa·vor

32E Could I have my valuables, please?
¿Me puede dar mis objetos   me pwe·de dar mees ob·khe·tos
de valor, por favor?   de va·lor por fa·vor

I'll be back ...	*Volveré ...*	vol·ve·re ...
in (three) days	*en (tres) días*	en (tres) dee·as
on (Tuesday)	*el (martes)*	el (mar·tes)

I had a great stay, thank you.
   He tenido una estancia   e te·*nee*·do oo·na es·*tan*·thya
   muy agradable, gracias.   mooy a·gra·*da*·ble gra·thyas

You've been terrific.
   Han sido estupendos.   an *see*·do es·too·*pen*·dos

I'll recommend it to my friends.
   Se lo recomendaré a   se lo re·ko·men·da·*re* a
   mis amigos.   mees a·*mee*·gos

camping

acampando

Where's the nearest ...?	*¿Dónde está ...?*	*don*·de es·*ta* ...
camp site	*el terreno de*	el te·*re*·no de
	cámping	*kam*·peeng
	más cercano	mas ther·*ka*·no
shop	*la tienda*	la *tyen*·da
	más cercana	mas ther·*ka*·na
I'm looking for the nearest ...	*Estoy buscando ...*	es·*toy* boos·*kan*·do ...
showers	*las duchas*	las *doo*·chas
	más cercanas	mas ther·*ka*·nas
toilet block	*los servicios*	los ser·*vee*·thyos
	más cercanos	mas ther·*ka*·nos

Is it coin-operated?
   ¿Funciona con monedas?   foon·*thyo*·na kon mo·*ne*·das

Is the water drinkable?
   ¿Se puede beber el agua?   se *pwe*·de be·ber el *a*·gwa

26E Am I allowed to camp here?
   ¿Se puede acampar aquí?   se *pwe*·de a·kam·*par* a·*kee*

Can I park next to my tent?
   ¿Se puede aparcar al lado   se *pwe*·de a·par·*kar* al *la*·do
   de la tienda?   de la *tyen*·da

Do you have ...?	¿Tiene ...?	tye·ne ...
electricity	electricidad	e·lek·tree·thee·da
shower facilities	duchas	doo·chas
a site	un sitio	oon see·tyo
tents for hire	tiendas de	tyen·das de
	campaña para	kam·pa·nya pa·ra
	alquilar	al·kee·lar

How much is it	¿Cuánto vale	kwan·to va·le
per ...?	por ...?	por ...
caravan	caravana	ka·ra·va·na
person	persona	per·so·na
tent	tienda	tyen·da
vehicle	vehículo	ve·ee·koo·lo

Whom do I ask to stay here?
    ¿Con quién tengo que hablar   kon kyen *ten*·go ke a·*blar*
    para quedarme aquí?   pa·ra ke·*dar*·me a·*kee*

Could I borrow ...?
    ¿Me puede prestar ...?   me *pwe*·de pres·*tar* ...

For cooking utensils, see **self-catering**, page 155.

renting

alquilando

Do you have	¿Tiene ... para	tye·ne ... pa·ra
a/an ... for rent?	alquilar?	al·kee·lar
apartment	un piso	oon pee·so
cabin	una cabaña	oo·na ka·ba·nya
house	una casa	oo·na ca·sa
room	una habitación	oo·na a·bee·ta·thyon
villa	un chalet	oon cha·le

furnished	amueblado/a m/f	a·mwe·bla·do/a
partly furnished	semi	se·mee
	amueblado/a m/f	a·mwe·bla·do/a
unfurnished	sin amueblar	seen a·mwe·blar

staying with locals

Can I stay at your place?
¿Me puedo quedar en   me *pwe*·do ke·*dar* en
tu casa?   too *ka*·sa

Can I help?
¿Puedo ayudar?   *pwe*·do a·yoo·*dar*

Can I use your telephone?
¿Puedo usar vuestra   *pwe*·do oo·*sar* vwe·stra
teléfono?   te·*le*·fo·no

Thanks for your hospitality.
Gracias por tu   *gra*·thyas por too
hospitalidad.   os·pee·ta·lee·*da*

I have my own ...	*Tengo mi propio ...*	*ten*·go mee *pro*·pyo ...
mattress	*colchón*	kol·*chon*
sleeping bag	*saco de dormir*	*sa*·ko de dor·*meer*

Can I ...?	*¿Puedo ...?*	*pwe*·do ...
bring anything	*traer algo para*	tra·*er al*·go *pa*·ra
for the meal	*la comida*	la ko·*mee*·da
do the dishes	*lavar los platos*	la·*var* los *pla*·tos
set/clear the table	*poner/quitar*	po·*ner*/kee·*tar*
	la mesa	la *me*·sa
take out the	*sacar*	sa·*kar*
rubbish	*la basura*	la ba·*soo*·ra

For compliments to the chef, see **food**, page 147.

signs		
Caballeros	ka·ba·*lye*·ros	**Men**
Caliente	ka·*lyen*·te	**Hot**
Dirección	dee·rek·*thyon*	**No Entry**
Prohibida	pro·hee·*bee*·da	
Frío	*free*·o	**Cold**
Señoras	se·*nyo*·ras	**Women**

PRACTICAL

60

Excuse me.
Perdone.   per·*do*·ne

Could you help me, please?
¿Perdone, puede   per·*do*·ne *pwe*·de
ayudarme por favor?   a·yoo·*dar*·me por fa·*vor*

21A **Where's …?**
¿Dónde está …?   *don*·de es·*ta* …

I'm looking for …
Busco …   *boos*·ko …

Which way is …?
¿Por dónde se va a …?   por *don*·de se va a …

21C **How can I get there?**
¿Cómo se puede ir?   *ko*·mo se *pwe*·de eer

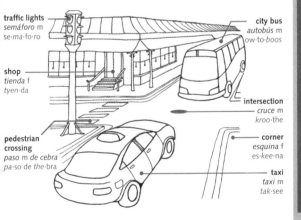

traffic lights
semáforo m
se·*ma*·fo·ro

shop
tienda f
tyen·da

pedestrian crossing
paso m *de cebra*
pa·so de *the*·bra

city bus
autobús m
ow·to·*boos*

intersection
cruce m
kroo·the

corner
esquina f
es·*kee*·na

taxi
taxi m
tak·see

21D	How far is it?		
	¿A qué distancia está?		a ke dees·*tan*·thya es·*ta*
21E	Can you show me (on the map)?		
	¿Me lo puede indicar (en el mapa)?		me lo *pwe*·de een·dee·*kar* (en el *ma*·pa)

22A	It's far.	*Está lejos.*	es·*ta le*·khos
22B	It's near.	*Está cerca.*	es·*ta ther*·ka
22C	here	*aquí*	a·*kee*
22D	there	*allí*	a·*yee*
22E	It's next to ...	*Está al lado de ...*	es·*ta* al *la*·do de ...
22F	opposite ...	*frente a ...*	*fren*·te a ...
22G	straight ahead	*todo recto*	*to*·do *rek*·to

It's behind ...	*Está detrás de ...*	es·*ta* de·*tras* de ...
It's in front of ...	*Está enfrente de ...*	es·*ta* en·*fren*·te de ...
It's left.	*Está por la izquierda.*	es·*ta* por la eeth·*kyer*·da
It's right.	*Está por la derecha.*	es·*ta* por la de·*re*·cha

23A	Turn at the corner.	*Doble en la esquina.*	*do*·ble en la es·*kee*·na
23B	Turn at the traffic lights.	*Doble en el semáforo.*	*do*·ble en el se·*ma*·fo·ro
23C	Turn left.	*Doble a la izquierda.*	*do*·ble a la eeth·*kyer*·da
23D	Turn right.	*Doble a la derecha.*	*do*·ble de·*re*·cha

24A	by bus	*en autobús*	en ow·to·*boos*
24B	by taxi	*en taxi*	en *tak*·see
24C	by train	*en tren*	en tren
24D	on foot	*a pie*	a pye

25A	north	*norte*	*nor*·te
25B	south	*sur*	soor
25C	east	*este*	*es*·te
25D	west	*oeste*	o·*es*·te

For locations and compass directions, see the **dictionary**.

shopping

looking for ...

buscando ...

Where's ...?
¿Dónde está …? — don·de es·ta …

33A **Where can I buy (a padlock)?**
¿Dónde puedo comprar (un candado)? — don·de pwe·do kom·prar (oon kan·da·do)

bank	*banco* m	*ban·ko*
camping store	*tienda* f *de provisiones de camping*	*tyen·da de pro·vee·syo·nes de kam·peeng*
supermarket	*supermercado* m	*soo·per·mer·ka·do*

For more on shops and how to get there, see **directions**, page 61 and the **dictionary**.

making a purchase

comprando algo

33B **How much is it?**
¿Cuánto cuesta? — kwan·to kwes·ta

34A **I'm looking for ...**
Quisiera comprar … — kee·sye·ra kom·prar …

I'm just looking.
Sólo estoy mirando. — so·lo es·toy mee·ran·do

34B **Can I look at it?**
¿Puedo verlo? — pwe·do ver·lo

34C **Do you have any others?**
¿Tiene otros? — tye·ne o·tros

Do you have something cheaper?
¿Tiene algo más barato? — tye·ne al·go mas ba·ra·to

35A Do you accept credit cards?
¿Aceptan tarjetas de crédito?
a·*thep*·tan tar·*khe*·tas de kre·dee·to

35B Do you accept debit cards?
¿Aceptan tarjetas de débito?
a·*thep*·tan tar·*khe*·tas de *de*·bee·to

35C Do you accept travellers cheques?
¿Aceptan cheques de viajero?
a·*thep*·tan *che*·kes de vya·*khe*·ro

35D Could I have a bag, please?
¿Podría darme una bolsa, por favor?
po·*dree*·a *dar*·me oo·na *bol*·sa por fa·*vor*

35E Could I have a receipt, please?
¿Podría darme un recibo, por favor?
po·*dree*·a *dar*·me oon re·*thee*·bo por fa·*vor*

33C Can you write down the price?
¿Puede escribir el precio?
pwe·de es·kree·*beer* el *pre*·thyo

Could I have it wrapped?
¿Me lo podría envolver?
me lo po·*dree*·a en·vol·*ver*

34D Does it have a guarantee?
¿Tiene garantía?
tye·ne ga·ran·*tee*·a

PRACTICAL

64

Can I have it sent overseas?
¿Pueden enviarlo por correo a otro país? — pwe·den en·vee·ar·lo por ko·re·o a o·tro pa·ees

Can you order it for me?
¿Me lo puede pedir? — me lo pwe·de pe·deer

Can I pick it up later?
¿Puedo recogerlo más tarde? — pwe·do re·ko·kher·lo mas tar·de

35F **I'd like my change, please.**
Quisiera mi cambio, por favor. — kee·sye·ra mee kam·byo por fa·vor

36A **It's faulty.**
Es defectuoso. — es de·fek·too·o·so

36B **I'd like a refund.**
Quisiera que me devuelva el dinero, por favor. — kee·sye·ra ke me de·vwel·va el dee·ne·ro por fa·vor

36C **I'd like to return this.**
Quisiera devolver esto, por favor. — kee·sye·ra mee kam·byo de·vol·ver es·to por fa·vor

local talk		
bargain	*ganga* f	gan·ga
rip-off	*estafa* f	es·ta·fa
sale	*ventas* f pl	ven·tas
specials	*rebajas* f pl	re·ba·khas

bargaining

el regateo

33D **That's too expensive.**
Es muy caro. — es mooy ka·ro

33E **Can you lower the price?**
¿Podría bajar el precio? — po·dree·a ba·khar el pre·thyo

I'll give you ...
Te daré ... — te da·re ...

clothes

la ropa

37A Can I try it on?
¿Me lo puedo probar? me lo *pwe*·do pro·*bar*

37B My size is (32).
Uso la talla *oo*·so la *ta*·lya
(treinta y dos). (*treyn*·ta ee dos)

37C It doesn't fit.
No me queda bien. no me *ke*·da byen

repairs

reparaciones

Can I have my	*¿Puede reparar mi*	*pwe*·de re·pa·*rar* mee
... repaired here?	*... aquí?*	... a·*kee*
backpack	*mochila*	mo·*chee*·la
camera	*cámara*	*ka*·ma·ra
When will my	*¿Cuándo estarán*	*kwan*·do es·ta·*ran*
... be ready?	*listos/as mis ...?* m/f	*lees*·tos/as mees ...
(sun)glasses	*gafas (de sol)* f	*ga*·fas (de sol)
shoes	*zapatos* m	tha·*pa*·tos

For more clothing items, see the **dictionary**.

darn holes		
buttons	*botónes* m pl	bo·*to*·nes
needle	*aguja* f	a·*goo*·kha
scissors	*tijeras* f pl	tee·*khe*·ras
thread	*hilo* m	*ee*·lo

PRACTICAL

hairdressing

I'd like (a) ...	*Quisiera ...*	kee·*sye*·ra ...
blow wave	*un secado a mano*	oon se·*ka*·do a *ma*·no
colour	*un tinte de pelo*	oon *teen*·te de *pe*·lo
haircut	*un corte de pelo*	oon *kor*·te de *pe*·lo
highlights	*reflejos*	re·*fle*·khos
my beard	*que me recorte*	ke me re·*kor*·te
trimmed	*la barba*	la *bar*·ba
shave	*que me afeite*	ke me a·*fey*·te
trim	*que me recorte*	ke me re·*kor*·te
	el pelo	el *pe*·lo

Don't cut it too short.
No me lo corte   no me lo *kor*·te
demasiado corto.   de·ma·*sya*·do *kor*·to

Shave it all off!
¡Aféitelo todo!   a·*fey*·te·lo *to*·do

Please use a new blade.
Por favor, use una   por fa·*vor* oo·*se* oo·na
cuchilla nueva.   koo·*chee*·lya *nwe*·va

worth a read

Spanish literature has a long history (dating from the 12th century), resulting in a thriving writing industry today. Look out for authors Ana María Matute, Jorge Luis Borges, Miguel de Unamuno, Carmen Martín Gaite, Juan Goytisolo, Miguel Delibes, Gabriel García Marquez and the 1989 Nobel Prize winner, Camilo José Cela.

books & reading

Is there a/an (English-language) ...?	¿Hay algún/ alguna ... en inglés? m/f	ai al·goon/ al·goo·na ... en een·gles
book by ...	libro m de ...	lee·bro de ...
bookshop	librería m	lee·bre·ree·a
entertainment guide	guía f del ocio	gee·a del o·thyo
section	sección f	sek·thyon

I (don't) like ...
(No) Me gusta/gustan ... sg/pl (no) me goos·ta/goos·tan ...

Do you have Lonely Planet guidebooks?
¿Tiene libros de Lonely   tye·ne lee·bros de lon·lee
Planet?   pla·net

Do you have a better phrasebook than this?
¿Tiene algún libro de   tye·ne al·goon lee·bro de
frases mejor que éste?   fra·ses me·khor ke es·te

For more on books, see **interests**, page 109.

music

I heard a band called ...
Escuché a un grupo   es·koo·che a oon groo·po
que se llama ...   ke se lya·ma ...

I heard a singer called ...
Escuché a un/una   es·koo·che a oon/oo·na
cantante que se llama ... m/f kan·tan·te ke se lya·ma ...

What's their best recording?
¿Cuál es su mejor disco?   kwal es soo me·*khor* dees·ko

Can I listen to this?
¿Puedo escuchar   pwe·do es·koo·char
este ... aquí?   es·te ... a·kee

Is this a pirated copy?
¿Es copia pirata?   es *ko*·pya pee·*ra*·ta

I'd like (a) ...	*Quisiera ...*	kee·*sye*·ra ...
blank tape	*una cinta*	*oo*·na *theen*·ta
	virgen	*veer*·khen
CD	*un cómpac*	oon *kom*·pak
headphones	*unos*	*oo*·nos
	auriculares	ow·ree·koo·*la*·res

photography

I need a passport photo taken.
Necesito fotos de   ne·the·*see*·to *fo*·tos de
pasaporte.   pa·sa·*por*·te

How much is it to develop this film?
¿Cuánto cuesta revelar   *kwan*·to *kwes*·ta re·ve·*lar*
este carrete?   es·te ka·*re*·te

38A Could you load my film?
¿Puede cargar   *pwe*·de kar·*gar*
el carrete?   el ka·*re*·te

I'd like double copies.
Quisiera dos copias.   kee·*sye*·ra dos *ko*·pyas

I'm not happy with these photos.

No estoy contento/a con estas fotos. m/f   no es·*toy* kon·*ten*·to/a kon es·tas *fo*·tos

I don't want to pay the full price.

No quiero pagar el precio íntegro.   no *kye*·ro pa·*gar* el *pre*·thyo *een*·te·gro

Do you have slide film?

¿Tiene diapositivas?   *tye*·ne dya·po·see·*tee*·vas

38B I need a B&W film for this camera.

Necesito película blanco y negro para esta cámara.   ne·the·*see*·to pe·*lee*·koo·la *blan*·ko y *ne*·gro *pa*·ra es·ta *ka*·ma·ra

38C I need a colour film for this camera.

Necesito película color para esta cámara.   ne·the·*see*·to pe·*lee*·koo·la ko·*lor pa*·ra es·ta *ka*·ma·ra

I need an APS film for this camera.

Necesito película APS para esta cámara.   ne·the·*see*·to pe·*lee*·koo·la a pe *e*·se *pa*·ra es·ta *ka*·ma·ra

I need a (400) speed film for this camera.

Necesito película de sensibilidad (cuatrocientos) para esta cámara.   ne·the·*see*·to pe·*lee*·koo·la de sen·see·bee·lee·*da* (kwa·tro·*thyen*·tos) *pa*·ra es·ta *ka*·ma·ra

38D When will it be ready?

¿Cuándo estará listo?   kwan·do es·ta·ra *lees*·to

batteries	*pilas* f pl	*pee*·las
camera	*cámara* f (*fotográfica*)	*ka*·ma·ra (fo·to·*gra*·fee·ka)
disposable camera	*cámara* f *desechable*	*ka*·ma·ra de·se·*cha*·ble
flash	*flash* f	flash
underwater camera	*cámara* f *submarina*	*ka*·ma·ra soob·ma·*ree*·na

communications
las comunicaciones

post office

correos

39A I want to send a fax.
Quisiera enviar un fax. kee·sye·ra en·vee·ar oon faks

39B I want to send a parcel.
Quisiera enviar kee·sye·ra en·vee·ar
un paquete. oon pa·ke·te

39C I want to send a postcard.
Quisiera enviar una postal. kee·sye·ra en·vee·ar oo·na pos·tal

I want to buy an aerogram.
Quisiera comprar kee·sye·ra kom·prar
un aerograma. oon ae·ro·gra·ma

39D I want to buy an envelope.
Quisiera comprar un sobre. kee·sye·ra kom·prar oon so·bre

39E I want to buy stamps.
Quisiera comprar sellos. kee·sye·ra kom·prar se·lyos

airmail	*por vía aérea*	por vee·a a·e·re·a
customs declaration	*declaración f de aduana*	de·kla·ra·thyon de a·dwa·na
domestic	*nacional*	na·thyo·nal
express mail	*correo m urgente*	ko·re·o oor·khen·te
fragile	*frágil*	fra·kheel
international	*internacional*	een·ter·na·thyo·nal
mail box	*buzón m*	boo·thon
postcode	*código m postal*	ko·dee·go pos·tal
registered mail	*correo m certificado*	ko·re·o ther·tee·fee·ka·do
surface mail	*por vía terrestre*	por vee·a te·res·tre

Please send it by air/surface mail to ...
Por favor, mándelo por por fa·vor man·de·lo por
vía aérea/terrestre a ... vee·a a·e·re·a/te·res·tre a ...

communications

71

It contains …
Contiene …   kon·*tye*·ne …

Where's the poste restante section?
¿Dónde está la lista de   *don*·de es·*ta* la *lees*·ta de
correos?   ko·*re*·os

Is there any mail for me?
¿Hay alguna carta para mí?   ai al·*goo*·na *kar*·ta *pa*·ra mee

phone

40A What's your phone number?
¿Cuál es su número de   kwal es soo *noo*·me·ro de
teléfono?   te·*le*·fo·no

40B Where's the nearest public phone?
¿Dónde hay una cabina   *don*·de ai *oo*·na ka·*bee*·na
telefónica?   te·le·fo·*nee*·ka

40C I'd like to buy a phone card.
Quisiera comprar una   kee·*sye*·ra kom·*prar oo*·na
tarjeta telefónica.   tar·*khe*·ta te·le·*fo*·nee·ka

I'd like to speak for (three) minutes.
Quiero hablar por (tres)   *kye*·ro ab·*lar* por (tres)
minutos.   mee·*noo*·tos

I want to make a … (to Singapore).	*Quiero hacer … (a Singapur).*	*kye*·ro a·*ther* … (a seen·ga·*poor*)
call	*una llamada*	*oo*·na lya·*ma*·da
reverse-charge/ collect call	*una llamada a cobro revertido*	*oo*·na lya·*ma*·da a *ko*·bro re·ver·*tee*·do

How much does … cost?	*¿Cuánto cuesta …?*	*kwan*·to *kwes*·ta…
a (three)- minute call	*una llamada de (tres) minutos*	*oo*·na lya·*ma*·da de (tres) mee·*noo*·tos
each extra minute	*cada minuto extra*	*ka*·da mee·*noo*·to *ek*·stra

The number is ...	
El número es ...	el *noo*·me·ro es ...

What's the area code for ...?	
¿Cuál es el prefijo de la zona ...?	kwal es el pre·*fee*·kho de la *tho*·na ...

What's the country code for ...?	
¿Cuál es el prefijo del país ...?	kwal es el pre·*fee*·kho del pa·*ees* ...

It's engaged.	
Está comunicando.	es·*ta* ko·moo·nee·*kan*·do

I've been cut off.	
Me han cortado (la comunicación).	me an kor·*ta*·do (la ko·moo·nee·ka·*thyon*)

The connection's bad.	
Es mala conexión.	es *ma*·la ko·nek·*syon*

Hello. (making a call)	*Hola.*	o·la
Hello? (answering a call)	*¿Diga?*	dee·ga
Can I speak to ...?	*¿Está ...?*	es·*ta* ...
It's ...	*Soy ...*	soy ...

Can I leave a message?
¿Puedo dejar un mensaje?
pwe·do de·*khar* oon men·*sa*·khe

Please tell him/her I called.
Sí, por favor, dile que he llamado.
see por fa·*vor* dee·le ke e lya·*ma*·do

I'll call back later.
Ya llamaré más tarde.
ya lya·ma·*re* mas *tar*·de

mobile/cell phone

el teléfono móvil

I'd like a/an ...	*Quisiera ...*	kee·*sye*·ra ...
adaptor plug	*un adaptador*	oon a·dap·ta·*dor*
charger for my phone	*un cargador para mi teléfono*	oon kar·ga·*dor pa*·ra mee te·*le*·fo·no
mobile/cell phone for hire	*un móvil para alquilar*	oon *mo*·veel *pa*·ra al·kee·*lar*
prepaid phone	*una tarjeta prepagada*	*oo*·na tar·*khe*·ta pre·pa·*ga*·da

40D **I'd like a SIM card for your network.**
Quisiera una tarjeta SIM para su red.
kee·*sye*·ra *oo*·na tar·*khe*·ta seem *pa*·ra soo red

What are the rates?
¿Cuál es la tarifa?
kwal es la ta·*ree*·fa

(30c) per (30) seconds.
(Treinta centavos) por (treinta) segundos.
(*treyn*·ta then·*ta*·vos) por (*treyn*·ta) se·*goon*·dos

the internet

41A **Where's the local Internet cafe?**
¿Dónde hay un cibercafé   *don*·de ai oon thee·ber·ka·*fe*
cercano?   ther·*ka*·no

41B **I'd like to get Internet access.**
Quisiera usar el Internet.   kee·sye·ra oo·*sar* el *een*·ter·net

I'd like to check my email.
Quisiera revisar mi   kee·sye·ra re·vee·*sar* mee
correo electrónico.   ko·*re*·o e·lek·*tro*·nee·ko

41C **I'd like to use a printer.**
Quisiera usar una   kee·sye·ra oo·*sar* oo·na
impresora.   eem·pre·*so*·ra

I'd like to use a scanner.
Quisiera usar un escáner.   kee·sye·ra oo·*sar* oon es·*ka*·ner

How much is it per hour?
¿Cuánto cuesta por hora?   kwan·to kwes·ta por *o*·ra

How much per ...?	¿Cuánto cuesta por ...?	kwan·to kwes·ta por ...
CD	cómpact	kom·pakt
(five) minutes	(cinco)	(theen·ko)
	minutos	mee·noo·tos
page	página	pa·khee·na
Do you have ...?	¿Tiene ...?	tye·ne ...
Macs	Apples	a·pels
PCs	PCs	pe thes
a Zip drive	unidad de Zip	oo·nee·da de theep

How do I log on?
¿Cómo entro al sistema?   ko·mo en·tro al sees·te·ma

It's crashed.
Se ha quedado colgado.   se a ke·da·do kol·ga·do

I've finished.
He terminado.   e ter·mee·na·do

a spangled web

Nowhere is the rise of 'Spanglish' (anglicised Spanish) more evident than on the Internet. New verbs such as *chatear*, *downloar*, *emailar*, *postear* and *surfear* are beginning to circulate freely in Hispanic cyberspace. In many cases, however, there are Spanish substitutes for common net-related terms. Here are just some of the officially-endorsed alternatives:

chat	*charlar*	char·lar
cyberspace	*ciberespacio*	see·ber·e·spa·thyo
download	*descargar*	des·kar·gar
homepage	*página Web inicial*	pa·jee·na web ee·nee·thyal
online	*en línea*	en lee·ne·a
search engine	*sistema de búsqueda*	sees·te·ma de boos·ke·da
surf	*correr tabla por la red*	ko·rer ta·bla por la re
username	*nombre de usuario*	nom·bre de oo·swa·ryo
website	*sitio Web*	see·tyo web

People usually shoot the breeze for a while before they get down to business.

I'm attending a ...	Asisto a ...	a·sees·to a ...
conference	un congreso	oon kon·gre·so
course	un curso	oon koor·so
meeting	una reunión	oo·na re·oo·nyon
trade fair	una feria de muestras	oo·na fe·rya de mwes·tras

I'm with ...	Estoy con ...	es·toy kon ...
my company	mi compañía	mee kom·pa·nyee·a
my colleagues	mis colegas	mees ko·le·gas
(two) others	otros (dos)	ot·ros (dos)

using your manners

If you're in a formal situation or you want to show respect to someone much older than yourself, you should use the polite form of address (see below). The best approach is to take the lead from how people address you and respond in the same way. It's always a good idea to use the polite form in business, and also with any service providers (be they kiosk attendants or doctors).

you sg	Usted	oo·ste
you pl	Ustedes	oo·ste·des

What's your name?
¿Cómo se llama Usted? sg pol	ko·mo se lya·ma oos·te

For more on polite forms, see **you** in the **a–z phrasebuilder**, page 26.

Where's the ...?
¿Dónde está ...?
don·de es·ta ...

    business centre
    el centro
    financiero
    el *then*·tro
    fee·nan·*thye*·ro

    conference
    el congreso
    el kon·*gre*·so

Where's the meeting?
¿Dónde es a reunión?
don·de es la re·oo·*nyon*

I'm alone.
Estoy solo/a. m/f
es·*toy* so·lo/a

Let me introduce my colleague.
¿Puedo presentarle a mi
compañero/a? m/f
pwe·do pre·sen·*tar*·le a mee
kom·pa·*nye*·ro/a

I'm staying at ..., room ...
Me estoy alojando en ...,
la habitación ...
me es·*toy* a·lo·*khan*·do en ...,
la a·bee·ta·*thyon* ...

I'm here for ... days/weeks.
Estoy aquí por ... días/
semanas.
es·*toy* a·*kee* por ... dee·as/
se·*ma*·nas

Here's my business card.
Aquí tiene mi tarjeta
de visita.
a·*kee* tye·ne mee tar·*khe*·ta
de vee·*see*·ta

I have an appointment with ...
Tengo una cita con ...
ten·go oo·na *thee*·ta kon ...

That went very well.
Eso fue muy bien.
e·so fwe mooy byen

Shall we go for a drink/meal?
¿Vamos a tomar/
comer algo?
va·mos a to·*mar*/
ko·*mer* al·go

It's on me.
Invito yo.
een·*vee*·to yo

bank

el banco

43A I'd like to cash a cheque.
Me gustaría cambiar un cheque.
me goos·ta·*ree*·a kam·*byar* oon *che*·ke

43B I'd like to change money.
Me gustaría cambiar dinero.
me goos·ta·*ree*·a kam·*byar* dee·*ne*·ro

43C I'd like to change a travellers cheque.
Me gustaría cobrar un cheque de viajero.
me goos·ta·*ree*·a ko·*brar* oon *che*·ke de vee·a·*khe*·ro

43D I'd like to withdraw money.
Me gustaría sacar dinero.
me goos·ta·*ree*·a sa·*kar* dee·*ne*·ro

42A What time does the bank open?
¿A qué hora abre el banco?
a ke *o*·ra *a*·bre el *ban*·ko

Can I arrange a transfer?
¿Puedo hacer una transferencia?
pwe·do ha·*ther* oo·na trans·fe·*ren*·thya

42C Where's the nearest foreign exchange office?
¿Dónde está la oficina de cambio más cercana?
don·de es·*ta* la o·fee·*thee*·na de *kam*·byo mas ther·*ka*·na

The ATM took my card.
El cajero automático se ha tragado mi tarjeta.
el ka·*khe*·ro ow·to·*ma*·tee·ko se a tra·*ga*·do mee tar·*khe*·ta

I've forgotten my PIN.
Me he olvidado del NPI.
me e ol·vee·*da*·do del *e*·ne pe ee

What's the charge for that?
¿Cuánto hay que pagar por eso?
kwan·to ai ke pa·*gar* por *e*·so

Can I have smaller notes?

¿Me lo puede dar en billetes más pequeños?

me lo *pwe*·de dar en bee·*lye*·tes mas pe·*ke*·nyos

Has my money arrived yet?

¿Ya ha llegado mi dinero?

ya a lye·*ga*·do mee dee·*ne*·ro

How long will it take to arrive?

¿Cuánto tiempo tardará en llegar?

kwan·to *tyem*·po tar·da·ra en lye·*gar*

43E What's the exchange rate?

¿Cuál es el tipo de cambio?

kwal es el *tee*·po de *kam*·byo

listen for ...

ai oon pro·*ble*·ma kon soo *kwen*·ta
Hay un problema con su cuenta.

There's a problem with your account.

no le *ke*·dan fon·dos
No le quedan fondos.

You have no funds left.

no po·*de*·mos a·ther e·so
No podemos hacer eso.

We can't do that.

por fa·*vor* feer·me a·*kee*
Por favor firme aquí.

Please sign here.

pwe·de es·kree·*beer*·lo
¿Puede escribirlo?

Could you write it down?

pwe·do ver soo ee·den·tee·fee·ka·*thyon*/
pa·sa·*por*·te por fa·*vor*
¿Puedo ver su identificación/ pasaporte, por favor?

Can I see some ID/your passport, please?

tye·ne oon des·koo·*byer*·to
Tiene un descubierto.

You're overdrawn.

en ...	En ...	In ...
(kwa·tro) dee·as la·bo·*ra*·bles oo·na se·*ma*·na	(cuatro) días laborables una semana	(four) working days one week

PRACTICAL

44A I'd like a (local) map.
Quisiera un mapa (de la zona).
kee·*sye*·ra oon *ma*·pa (de la *tho*·na)

I'd like a/an ...	*Quisiera ...*	kee·*sye*·ra ...
audio set	*un equipo audio*	oon e·*kee*·po *ow*·dyo
catalogue	*un catálogo*	oon ka·*ta*·lo·go
guidebook in English	*una guía turística en inglés*	*oo*·na *gee*·a too·*rees*·tee·ka en een·*gles*

Do you have information on ... sights?	*¿Tiene información sobre los lugares de interés ...?*	*tye*·ne een·for·ma·*thyon so*·bre los loo·*ga*·res de een·te·*res* ...
cultural	*cultural*	kool·too·*ral*
local	*local*	lo·*kal*
religious	*religioso*	re·lee·*khyo*·so
unique	*único*	*oo*·nee·ko

Can we hire a guide?
¿Podemos alquilar un guía?
po·*de*·mos al·kee·*lar* oon *gee*·a

44B I'd like to see ...
Me gustaría ver ...
me goos·ta·*ree*·a ver ...

44C What's that?
¿Qué es eso?
ke es *e*·so

Who made it?
¿Quién lo hizo?
kyen lo *ee*·tho

How old is it?
¿De qué época es?   de ke e·po·ka es

Could you take a photograph of me?
¿Me puede hacer una foto?   me pwe·de a·ther oo·na fo·to

44D Can I take a photo?
¿Puedo tomar fotos?   pwe·do to·mar fo·tos

getting in

la entrada

45A What time does it open?
¿A qué hora abre?   a ke o·ra ab·re

45B What time does it close?
¿A qué hora cierra?   a ke o·ra thye·ra

45C What's the admission charge?
¿Cuánto cuesta la entrada?   kwan·to kwes·ta la en·tra·da

It costs ...
Cuesta ...   kwes·ta ...

45D Is there a discount for children?
¿Hay descuentos   ai des·kwen·tos
para niños?   pa·ra nee·nyos

45E Is there a discount for students?
¿Hay descuentos   ai des·kwen·tos
para estudiantes?   pa·ra es·too·dyan·tes

Is there a discount for ...?	¿Hay descuentos para ...?	ai des·kwen·tos pa·ra ...
families	familias	fa·mee·lee·as
groups	grupos	groo·pos
pensioners	pensionistas	pen·syo·nees·tas

signs		
Abierto	a·byer·to	**Open**
Cerrado	the·ra·do	**Closed**

tours

46A **When's the next day trip?**
¿Cuándo es la próxima excursión de un día?
kwan·do es la *prok*·see·ma eks·koor·*syon* de oon *dee*·a

46B **When's the next tour?**
¿Cuándo es el próximo recorrido?
kwan·do es el *prok*·see·mo re·ko·*ree*·do

When's the next boat trip?
¿Cuándo es el próximo paseo en barca?
kwan·do es el *prok*·see·mo pa·*se*·o en *bar*·ka

Is equipment included?
¿Incluye equipo?
een·*kloo*·ye e·*kee*·po

46C **Is food included?**
¿Incluye comida?
een·*kloo*·ye ko·*mee*·da

46D **Is transport included?**
¿Incluye transporte?
een·*kloo*·ye trans·*por*·te

The guide will pay.
El guía va a pagar.
el *gee*·a va a pa·*gar*

The guide has paid.
El guía ha pagado.
el *gee*·a a pa·*ga*·do

46E **How long is the tour?**
¿Cuánto dura el recorrido?
kwan·to *doo*·ra el re·ko·*ree*·do

46F **What time should we be back?**
¿A qué hora debo regresar?
a ke *o*·ra *de*·bo reg·re·*sar*

Be back here at ...
Vuelva ...   vwel·va ...

I'm with them.
Voy con ellos.   voy kon e·lyos

I've lost my group.
He perdido a mi grupo.   e per·dee·do a mee groo·po

the royal lisp

According to a popular legend, one of the Spanish kings
– some say Felipe IV, others Ferdinand I – had a slight
speech impediment. Unable to pronounce the sound s
properly, he lisped his way through conversation. In an
epic act of flattery, the entire court, and eventually all of
Spain, mimicked his lisp. This story provides a colourful
explanation as to why Spaniards pronounce the word
cerveza (beer) as ther·ve·tha, while Latin Americans
continue to pronounce it ser·ve·sa.

It so happens, the story of the lisping king is a myth.
After all, only the letters c and z are pronounced th (when
they precede an i or an e), while the letter s remains the
same as in English. The reason for this selectiveness is due
to the way Spanish evolved from Latin and has nothing
to do with lisping monarchs at all. In fact, when you hear
someone say gracias, gra·thyas, they are no more lisping
as when you say 'thank you' in English.

I'm disabled.
Soy minusválido/a. m/f   soy mee·noos·va·lee·do/a

What services do you have for disabled people?
¿Qué servicios tienen   ke ser·vee·thyos tye·nen
para minusválidos/as? m/f   pa·ra mee·noos·va·lee·dos/as

Is there wheelchair access?
¿Hay acceso para la silla   ai ak·the·so pa·ra la see·lya
de ruedas?   de rwe·das

Speak more loudly, please.
Hable más alto, por favor.   ab·le mas al·to por fa·vor

I'm deaf.
Soy sordo/a. m/f   soy sor·do/a

Are guide dogs permitted?
¿Se permite la entrada a   se per·mee·te la en·tra·da a
los perros lazarillos?   los pe·ros la·tha·ree·lyos

Could you help me cross this street?
¿Me puede ayudar a   me pwe·de a·yoo·dar a
cruzar la calle?   kroo·thar la ka·lye

I need assistance.
Necesito asistencia.   ne·the·see·to a·sees·ten·thya

Braille library	*biblioteca* f	bee·blee·o·*te*·ka
	Braille	*brai*·lye
disabled person	*persona* f	per·*so*·na
	minusválida	mee·noos·*va*·lee·da
guide dog	*perro* m *lazarillo*	*pe*·ro la·tha·*ree*·lyo
wheelchair	*silla* f *de ruedas*	*see*·lya de *rwe*·das
ramp	*rampa* f	*ram*·pa
space	*espacio* m	es·*pa*·thyo

signs

Acceso para	ak·*the*·so *pa*·ra	**Wheelchair**
Sillas de	*thee*·lyas de	**Entrance**
Ruedas	ru·e·das	
Ascensor	as·then·*sor*	**Elevator/Lift**
Aseos para	a·*the*·os *pa*·ra	**Disabled**
Minusválidos	mee·nus·va·lee·dos	**Toilets**
Carros de	*ka*·ros de	**Disabled**
Minusválidos	mee·nus·va·lee·dos	**Trolleys**
		(in major
		supermarkets)

Is there a/an ...?	*¿Hay ...?*	ai ...
baby change room	*una sala en la que cambiarle el pañal al bebé*	oo·na sa·la en la ke kam·byar·le el pa·nyal al be·be
(English-speaking) babysitter	*canguro (de habla inglésa)*	kan·goo·ro (de ab·la een·gle·sa)
child-minding service	*servicio de cuidado de niños*	ser·vee·thyo de kwee·da·do de nee·nyos
children's menu	*menú infantil*	me·noo een·fan·teel
family discount	*descuento familiar*	des·kwen·to fa·mee·lyar
highchair	*trona*	tro·na

Do you mind if I breastfeed here?
¿Le molesta que dé de pecho aquí?
le mo·les·ta ke de de pe·cho a·kee

Are children allowed?
¿Se admiten niños?
se ad·mee·ten nee·nyos

Is this suitable for ... year old children?
¿Es apto para niños de ... años?
es ap·to pa·ra nee·nyos de ... a·nyos

I need a ...	Necesito un...	ne·the·*see*·to oon ...
baby seat	asiento m de seguridad para bebés	a·*syen*·to de se·goo·ree·*da* pa·ra be·*bes*
booster seat	asiento m de seguridad para niños	a·*syen*·to de se·goo·ree·*da* pa·ra *nee*·nyos
potty	orinal m de niños	o·ree·*nal* de *nee*·nyos
stroller	cochecito m	ko·che·*thee*·to
creche	guardería f	gwar·de·ree·a
park	parque m	*par*·ke
playground	parque m infantil	*par*·ke een·fan·*teel*
slide	tobogán m	to·bo·*gan*
swings	columpios m pl	ko·*loom*·pyos
theme park	parque m de atracciones	*par*·ke de a·trak·*thyo*·nes
toyshop	juguetería f	khoo·ge·te·*ree*·a

bless you!

In Spain, a polite way to respond to someone sneezing is by saying ¡Salud!, sa·*loo*, (health) or even ¡Jesús! khe·*soos* (Jesus).

basics

lo básico

2A	Yes.	*Sí.*	see
2B	No.	*No.*	no
2C	Please.	*Por favor.*	por fa·*vor*
2D	Thank you (very much).	*(Muchas) Gracias.*	(moo·chas) *gra*·thyas
2E	You're welcome.	*De nada.*	de *na*·da
2F	Excuse me.	*Perdón/*	per·*don/*
		Discúlpeme.	dees·*kool*·pe·me
2G	Sorry.	*Lo siento.*	lo *syen*·to

greetings

los saludos

In Spain people are often quite casual in their interactions. It's fine to use the following expressions in both formal and informal situations.

47A	Hello/Hi.	*Hola.*	o·la
	Good morning.	*Buenos días.*	*bwe*·nos *dee*·as
	Good afternoon. (until 8pm)	*Buenas tardes.*	*bwe*·nas *tar*·des
	Good evening.	*Buenas noches.*	*bwe*·nas *no*·ches
47B	See you later.	*Hasta luego.*	*as*·ta *lwe*·go
47C	Goodbye/Bye.	*Adiós.*	a·*dyos*
47D	How are you?	*¿Qué tal?*	ke tal
47E	Fine, thanks.	*Bien, gracias.*	byen *gra*·thyas

meeting people

89

48A What's your name?

¿Cómo se llama Usted? pol   ko·mo se *lya*·ma oos·*te*

48B What's your name?

¿Cómo te llamas? inf   ko·mo te *lya*·mas

48C My name is ...

Me llamo ...   me *lya*·mo ...

I'd like to introduce you to ...

     Quisiera presentarte a ... inf   kee·*sye*·ra pre·sen·*tar*·te a ...

     Quisiera presentarle a ... pol   kee·*sye*·ra pre·sen·*tar*·le a ...

48D I'm pleased to meet you.

Mucho gusto.   moo·cho *goos*·to

titles & addressing people

Señor and *Señora* tend to be used in everyday speech. *Doña*, although rare, is used as a mark of respect towards older women, while *Don* is sometimes used to address men. An elderly neighbour, for example, might be called *Doña Lola*.

49A Mr	*Señor*	se·*nyor*
49B Mrs/Ms	*Señora*	se·*nyo*·ra
49C Miss	*Señorita*	se·nyo·*ree*·ta
Sir	*Don*	don
Madam	*Doña*	*do*·nya

call a friend

You may hear friends calling each other *tío* m, *tee*·o, or *tía* f, *tee*·a, but these words are usually used when talking about others. They're a bit crass (a little like using 'sheila' to describe a girl in Australia). Guys use *colega*, ko·*le*·ga, and *hombre*, *om*·bre, to address their workmates or male friends. In the south, people call their friends *pixas*, *pee*·chas or *xoxos*, *cho*·chos.

making conversation

Spain is known for its distinct regional areas. A great conversation starter in Spain is to ask someone where they come from. Other good topics are sport, politics, history and travel.

Do you live here?
¿Vives aquí?   vee·ves a·kee

Where are you going?
¿Adónde vas?   a·don·de vas

What are you doing?
¿Qué haces?   ke a·thes

Are you waiting (for a city bus)?
¿Estás esperando   es·tas es·pe·ran·do
(un autobús)?   (oon ow·to·boos)

Can I have a light, please?
¿Tienes fuego, por favor?   tye·nes fwe·go por fa·vor

Do you like this?
¿Te gusta esto?   te goos·ta es·to

I love this.
Me encanta esto.   me en·kan·ta es·to

I'm here ...	Estoy aquí ...	es·toy a·kee ...
for a holiday	de vacaciones	de va·ka·thyo·nes
on business	en viaje de negocios	en vya·khe de ne·go·thyos
to study	estudiando	es·tu·dyan·do
with my family	con mi familia	kon mee fa·mee·lya
with my partner	con mi pareja m&f	kon mee pa·re·kha

---

listen for ...

es·tas a·kee de va·ka·thyo·nes
¿Estás aquí de   **Are you here on**
vacaciones?   **holiday?**

meeting people

91

What's this called?
¿Cómo se llama esto?   ko·mo se lya·ma es·to

What a gorgeous baby!
¡Qué niño/a más   ke nee·nyo/a mas
precioso/a! m/f   pre·thyo·so/a

Can I take a photo?
¿Puedo hacer una foto?   pwe·do a·ther oo·na fo·to

That's (beautiful), isn't it?
¿Es (precioso), no?   es (pre·thyo·so) no

How long are you here for?
¿Cuánto tiempo te vas   kwan·to tyem·po te vas
a quedar?   a ke·dar

I'm here for … weeks/days.
Estoy aquí por …   es·toy a·kee por …
semanas/días.   se·ma·nas/dee·as

50A This is my son.
Éste es mi hijo.   es·te es mee ee·kho

50B This is my daughter.
Ésta es mi hija.   es·ta es mee ee·kha

50C This is my friend.
Éste/a es mi amigo/a. m/f   es·te/a es mee a·mee·go/a

50D This is my husband.
Éste es mi marido.   es·te es mee ma·ree·do

50E This is my wife.
Ésta es mi esposa.   es·ta es mee es·po·sa

---

local talk

Drop a few casual expressions into your Spanish and see the difference it makes in interacting with locals:

Great!	¡Cojonudo!	ko·kho·noo·do
How cool!	¡Qué guay!	ke gwai
How interesting!	¡Qué interesante!	ke een·te·re·san·te
Really?	¿De veras?	de ve·ras
That's fantastic!	¡Estupendo!	es·too·pen·do
What's up?	¿Qué hay?	ke ai
You don't say!	¡No me digas!	no me dee·gas

nationalities

You'll find that many country names are similar to English. If you're not sure, try to say the name of your country with a Spanish flavour and it's more than likely you'll be understood.

51A Where are you from?
¿De dónde es Usted?   de *don*·de es oos·*te*

51B I'm from (Singapore).
Soy de (Singapur).   soy de (seen·ga·*poor*)

I'm from ...	Soy de ...	soy de ...
Australia	Australia	ow·*stra*·lya
Canada	Canadá	ka·na·*da*
Sweden	Suecia	swe·thya

For more countries, see the **dictionary**.

age

51C How old are you?
¿Cuántos años tiene?   *kwan*·tos *a*·nyos *tye*·ne

51D I'm (25) years old.
Tengo (veinticinco) años.   *ten*·go (veyn·tee·*theen*·ko) *a*·nyos

How old is your son/daughter?
¿Cuántos años tiene su hijo/a? m/f   *kwan*·tos *a*·nyos *tye*·ne soo ee·kho/a

He's/She's ... years old.
Tiene ... años.   *tye*·ne ... *a*·nyos

I'm younger than I look.
Soy más joven de lo que parezco.   soy mas *kho*·ven de lo ke pa·*reth*·ko

Too old!
¡Demasiado viejo!   de·ma·*sya*·do *vye*·kho

For your age, see **numbers**, page 29.

occupations & study

What do you do?
¿A qué te dedicas?
a ke te de·*dee*·kas

What are you studying?
¿Qué estudias?
ke es·*too*·dyas

I'm self-employed.
Soy trabajador/
soy tra·ba·kha·*dor*/
trabajadora
tra·ba·kha·*do*·ra
autónomo/a. m/f
ow·*to*·no·mo/a

I'm a/an ...	*Soy ...*	soy ...
architect	*arquitecto/a* m/f	ar·kee·*tek*·to/a
mechanic	*mecánico/a* m/f	me·*ka*·nee·ko/a
writer	*escritor/*	es·kree·*tor*/
	escritora m/f	es·kree·*to*·ra
I work in ...	*Trabajo en ...*	tra·*ba*·kho en ...
education	*enseñanza*	en·se·*nyan*·tha
hospitality	*hostelería*	os·te·le·*ree*·a
I'm ...	*Estoy ...*	es·*toy* ...
retired	*jubilado/a* m/f	khoo·bee·*la*·do/a
unemployed	*en el paro*	en el *pa*·ro
I'm studying ...	*Estudio ...*	es·*too*·dyo ...
business	*comercio*	ko·*mer*·thyo
languages	*idiomas*	ee·*dyo*·mas
science	*ciencias*	*thyen*·thyas

I'm studying at ...	Estudio en ...	es·too·dyo en ...
college	el instituto	el eens·tee·too·to
school	el colegio	el ko·le·khyo
trade school	el instituto de formación profesional	el eens·tee·too·to de for·ma·thyon pro·fe·syo·nal
university	la universidad	la oo·nee·ver·see·da

For more occupations and studies, see the **dictionary**.

family

la familia

Do you have a ...?	¿Tienes ...?	tye·nes ...
I (don't) have a ...	(No) Tengo ...	(no) ten·go ...
brother	un hermano	oon er·ma·no
family	una familia	oo·na fa·mee·lya
partner	una pareja m&f	oo·na pa·re·kha

Do you live with your ...?
¿Vives con tu ...?   vee·ves kon too ...

I live with my ...
Vivo con mi ...   vee·vo kon mee ...

This is my ...
Éste/a es mi ... m/f   es·te/a es mee ...

52A Are you married?
¿Está casado/a? m/f   es·ta ka·sa·do/a

52B I'm married.
Estoy casado. m   es·toy ka·sa·do

52C I'm married.
Estoy casada. f   es·toy ka·sa·da

52D I'm single.
Soy soltero. m   soy sol·te·ro

52E I'm single.
Soy soltera. f   soy sol·te·ra

I live with someone.
Vivo con alguien.   vee·vo kon al·gyen

children

When's your birthday?
¿Cuándo es tu cumpleaños?
kwan·do es too koom·ple·a·nyos

Do you go to school or kindergarten?
¿Vas al colegio o a la guardería?
vas al ko·le·khyo o a la gwar·de·ree·a

What grade are you in?
¿En qué curso estás?
en ke koor·so es·tas

Do you like …?   *¿Te gusta …?*   te goos·ta …
  school   *el colegio*   el ko·le·khyo
  sport   *el deporte*   el de·por·te
  your teacher   *tu profesor/ profesora* m/f   too pro·fe·sor/ pro·fe·so·ra

What do you do after school?
¿Qué haces después del colegio?
ke a·thes des·pwes del ko·le·khyo

Do you learn English?
¿Aprendes inglés?
a·pren·des een·gles

I come from very far away.
Vengo de muy lejos.
ven·go de mooy le·khos

Are you lost?
¿Estás perdido/a? m/f
es·tas per·dee·do/a

Show me how to play.
Dime cómo se juega.
dee·me ko·mo se khwe·ga

Well done!
¡Muy bien!
mooy byen

farewells

Tomorrow is my last day here.
*Mañana es mi último
día aquí.*
ma·*nya*·na es mee *ool*·tee·mo
dee·a a·*kee*

It's been great meeting you.
*Me ha encantado
conocerte.*
me a en·kan·*ta*·do
ko·no·*ther*·te

Keep in touch!
*¡Nos mantendremos en
contacto!*
nos man·ten·*dre*·mos en
kon·*tak*·to

I'll send you copies of the photos.
*Te enviaré copias de
las fotos.*
te en·vee·a·*re* ko·pyas de
las *fo*·tos

spanish grannies

Even idioms translate across languages. Here are a few
golden oldies:

It's like casting pearls before swine.
*Es como echar
margaritas a los
cerdos.*
es ko·mo e·*char*
ma·ga·*ree*·tas a los
ther·dos

(lit: it's like feeding daisies to the pigs)

It doesn't rain, it pours.
*Éramos pocos y
parió la abuela.*
e·*ra*·mos *po*·kos y
pa·ree·o la a·*bwe*·la

(lit: there were a few of us and then granny gave birth)

This is like watching grass grow.
*Es más largo que un
día sin pan.*
es mas *lar*·go ke oon
dee·a seen pan

(lit: it's longer than a day without bread)

If you ever visit (Scotland) you can …	Si algún día visitas (Escocia) …	see al·*goon* dee·a vee·*see*·tas (es·*ko*·thya) …
come and visit	ven a visitarnos	ven a vee·see·*tar*·nos
stay with me	te puedes quedar conmigo	te *pwe*·des ke·*dar* kon·*mee*·go

53A Here's my address.
Ésta es mi dirección. · es·ta es mee dee·rek·*thyon*

53B What's your address?
¿Cuál es su dirección de email? · kwal es soo dee·rek·*thyon* de ee·mayl

53C Here's my email address.
Ésta es mi dirección de email. · es·ta es mee dee·rek·*thyon* de ee·mayl

53D What's your email address?
¿Cuál es su dirección? · kwal es soo dee·rek·*thyon*

Here's my phone number.
Éste es mi número de teléfono. · es·te es mee *noo*·me·ro de te·*le*·fo·no

What's your phone number?
¿Cuál es su número de teléfono? · kwal es soo *noo*·me·ro de te·*le*·fo·no

For more on addresses, see **directions**, page 61.

brave new world

With Columbus' discovery of the New World in 1492 began an era of Spanish expansion in America, which is reflected in the language. *Patata*, *tomate*, *cacao* and *chocolate* are some of the words taken from the indigenous American languages. Bear in mind that Spanish has evolved differently and it's a good idea to take the *Latin American Spanish phrasebook* with you, rather than this one, if you're travelling there.

writing to people

If you want to impress your new friends by writing to them in Spanish when you get back home, here are some useful words and phrases:

Dear ...
Querido/a ... m/f

I'm sorry it's taken me so long to write.
Siento haber tardado tanto en escribir.

It was great to meet you.
Me encantó conocerte.

Thank you so much for your hospitality.
Muchísimas gracias por tu hospitalidad.

I miss you a lot.
Te echo mucho de menos.

I had a fantastic time in ...
Me lo pasé genial en ...

My favourite place was ...
Mi lugar preferido fue ...

I hope to visit ... again.
Espero visitar otra vez ...

Say 'hi' to ... (and ...) for me.
Saluda a ... (y a ...) de mi parte.

I'd love to see you again.
Tengo ganas de verte otra vez.

Write soon!
¡Escríbeme pronto!

With love,
Un beso,

Regards, ...
Saludos, ...

basque

Basque, or *Euskara*, is spoken at the western end of the Pyrenees and along the Bay of Biscay – from Bayonne in France to Bilbao in Spain, and then inland, almost to Pamplona.

No one quite knows its origin. Some have related it to the Sioux language, to Japanese, and even to the language of the Atlanteans. To complicate matters, dialects are also spoken in the Basque country, including Bizkaian, Gipuzkoan, High Navarrese, Aezkoan, Salazarese, Lapurdian, Low Navarrese and Suberoan. The most likely theory is that Basque is the lone survivor of a language family which once extended across Europe, and was wiped out by the languages of the Celts, the Germanic tribes and the Romans. It's amazing that Basque has survived so close to its original form.

Speaking Spanish in the Basque-speaking towns might be expected from a foreigner, but is not as warmly received as an attempt at one of the most ancient languages of Europe.

> greetings & civilities

Hi!	*Kaixo!*	kai·sho
Good morning.	*Egun on.*	e·goo *non*
Good afternoon/ evening.	*Arratsalde on.*	a·ra·chyal·de *on*
Goodbye.	*Agur.*	a·*goor*
Take care.	*Ondo ibili.*	on·do ee·*beel*·ee
How are you?	*Zer moduz?*	ser mo·*doos*
Fine, thank you.	*Ongi, eskerrik asko.*	on·gee e·*ske*·reek *as*·ko
Excuse me.	*Barkatu.*	bar·*ka*·too
Please.	*Mesedez.*	me·*se*·des
Thank you.	*Eskerrik asko.*	es·*ke*·reek *kas*·ko
You're welcome.	*Ez horregatik.*	es o·*re*·ga·teek

> language difficulties

Do you speak English?
Ingelesez ba al dakizu?
een·ge·le·ses ba al da·kee·soo

I know a little Basque.
Euskara apur bat badakit.
e·oos·ka·ra a·poor bat ba·da·keet

I don't understand.
Ez dut ulertzen.
es toot oo·ler·tzen

Could you speak in Castillian please?
Erdaraz egingo al didazu, mesedez?
er·da·ras e·geen·go al dee·da·soo me·se·des

How do you say that in Basque?
Nola esaten da hori euskaraz?
no·la e·sa·ten da o·ree e·oo·ska·ras

meeting people

101

catalan

Catalan is spoken by up to 10 million people in the north-east of Spain, a territory that comprises Catalonia, coastal Valencia and the Balearic Islands (Majorca, Minorca and Ibiza). Outside Spain, Catalan is also spoken in Andorra, the south of France and the town of Alguer in Sardinia.

Many famous creative types have been Catalan speakers: painters like Dalí, Miró and Picasso, architects like Gaudí and writers like Mercé Rodoreda.

Despite the fact that almost all Catalan speakers from Spain are bilingual, they appreciate it when visitors attempt to communicate, if even in the simplest way, in Catalan.

> greetings & civilities

Hello!	*Hola!*	o·la
Good morning.	*Bon dia.*	bon *dee*·a
Good afternoon.	*Bona tarda.*	bo·na *tar*·da
Good evening.	*Bon vespre.*	bon *bes*·pra
Goodbye.	*Adéu.*	a·*the*·oo
How are you?	*Com estàs?*	kom as·*tas*
(Very) Well.	*(Molt) Bé.*	(mol) be
Excuse me.	*Perdoni.*	par·*tho*·nee
Sorry.	*Ho sento.*	oo *sen*·to
Please.	*Sisplau.*	sees·*pla*·oo
Thank you.	*Gràcies.*	gra·*see*·as
Yes/No.	*Sí/No.*	see/no

> language difficulties

Do you speak English?
Parla anglès?   par·la an·*gles*

Could you speak in Castilian please?
Pot parlar castellà   pot par·*la* kas·ta·*lya*
sisplau?   sees·*pla*·oo

I (don't) understand.
(No) Ho entenc.   (no) oo an·teng

How do you say ...?
Com es diu ...?   kom az *dee*·oo

local talk

No problem!
Això rai!   a·*sho* ra·ee

What a laugh!
Quin tip de riure!   kin tip da ri·a·oo·ra

galician

Galician, or *Galego*, is an official language of the Autonomous Community of Galicias and is also widely understood in neighbouring regions Asturias and Castilla-Léon. It's very similar to Portuguese, as the two languages have roots in Vulgar Latin.

Galicians are likely to revert to Spanish when addressing a stranger, especially a foreigner, but making a small effort to communicate in Galician will always be welcomed.

> greetings & civilities

Hello!	*Ola!*	o·la
Good day.	*Bon dia.*	bon dee·a
Good afternoon/ evening.	*Boa tarde.*	bo·a tar·de
Goodbye.	*Adeus.*	a·de·oos
	Até logo.	a·te lo·go
Excuse me.	*Perdón.*	per·don
Please.	*Por favor.*	por fa·vor
Thank you.	*Grácias.*	gra·see·as
Many thanks.	*Moitas grácias.*	moy·tas gra·see·as
That's fine.	*De nada.*	de na·da
Yes/No.	*Si/Non.*	see/non

> language difficulties

Do you speak English?
Fala inglés? — fa·la een·gles

Could you speak in Castilian please?
Pode falar en español, por favor? — po·de fa·la en e·spa·nyol por fa·bor

I (don't) understand.
(Non) Entendo. — (non) en·ten·do

What's this called in Galician?
Como se chama iso en galego? — ko·mo se cha·ma ee·so en ga·le·go

common interests

los intereses en común

**What do you do in your
spare time?**

*¿Qué te gusta hacer en tu
tiempo libre?*

ke te *goos*·ta a·*ther* en too
tyem·po *lee*·bre

54A Do you like ...?

¿Te gusta ...?

te *goos*·ta ...

54B **I like ...**	*Me gusta ...*	me *goos*·ta ...
54C **I don't like ...**	*No me gusta ...*	no me *goos*·ta ...
cooking	*cocinar*	ko·thee·*nar*
dancing	*ir a bailar*	eer a bai·*lar*
films	*el cine*	el *thee*·ne
gardening	*jardinería*	kha·dee·ne·*ree*·a
hiking	*el excursio-nismo*	el eks·koor·syo·*nees*·mo
music	*la música*	la *moo*·see·ka
painting	*la pintura*	la peen·*too*·ra
photography	*la fotografía*	la fo·to·gra·*fee*·a
pub crawls	*ir de bar en bar*	eer de bar en bar
reading	*leer*	le·*er*
shopping	*ir de compras*	eer de *kom*·pras
socialising	*salir*	sa·*leer*
sport	*el deporte*	el de·*por*·te
travelling	*viajar*	vya·*khar*

For sporting activities, see **sport**, page 129.

music

Do you like to ...?	¿Te gusta ...?	te goos·ta ...
go to concerts	ir a conciertos	eer a kon·thyer·tos
listen to music	escuchar	es·koo·char
	música	moo·see·ka
play an	tocar algún	to·kar al·goon
instrument	instrumento	eens·troo·men·to
sing	cantar	kan·tar
What ... do you like?	¿Qué ... te gusta/gustan? sg/pl	ke ... te goos·ta/goos·tan
music	música sg	moo·see·ka
bands	grupos pl	groo·pos
classical music	música f clásica	moo·see·ka kla·see·ka
electronic music	música f electrónica	moo·see·ka e·lek·tro·nee·ka
jazz	jazz m	khath
metal	metal m	me·tal
pop	música f pop	moo·see·ka pop
punk	música f punk	moo·see·ka poonk
rock	música f rock	moo·see·ka rok
R&B	rhythm and blues m	ree·dem and bloos
traditional music	música f popular	moo·see·ka po·pu·lar
world music	música f étnica	moo·see·ka et·nee·ka

art

When's the gallery open?
  ¿A qué hora abre la galería?   a ke o·ra a·bre la ga·le·ree·a

What's in the collection?
  ¿Qué hay en la colección?   ke ai en la ko·lek·thyon

What kind of art are you interested in?
¿Qué tipo de arte te interesa?
ke *tee*·po de *ar*·te te een·te·*re*·sa

I'm interested in ...
Me interesa/ interesan ... sg/pl
me een·te·*re*·sa/ een·te·*re*·san ...

What do you think of ...?
¿Qué piensas de ...?
ke *pyen*·sas de ...

It's a/an ... exhibition.
Es una exposición de ...
es *oo*·na eks·po·see·*thyon* de ...

I like the works of ...
Me gustan las obras de ...
me *goos*·tan las *o*·bras de ...

It reminds me of ...
Me recuerda a ...
me re·*kwer*·da a ...

... art	*arte* m ...	*ar*·te ...
graphic	*gráfico*	*gra*·fee·ko
impressionist	*impresionista*	eem·pre·syo·*nees*·ta
modernist	*modernista*	mo·der·*nees*·ta
Renaissance	*renacentista*	re·na·then·*tees*·ta

cinema & theatre

el cine & el teatro

I feel like going to (a comedy).
 Tengo ganas de ir
 a (una comedia).
 ten·go ga·nas de eer
 a (oo·na ko·me·dya)

What's showing at the cinema (tonight)?
 ¿Qué película dan en el
 cine (esta noche)?
 ke pe·lee·koo·la dan en el
 thee·ne (es·ta no·che)

Is it in English?
 ¿Es en inglés?
 es en een·gles

Does it have (English) subtitles?
 ¿Tiene subtítulos
 (en inglés)?
 tye·ne soob·tee·too·los
 (en een·gles)

I want to sell this ticket.
 Quiero vender esta entrada.
 kye·ro ven·der es·ta en·tra·da

Are those seats taken?
 ¿Están ocupados estos
 asientos?
 es·tan o·koo·pa·dos es·tos
 a·syen·tos

Have you seen ...?
 ¿Has visto ...?
 as vees·to ...

Who's in it?
 ¿Quién actúa?
 kyen ak·too·a

It stars ...
 Actúa ...
 ak·too·a ...

Did you like the ...?	¿Te gustó el ...?	te goos·to el ...
ballet	ballet	ba·le
film	cine	thee·ne
play	teatro	te·a·tro

SOCIAL

I (don't) like ...		
	(No) me gusta/gustan ... sg/pl	(no) me *goos*·ta/*goos*·tan ...

I thought it was ...	*Pienso que fue ...*	*pyen*·so ke fwe ...
excellent	*excelente*	eks·the·*len*·te
long	*largo*	*lar*·go
OK	*regular*	re·goo·*lar*

animated films	*películas* f pl *de*	pe·*lee*·koo·las de
	dibujos	dee·*boo*·khos
	animados	a·nee·*ma*·dos
comedy	*comedia* f	ko·*me*·dya
documentary	*documentales* m pl	do·koo·men·*ta*·les
drama	*drama* m	*dra*·ma
film noir	*cine* m *negro*	*thee*·ne *ne*·gro
(Spanish) cinema	*cine* m *(español)*	*thee*·ne (es·pa·*nyol*)
horror movies	*cine* m *de terror*	*thee*·ne de te·*ror*
sci-fi	*cine* m *de*	*thee*·ne de
	ciencia ficción	*thyen*·thya feek·*thyon*
short films	*cortos* m pl	*kor*·tos
thrillers	*cine* m *de*	*thee*·ne de
	suspenso	soos·*pen*·so

reading

la lectura

What kind of books do you read?
¿Qué tipo de libros lees?   ke *tee*·po de *lee*·bros *le*·es

Which (Spanish) author do you recommend?
¿Qué autor (español) recomiendas?   ke ow·*tor* (es·pa·*nyol*) re·ko·*myen*·das

interests

Have you read …?
¿Has leído …? as le·*ee*·do …

On this trip I'm reading …
En este viaje estoy
leyendo … en *es*·te *vya*·khe es·*toy*
le·*yen*·do …

I'd recommend …
Recomiendo a … re·ko·*myen*·do a …

Where can I exchange books?
¿Dónde puedo cambiar
libros? don·de *pwe*·do kam·*byar*
lee·bros

For more on books, see **shopping**, page 68.

For more on books, see **shopping**, page 68.

dog in the manger

Proverbs are big in Spain. The Marques de Santilllana compiled a national collection in the second half of the 15th century, and one of the characters in *Don Qixote*, Sancho Panza, speaks almost entirely in proverbs.

The author Cervantes described these popular sayings as 'short sentences based on long experience', or is that long-windedness?

ser como el perro del hortelano, que ni come las
berzas, ni las deja comer al amo

(lit: to be like the market gardener's dog who doesn't eat the cabbages and won't let his master eat them either)

feelings

los sentimientos

55A	I'm cold.	Tengo frío.	ten·go free·o
55B	I'm not cold.	No tengo frío.	no ten·go free·o
55C	Are you cold?	¿Tienes frío?	tye·nes free·o
56A	I'm hot.	Tengo calor.	ten·go ka·lor
56B	I'm not hot.	No tengo calor.	no ten·go ka·lor
56C	Are you hot?	¿Tienes calor?	tye·nes ka·lor
57A	I'm hungry.	Tengo hambre.	ten·go am·bre
57B	I'm not hungry.	No tengo hambre.	no ten·go am·bre
57C	Are you hungry?	¿Tienes hambre?	tye·nes am·bre
58A	I'm thirsty.	Tengo sed.	ten·go se
58B	I'm not thirsty.	No tengo sed.	no ten·go se
58C	Are you thirsty?	¿Tienes sed?	tye·nes se
59A	I'm tired.	Estoy cansado. m	es·toy kan·sa·do
59B	I'm tired.	Estoy cansada. f	es·toy kan·sa·da
59C	I'm not tired.	No estoy cansado. m	no es·toy kan·sa·do
59D	I'm not tired.	No estoy cansada. f	no es·toy kan·sa·da
59E	Are you tired?	¿Estás cansado?	es·tas kan·sa·do
60A	I'm OK.	Estoy bien.	es·toy byen
60B	I'm not OK.	No estoy bien.	no es·toy byen
60C	Are you OK?	¿Estás bien?	es·tas byen

For health-related feelings, see **health**, page 182.

opinions

las opiniones

Did you like it?
   ¿Te gustó?   te goos·to

What did you think of it?
   ¿Qué pensaste de eso?   ke pen·sas·te de e·so

I thought it was ...	*Pienso que fue ...*	pyen·so ke fwe ...
It's ...	*Es ...*	es ...
beautiful	*bonito/a* m/f	bo·*nee*·to/a
bizarre	*raro/a* m/f	*ra*·ro/a
crap	*un coñazo/a* m/f	oon ko·*nya*·tho/a
crazy	*loco/a* m/f	*lo*·ko/a
entertaining	*entretenido/a* m/f	en·tre·te·*nee*·do/a
excellent	*fantástico/a* m/f	fan·*tas*·tee·ko/a
full on	*heavy*	*khe*·vee
horrible	*horrible*	o·*ree*·ble

by degrees

a little	*un poco*	oon *po*·ko
I'm a little sad.	*Estoy un poco triste.*	es·*toy* oon *po*·ko *trees*·te
quite	*bastante*	bas·*tan*·te
I'm quite disappointed.	*Estoy bastante decepcionado/a.* m/f	es·*toy* bas·*tan*·te de·thep·thyo·*na*·do/a
very	*muy*	mooy
I feel very lucky.	*Me siento muy afortunado/a.* m/f	me *syen*·to mooy a·for·too·*na*·do/a

politics & social issues

la política & los temas sociales

Who do you vote for?
¿A quién votas?   a kyen *vo*·tas

I support the ... party.
Apoyo al partido ...   a·*po*·yo al par·*tee*·do ...

Did you hear about ...?
¿Has oído que ...? as o·ee·do ke ...

Are you in favour of ...?
¿Estás a favor de ...? es·tas a fa·vor de ...

How do people feel about ...?
¿Cómo se siente la ko·mo se syen·te la
gente de ...? khen·te de ...

drugs	*drogas* f pl	*dro*·gas
the economy	*economía* f	e·ko·no·*mee*·a
immigration	*inmigración* f	een·mee·gra·*thyon*
racism	*racismo* m	ra·*thees*·mo
unemployment	*desempleo* m	de·sem·*ple*·o

octopus in the garage

Keeping the attention of your audience can be a challenge in a foreign language. Try emphasising your opinion with some of these colourful expressions:

He's/She's the best.
Es un trozo de pan. es oon *tro*·tho de pan
(lit: he's/she's a piece of bread)

**You can't make a silk purse
out of a sow's ear.**
Aunque el mono se a·*oon*·ke el *mo*·no se
vista de seda, *vees*·ta de *se*·da
mono se queda. *mo*·no se *ke*·da
(lit: though the monkey may wear silk, it's still a monkey)

He's/She's a fish out of water.
Se encuentra se en·koo·*en*·tra
como un pulpo en *ko*·mo oon *pool*·po en
un garaje. oon ga·*ra*·khe
(lit: he's/she's like an octopus in a garage)

the environment

el medio ambiente

Is there an environmental problem here?

¿Aquí hay un problema   a·*kee* ai oon pro·*ble*·ma
con el medio ambiente?   kon el *me*·dyo am·*byen*·te

Is this (forest) protected?

¿Está este (bosque)   es·*ta* es·te (*bos*·ke)
protegido?   pro·te·*khee*·do

biodegradable	biodegradable	bee·o·de·gra·*da*·ble
deforestation	deforestación f	de·fo·res·ta·*thyon*
hunting	caza f	*ka*·tha
oil spill	fuga f de petróleo	*foo*·ga de pe·*tro*·le·o
pollution	contaminación f	kon·ta·mee·na·*thyon*

perhaps, perhaps, perhaps

Don't feel you're limited to a plain 'yes' or 'no'.

Maybe.	Quizás.	kee·*thas*
OK.	Vale.	*va*·le
No way!	¡De ningún modo!	de neen·*goon mo*·do
It's/I'm OK.	Está/Estoy bien.	es·*ta*/es·*toy* byen
Just a minute.	Un momento.	oon mo·*men*·to
No problem.	Sin problema.	seen pro·*ble*·ma
Of course!	¡Claro (que sí)!	*kla*·ro (ke see)
Sure.	Claro.	*kla*·ro
You bet!	¡Ya lo creo!	ya lo *kre*·o
Just joking.	Era broma.	e·ra *bro*·ma

where to go

adónde ir

What's there to do in the evenings?
¿Qué se puede hacer
por las noches?
ke se *pwe*·de a·*ther*
por las *no*·ches

What's on ...?	*¿Qué hay ...?*	ke ai ...
locally	*en la zona*	en la *tho*·na
this weekend	*este fin de semana*	*es*·te feen de se·*ma*·na
today	*hoy*	oy
tonight	*esta noche*	*es*·ta *no*·che

61A Where can I find ...?
¿Dónde hay ...?   *don*·de ai ...

61B Where can I find gay venues?
¿Dónde hay lugares gay?   *don*·de ai loo·*ga*·res gai

61C Where can I find pubs?
¿Dónde hay pubs?   *don*·de ai poobs

Where can I find restaurants?
¿Dónde hay restaurantes?   *don*·de ai res·tow·*ran*·tes

Is there a local ...	*¿Hay una guía ...*	ai oo·na gee·a ...
guide?	*de la zona?*	de la *tho*·na
entertainment	*del ocio*	del *o*·thyo
film	*de cine*	de *thee*·ne
gay	*de lugares gay*	de loo·*ga*·res gai
music	*de música*	de *moo*·see·ka

read my lips

Foreign movies are usually dubbed into Spanish, but in bigger cities you'll find some films have Spanish subtitles. Look for *v.o.* (*version original*, 'original version') or *v.o.s.* (*version original subtitulada*, 'original version with subtitles') in listings.

62A I feel like going to a concert.
Tengo ganas de ir   ten·go ga·nas de eer
a un concierto.   a oon kon·*thyer*·to

62B I feel like going to the movies.
Tengo ganas de ir al cine.   ten·go ga·nas de eer al *thee*·ne

62C I feel like going to a party.
Tengo ganas de ir   ten·go ga·nas de eer
a una fiesta.   a oo·na fyes·ta

62D I feel like going to the theatre.
Tengo ganas de ir al teatro.   ten·go ga·nas de eer al te·a·tro

I feel like going to a/the …	*Tengo ganas de ir …*	ten·go ga·nas de eer …
ballet	*al ballet*	al ba·*le*
(karaoke) bar	*a un bar (de karaoke)*	a oon bar (de ka·ra·o·ke)
cafe	*a un café*	a oon ka·fe
nightclub	*a una discoteca*	a oo·na dees·ko·te·ka
restaurant	*a un restaurante*	a oon res·tow·ran·te

invitations

las invitaciones

What are you doing this evening?
¿Qué haces esta noche?   ke a·thes es·ta no·che

What are you up to (right now)?
¿Qué haces (ahora)?   ke a·thes (a·o·ra)

Would you like to go for a …?	*¿Quieres que vayamos a …?*	kye·res ke va·ya·mos a …
coffee	*tomar un café*	to·mar oon ka·fe
drink	*tomar algo*	to·mar al·go
meal	*comer*	ko·mer
walk	*pasear*	pa·se·ar

I feel like going …	*Me apetece ir a …*	me a·pe·te·the eer a …
dancing	*bailar*	bai·lar
out somewhere	*salir*	sa·leer

My round.
Invito yo.
een·*vee*·to yo

Do you know a good restaurant?
¿Conoces algún buen restaurante?
ko·*no*·thes al·*goon* bwen res·tow·*ran*·te

Do you want to come to the (...) concert with me?
¿Quieres venir conmigo al concierto (de ...)?
kye·res ve·*neer* kon·*mee*·go al kon·*thyer*·to (de ...)

We're having a party.
Vamos a dar una fiesta.
va·mos a dar *oo*·na *fyes*·ta

Do you want to come?
¿Por qué no vienes?
por ke no *vye*·nes

Are you ready?
¿Estás listo/a? m/f
es·*tas lees*·to/a

are you my type?

If jobs, age and nationality don't really cut it when trying to describe yourself (and others), see if these words help:

activist	*activista* m&f	ak·tee·*vees*·ta
alcoholic	*alcohólico/a* m/f	al·ko·o·lee·ko/a
artistic	*artísticó/a* m/f	ar·*tees*·tee·ko/a
creative	*creador/ creadora* m/f	kre·a·*dor/* kre·a·*do*·ra
daggy/dorky	*hortera* m&f	or·*te*·ra
goth	*siniestra* m&f	see·*nye*·stra
heavy	*heavy* m&f	*khe*·vee
intellectual	*intelectual* m&f	een·te·*lek*·twal
progressive	*progre* m&f	*pro*·gre
sporty	*deportivo/a* m/f	de·por·*tee*·vo/a
trendy/stylish	*moderno/a* m/f	mo·*der*·no/a
workaholic	*adícto/a* m/f al trabajo	a·*deek*·to/a al tra·*ba*·kho
yuppie	*yupi* m&f	*yoo*·pee

responding to invitations

Sure!
¡Por supuesto!   por soo·*pwes*·to

Yes, I'd love to.
Me encantaría.   me en·kan·ta·*ree*·a

Where will we go?
¿A dónde vamos?   a *don*·de va·*mos*

That's very kind of you.
Es muy amable por   es mooy a·*ma*·ble por
tu parte.   *too par*·te

No, I'm afraid I can't.
Lo siento pero no puedo.   lo *syen*·to *pe*·ro no *pwe*·do

Sorry, I can't sing/dance.
Lo siento, no sé cantar/bailar.   lo *syen*·to no se kan·*tar*/bai·*lar*

What about tomorrow?
¿Qué tal mañana?   ke tal ma·*nya*·na

arranging to meet

What time shall we meet?
¿A qué hora quedamos?   a ke o·ra ke·*da*·mos

Where will we meet?
¿Dónde quedamos?   *don*·de ke·*da*·mos

Let's meet ...   *Quedamos ...*   ke·*da*·mos ...
   at (eight) o'clock   *a (las ocho)*   a (las *o*·cho)
   at the (entrance)   *en (la entrada)*   en (la en·*tra*·da)

I'll pick you up.
Paso a recogerte. — pa·so a re·ko·kher·te

I'll be coming later.
Iré más tarde. — ee·re mas tar·de

Where will you be?
¿Dónde estarás? — don·de es·ta·ras

If I'm not there by (nine), don't wait for me.
Si no estoy a (las nueve), — see no es·toy a (las nwe·ve)
no me esperes/esperéis. sg/pl — no me es·pe·res/es·pe·reys

OK!
¡Hecho! — e·cho

I'll see you then.
Nos vemos. — nos ve·mos

See you later/tomorrow.
Hasta luego/mañana. — as·ta lwe·go/ma·nya·na

I'm looking forward to it.
*Tengo muchas ganas
de ir.* — ten·go moo·chas ga·nas
de eer

Sorry I'm late.
Siento llegar tarde. — syen·to lye·gar tar·de

Never mind.
No pasa nada. — no pa·sa na·da

attention-getter

Hey!	*¡Eh, tú!*	e too
Look!	*¡Mira!*	mee·ra
Listen (to this)!	*¡Escucha (esto)!*	es·koo·cha (es·to)

nightclubs & bars

Where can we go (salsa) dancing?
*¿Dónde podemos ir a
bailar (la salsa)?*
don·de po·de·mos eer a
bai·lar (la sal·sa)

How do I get there?
¿Cómo se llega?
ko·mo se lye·ga

What type of music do you like?
*¿Qué tipo de música
prefieres?*
ke tee·po de moo·see·ka
pre·fye·res

I really like (reggae).
Me encanta (el reggae).
me en·kan·ta (el re·gai)

Come on!
¡Vamos!
va·mos

This place is great!
¡Este lugar me encanta!
es·te loo·gar me en·kan·ta

drugs

las drogas

I don't take drugs.
*No consumo ningún
tipo de drogas.*
no kon·soo·mo neen·goon
tee·po de dro·gas

I take ... occasionally.
Tomo ... de vez en cuando.
to·mo ... de veth en kwan·do

Do you want to have a smoke?
¿Nos fumamos un porro?
nos foo·ma·mos oon po·ro

I'm high.
Estoy colocado/a. m/f
es·toy ko·lo·ka·do/a

For more on bars, drinks and partying, see **eating out**, page 150.

asking someone out

saliendo con alguien

Don't be surprised if invitations come late in the day. Social life in Spain continues well into the night: sometimes people begin to eat dinner at 10pm and many clubs open at midnight.

Would you like to do something (tonight)?
*¿Quieres hacer algo
(esta noche)?*
kye·res a·*ther* al·go
(es·ta *no*·che)

Yes, I'd love to.
Me encantaría.
me en·kan·ta·*ree*·a

I'm busy.
Estoy ocupado/a. m/f
es·*toy* o·koo·*pa*·do/a

---

local talk

He's/She's hot.
*Él/Ella es
cachondo/a.* m/f
el/e·lya es
ka·*chon*·do/a

What a babe.
Vaya hembra.
va·ya em·bra

He/She gets around.
*Se va a la cama con
cualquiera.*
se va a la ka·ma kon
kwal·kye·ra

---

pick-up lines

frases para ligar

Would you like a drink?
¿Te apetece una copa?
te a·pe·te·the oo·na ko·pa

Do you have a light?
¿Tienes fuego?
tye·nes fwe·go

You're great.

Eres estupendo/a. m/f
e·res es·too·*pen*·do/a

You mustn't come here much, because I would have noticed you sooner.

No debes venir mucho
por aquí porque me habría
fijado en ti antes.

no *de*·bes ve·*neer* moo·cho
por a·*kee por*·ke me a·*bree*·a
fee·*kha*·do en tee *an*·tes

I've been watching you for a while, and you're (the best-looking girl) here.

Hace rato que te observo y
eres (la chica mas guapa)
aqui.

a·the *ra*·to ke te ob·*ser*·vo ee
e·res (la *chee*·ka mas *gwa*·pa)
a·*kee*

rejections

I'm here with my boyfriend/girlfriend.

Estoy aquí con mi
novio/a. m/f

es·*toy* a·*kee* kon mee
no·vyo/a

Excuse me, I have to go now.

Lo siento, pero me tengo
que ir.

lo *syen*·to *pe*·ro me *ten*·go
ke eer

Leave me alone!

Déjame en paz.
de·*kha*·me en path

Hey, I'm not interested in talking to you.

Mira tío/a, es que no me
interesa hablar
contigo. m/f

mee·ra *tee*·o/a es ke no me
een·te·*re*·sa ab·*lar*
kon·*tee*·go

Listen, why don't you go and get fucked.

Oye rico/a, por qué no
te vas a tomar por
el culo. m/f

o·ye *ree*·ko/a por ke no
te vas a to·*mar* por
el *koo*·lo

getting closer

Can I kiss you?
¿Te puedo besar?   te *pwe*·do be·*sar*

Do you want to come inside for a drink?
¿Quieres entrar a   *kye*·res en·*trar* a
tomar algo?   to·*mar* al·go

Do you want a massage?
¿Quieres un masaje?   *kye*·res oon ma·*sa*·khe

Let's go to bed!
¡Vámonos a la cama!   va·*mo*·nos a la *ka*·ma

sex

Kiss me!
¡Dame un beso!   *da*·me oon *be*·so

I want you.
Te deseo.   te de·*se*·o

I want to make love to you.
  Quiero hacerte el amor.   kye·ro a·ther·te el a·mor

Do you have a condom?
  ¿Tienes un condón?   tye·nes oon kon·don

Touch me here.
  Tócame aquí.   to·ka·me a·kee

Do you like this?
  ¿Esto te gusta?   es·to te goos·ta

I (don't) like that.
  Eso (no) me gusta.   e·so (no) me goos·ta

I think we should stop now.
  Pienso que deberíamos   pyen·so ke de·be·ree·a·mos
  parar.   pa·rar

Oh yeah!
  ¡Así!   a·see

faster	*rápido*	ra·pee·do
harder	*fuerte*	fwer·te
slower	*despacio*	des·pa·thyo
softer	*suave*	swa·ve

I can't get it up, sorry.
  Lo siento, no puedo   lo syen·to no pwe·do
  levantarla.   le·van·tar·la

Don't worry, I'll do it myself.
  No te preocupes, lo hago yo.   no te pre·o·koo·pes lo a·go yo

endearments

heart	*corazon* m&f	ko·ro·thon
little love	*amorcito/a* m/f	a·mor·thee·to/a
my life	*mi vida* m&f	mee vee·da
my love	*mi amor* m&f	mee a·mor
sky	*cielo* m&f	thye·lo
treasure	*tesoro* m&f	te·so·ro

SOCIAL

124

That was amazing.
  Eso fue increíble.   e·so fwe een·kre·ee·ble

Are you sleepy?
  ¿Tienes sueño?   tye·nes swe·nyo

Can I stay over?
  ¿Puedo quedarme?   pwe·do ke·dar·me

I love you.
  Te quiero.   te kye·ro

I think we're good together.
  Creo que estamos   kre·o ke es·ta·mos
  muy bien juntos.   mooy byen khoon·tos

problems

Are you seeing someone else?
  ¿Me estás engañando   me es·tas en·ga·nyan·do
  con alguien?   kon al·gyen

I never want to see you again.
  No quiero volver a verte.   no kye·ro vol·ver a ver·te

He's just a friend.
  Es un amigo   es oon a·mee·go
  nada más.   na·da mas

She's just a friend.
  Es una amiga   es oo·na a·mee·ga
  nada más.   na·da mas

I want to stay friends.

Me gustaría que quedáramos como amigos.

me goos·ta·*ree*·a ke ke·*da*·ra·mos *ko*·mo a·*mee*·gos

We'll work it out.

Lo resolveremos.

lo re·sol·ve·*re*·mos

passionate language

That's not true!	¡Eso no es verdad!	e·so no es ver·da
In your dreams!	¡En sueños!	en swe·nyos
Come off it!	¡No me jodas!	no me kho·das
Damn!	¡Hostia!	os·tya
Fuck!	¡Joder!	kho·der
Shit!	¡Mierda!	myer·da

SOCIAL

126

beliefs & cultural differences
creencias & diferencias culturales

religion

la religión

What's your religion?
¿Cuál es tu religión?   kwal es too re·lee·*khyon*

Can I pray here?
¿Puedo rezar aquí?   pwe·do re·*thar* a·*kee*

I'm (not) ...	(No) Soy ...	(no) soy ...
agnostic	*agnóstico/a* m/f	ag·*nos*·tee·ko/a
Buddhist	*budista*	boo·*dees*·ta
Catholic	*católico/a* m/f	ka·*to*·lee·ko/a
Christian	*cristiano/a* m/f	krees·*tya*·no/a
Hindu	*hindú*	een·*doo*
Jewish	*judío/a* m/f	khoo·*dee*·o/a
Muslim	*musulmán/*	moo·sool·*man/*
	musulmána m/f	moo·sool·*ma*·na
practising	*practicante*	prak·tee·*kan*·te
religious	*religioso/a* m/f	re·lee·*khyo*·so/a

I (don't) believe in ...	(No) Creo en ...	(no) kre·o en ...
God	*Dios*	dyos
destiny/fate	*el destino*	el des·*tee*·no

cultural differences

las diferencias culturales

Is this a local or national custom?
¿Esto es una costumbre   es·to es oo·na kos·*toom*·bre
local o nacional?   lo·*kal* o na·thyo·*nal*

I'm not used to this.
No estoy acostumbrado/a   no es·*toy* a·kos·toom·*bra*·do/a
a esto. m/f   a *es*·to

127

This is (very) ...	Esto es (muy) ...	es·to es (mooy) ...
fun	divertido	dee·ver·tee·do
interesting	interesante	een·te·re·san·te
different	diferente	dee·fe·ren·te

I'm sorry, it's against my beliefs.

Lo siento, eso va en contra de mis creencias.

lo *syen*·to *e*·so va en *kon*·tra de mees kre·*en*·thyas

I don't mind watching, but I'd rather not join in.

No me importa mirar, pero prefiero no participar.

no me eem·*por*·ta mee·*rar* pe·ro pre·*fye*·ro no par·tee·thee·*par*

I'll try it.

Lo probaré.

lo pro·ba·*re*

Sorry, I didn't mean to do something wrong.

Lo siento, lo hice sin querer.

lo *syen*·to lo ee·the seen ke·*rer*

sporting interests

los intereses deportivos

What sport do you play?
¿Qué deporte practicas?   ke de·*por*·te prak·*tee*·kas

What sport do you follow?
¿A qué deporte eres   a ke de·*por*·te e·res
aficionado/a? m/f   a·fee·thyo·*na*·do/a

I play/do ...
Practico ...   prak·*tee*·ko ...

I follow ...
Soy aficionado/a al ... m/f   soy a·fee·thyo·*na*·do/a al ...

basketball	*baloncesto* m	ba·lon·*thes*·to
cycling	*ciclismo* m	thee·*klees*·mo
football (soccer)	*fútbol* m	*foot*·bol
tennis	*tenis* m	*te*·nis
volleyball	*voleibol* m	bo·*lei*·bol

Do you like sport?
¿Te gustan los deportes?   te *goos*·tan los de·*por*·tes

Yes, very much.
Me encantan.   me en·*kan*·tan

Not really.
En realidad, no mucho.   en re·a·lee·*da* no *moo*·cho

I like watching it.
Me gusta mirar.   me *goos*·ta mee·*rar*

Who's your favourite sportsperson?

¿Quién es tu deportista
favorito/a? m/f

kyen es too de·por·tees·ta
fa·vo·ree·to/a

What's your favourite team?

¿Cuál es tu equipo
favorito?

kwal es too e·kee·po
fa·vo·ree·to

going to a game

ir al partido

Would you like to go to a (basketball) game?

¿Te gustaría ir a un
partido de (baloncesto)?

te goos·ta·ree·a eer a oon
par·tee·do de (ba·lon·thes·to)

Who are you supporting?

¿Con qué equipo vas?

kon ke e·kee·po vas

scoring

What's the score?	¿Cómo van?	ko·mo van
draw/even	empatados	em·pa·ta·dos
love (zero)	cero	the·ro
match-point	match point	mach poyn
nil (zero)	cero	the·ro

How much time is left?

¿Cuánto tiempo queda de
partido?

kwan·to tyem·po ke·da de
par·tee·do

Who's ...?	¿Quién ...?	kyen ...
playing	juega	khwe·ga
winning	va ganando	va ga·nan·do

That was a ... game!	¡Ese partido fue ...!	e·se par·tee·do fwe ...
boring	aburrido	a·boo·ree·do
great	cojonudo	ko·kho·noo·do

playing sport

Do you want to play?
¿Quieres jugar? — kye·res khoo·gar

Can I join in?
¿Puedo jugar? — pwe·do khoo·gar

Yeah, that'd be great.
Sí, me encantaría. — see me en·kan·ta·ree·a

Not at the moment, thanks.
Ahora mismo no, gracias. — a·o·ra mees·mo no gra·thyas

I have an injury.
Tengo una lesión. — ten·go oo·na le·syon

Where's the best place to run around here?
¿Cuál es el mejor sitio para hacer footing por aquí cerca? — kwal es el me·khor see·tyo pa·ra a·ther foo·teen por a·kee ther·ka

Do I have to be a member to attend?
¿Hay que ser socio/a para entrar? m/f — ai ke ser so·thyo/a pa·ra en·trar

Is there a women-only pool?
¿Hay alguna piscina sólo para mujeres? — ai al·goo·na pees·thee·na so·lo pa·ra moo·khe·res

Where are the change rooms?
¿Dónde están los vestuarios? — don·de es·tan los ves·twa·ryos

Can I have a locker?
¿Puedo usar una taquilla? — pwe·do oo·sar oo·na ta·kee·lya

Where's the nearest ...?	*¿Dónde está ... más cercano/a?* m/f	don·de es·ta ... mas ther·ka·no/a
gym	*el gimnasio* m	el kheem·na·syo
swimming pool	*la piscina* f	la pees·thee·na
tennis court	*la pista* f *de tenis*	la pees·ta de te·nees

What's the charge per ...?	¿Cúanto cobran por ...?	kwan·to ko·bran por ...
day	día	dee·a
game	partida	par·tee·da
hour	hora	o·ra
visit	visita	vee·see·ta
Can I hire a ...?	¿Es posible alquilar una ...?	es po·see·ble al·kee·lar oo·na ...
ball	pelota	pe·lo·ta
bicycle	bicicleta	bee·thee·kle·ta
court	cancha	kan·cha
racquet	raqueta	ra·ke·ta

fair play?

I disagree!	No estoy de acuerdo!	no es·toy de a·kwer·do
Yeah, sure!	Sí hombre!	see om·bre
Yes, but ...	Sí pero ...	see pe·ro ...
Whatever.	Lo que sea.	lo ke se·a

diving

el buceo

I'd like to (go) ...	Me gustaría ...	me goos·ta·ree·a ...
explore wrecks	explorar naufragios	eks·plo·rar now·fra·khyos
learn to dive	aprender a bucear	a·pren·der a boo·the·ar
scuba diving	hacer submarinismo	a·ther soob·ma·ree·nees·mo
snorkelling	bucear con tubo	boo·the·ar kon too·bo

Where are some good diving sites?

¿Dónde hay buenos lugares don·de ai bwe·nos loo·ga·res
para bucear? pa·ra boo·the·*ar*

Are there jellyfish?

¿Hay medusas? ai me·*doo*·sas

Where can we hire ...?

¿Dónde se puede alquilar ...? don·de se pwe·de al·kee·*lar* ...

diving course	*curso* m *de buceo*	*koor*·so de boo·*the*·o
diving equipment	*equipo* m *de buceo*	e·*kee*·po de boo·*the*·o
flippers	*aletas* f pl	a·*le*·tas
mask	*gafas* f pl	*ga*·fas
wetsuits	*trajes* m pl	*tra*·khes
	isotérmicos	ee·so·*ter*·mee·kos

extreme sports

los deportes extremos

Are you sure this is safe?

¿De verdad que esto es de ver·*da* ke *es*·to es
seguro? se·*goo*·ro

Is the equipment secure?

¿Está seguro el equipo? es·*ta* se·goo·ro el e·*kee*·po

This is insane!

¡Esto es una locura! *es*·to es oo·na lo·*koo*·ra

abseiling	*rappel* m	ra·*pel*
bungy-jumping	*puenting* m	*pwen*·teen
caving	*espeleología* f	es·pe·le·o·lo·*khee*·a
game fishing	*pesca* f *deportiva*	*pes*·ka de·por·*tee*·va
mountain biking	*ciclismo* m *de*	thee·*klees*·mo de
	montaña	mon·*ta*·nya
rock-climbing	*escalada* f	es·ka·*la*·da

soccer

el fútbol

Who plays for (Real Madrid)?
¿Quién juega en el
(Real Madrid)?

kyen *khwe*·ga en el
(re·*al* ma·*dree*)

What a terrible team!
¡Qué equipo más espantoso!

ke e·*kee*·po mas es·pan·*to*·so

He's a great player.
Es un gran jugador.

es oon gran khoo·ga·*dor*

He played brilliantly in the match against (Italy).
Jugó de fenomenal
en el partido contra
(Italia).

khoo·*go* de fe·no·me·*nal*
en el par·*tee*·do *kon*·tra
(ee·*ta*·lya)

Which team is at the top of the league?
¿Qué equipo está en
primera posición en
la liga?

ke e·*kee*·po es·*ta* en
pree·*me*·ra po·see·*thyon* en
la *lee*·ga

corner	saque m de esquina	sa·ke de es·kee·na
free kick	tiro m libre	tee·ro lee·bre
goalkeeper	portero m	por·te·ro
offside	fuera de juego	fwe·ra de khwe·go
penalty	penalty m	pe·nal·tee

sports talk

What a ...!	¡Qué ...!	ke ...
goal	gol	gol
pass	pase	pa·se

Your/My point.
Tu/Mi punto.　　　too/mee *poon*·to

Kick it to me!
¡Pásamelo!　　　pa·sa·me·lo

You're a good player.
Juegas bien.　　　khwe·gas byen

Thanks for the game.
Gracias por el partido.　　　gra·thyas por el par·tee·do

tennis

el tenis

Would you like to play tennis?
¿Quieres jugar al tenis?　　　kye·res khoo·gar al te·nees

Can we play at night?
¿Se puede jugar de noche?　　　se pwe·de khoo·gar de no·che

Game, Set, Match.
Juego, set y partido.　　　khwe·go set ee par·tee·do

ace	ace m	eys
advantage	ventaja f	ven·ta·kha
fault	falta f	fal·ta
play doubles (against)	jugar dobles (contra)	khoo·gar do·bles (kon·tra)
serve	saque m	sa·ke

sports

135

walking & mountaineering

trekking & alpinismo

For language on hiking, see **outdoors**, page 137.

water sports

los deportes acuáticos

Can I book a lesson?
¿Puedo reservar una clase?
pwe·do re·ser·var oo·na kla·se

Is safety gear provided?
¿Proporcionan el equipo
de seguridad?
pro·por·thyo·nan el e·kee·po
de se·goo·ree·da

Are there any ...?	¿Hay ...?	ai ...
reefs	arrecifes	a·re·thee·fes
rips	corrientes	ko·ryen·tes
water hazards	peligros en	pe·lee·gros en
	el agua	el a·gwa

motorboat	lancha f motora	lan·cha mo·to·ra
sail	vela f	ve·la
surfboard	tabla f de surf	ta·bla de soorf
surfing	surf m	soorf
water-skis	esquís m pl acuáticos	es·kees a·kwa·tee·kos
wave	ola f	o·la

local sports

If you hear the sounds of bat, ball and exertion, it may be
pelotari, pelota players, enjoying the traditional game of
pelota vasca, a type of handball. It's also known as *jai-alai*
in Basque.

ball	pelota f	pe·lo·ta
striker	delantero/a m/f	de·lan·te·ro/a
wall	frontón m	fron·ton

hiking

el excursionismo

There's plenty of walking, hiking and mountaineering to do in Spain. A recognised cross-country walking trail is known as *Gran Recorrido* (GR), gran re·ko·ree·do, while the shorter walking paths scattered throughout the country are called *Pequeños Recorridos* (PR), pe·ke·nyos re·ko·ree·dos.

Where can I ...?	¿Dónde puedo ...?	don·de pwe·do ...
buy supplies	*comprar viveres*	kom·*prar* vee·*ver*·es
find someone	*encontrar a*	en·kon·*trar* a
who knows	*alguien que*	*al*·gyen ke
this area	*conozca el área*	ko·*noth*·ka el *a*·re·a
get a map	*obtener un mapa*	ob·te·*ner* oon *ma*·pa
hire hiking gear	*alquilar un equipo para ir de excursion*	al·kee·*lar* oon e·*kee*·po *pa*·ra eer de eks·koor·*syon*

signs		
Por Aquí a ...	por a·*kee* a ...	This Way To ...
Terreno de Cámping	te·*re*·no de *kam*·peen	Camping Ground
Prohibido Acampar	pro·ee·*bee*·do a·*kam*·par	No Camping

Where can I find out about hiking trails?
¿Dónde hay información
sobre caminos rurales de
la zona?
*don·de ai een·for·ma·thyon
so·bre ka·mee·nos roo·ra·les
de la tho·na*

How long is the trail?
¿Cuántos kilómetros
tiene el camino?
*kwan·tos kee·lo·me·tros
tye·ne el ka·mee·no*

How high is the climb?
¿A qué altura se escala?
a ke al·too·ra se es·ka·la

Do we need a guide?
¿Se necesita un guía?
se ne·the·see·ta oon gee·a

Are there guided treks?
¿Se organizan
excursiones guiadas?
*se or·ga·nee·than
eks·koor·syo·nes gee·a·das*

Do we need to take ...?	¿Se necesita llevar ...?	se ne·the·see·ta lye·var ...
bedding	algo en que dormir	al·go en ke dor·meer
food	comida	ko·mee·da
water	agua	a·gwa
Is the track ...?	¿Es ... el sendero?	es ... el sen·de·ro
(well-)marked	(bien) marcado	(byen) mar·ka·do
open	abierto	a·byer·to
scenic	pintoresco	peen·to·res·ko
Which is the ... route?	¿Cuál es el camino más ...?	kwal es el ka·mee·no mas ...
easiest	fácil	fa·theel
shortest	corto	kor·to

Where's a ...?	¿Dónde hay ...?	don·de ai ...
camping site	un cámping	oon kam·peen
village	un pueblo	oon pwe·blo
Where are the ...?	¿Dónde hay ...?	don·de ai ...
showers	duchas	doo·chas
toilets	servicios	ser·vee·thyos

Where have you come from?
¿De dónde vienes? — de don·de vye·nes

How long did it take?
¿Cuánto ha tardado? — kwan·to a tar·da·do

Does this path go to ...?
¿Este camino va a ...? — es·te ka·mee·no va a ...

Can we go through here?
¿Se puede pasar por aquí? — se pwe·de pa·sar por a·kee

Is the water OK to drink?
¿Se puede beber el agua? — se pwe·de be·ber el a·gwa

I'm lost.
Estoy perdido/a. m/f — es·toy per·dee·do/a

Is it safe?
¿Es seguro? — es se·goo·ro

Is there a hut there?
¿Hay una cabaña allí? — ai oo·na ka·ba·nya a·lyee

When does it get dark?
¿A qué hora oscurece? — a ke o·ra os·koo·re·the

signs

| ¡Prohibido Nadar! | pro·ee·bee·do na·dar | No Swimming! |

outdoors

139

at the beach

en la playa

Where's the ... beach?	¿Dónde está la playa ...?	don·de es·ta la pla·ya ...
best	mejor	me·khor
nearest	más cercana	mas ther·ka·na
nudist	nudista	noo·dees·ta

Is it safe to dive/swim here?
¿Es seguro bucear/ nadar aquí?
es se·goo·ro boo·the·ar/ na·dar a·kee

What time is high/low tide?
¿A qué hora es la marea alta/baja?
a ke o·ra es la ma·re·a al·ta/ba·kha

Do we have to pay?
¿Hay que pagar?
ai ke pa·gar

How much to rent ...?	¿Cuánto por alquilar ... ?	kwan·to por al·kee·lar ...
a chair	una silla	oo·na see·lya
a hut	una cabaña	oo·na ka·ba·nya
an umbrella	un parasol	oon pa·ra·sol

listen for ...

kwee·da·do kon la re·sa·ka
Cuidado con la resaca.
Be careful of the undertow.

es pe·lee·gro·so
¡Es peligroso!
It's dangerous!

e·res mo·de·lo
¿Eres modelo?
Are you a model?

weather

9A **What's the weather like?**
¿Qué tiempo hace?   ke *tyem*·po a·the

Today it's ...	*Hoy hace ...*	oy a·the ...
Will it be ...	*Mañana*	ma·*nya*·na
tomorrow?	*hará ...?*	a·ra ...
freezing	*un frío*	oon *free*·o
	que pela	ke *pe*·la
sunny	*sol*	sol
warm	*calor*	ka·*lor*
windy	*viento*	*vyen*·to

9B **It's cold.**   *Hace frío.*   a·the *free*·o
9C **It's hot.**   *Hace calor.*   a·the ka·*lor*
9D **It's raining.**   *Está lloviendo.*   es·ta lyo·*vyen*·do

(Tomorrow) It will be raining.
(Mañana) Lloverá.   (ma·nya·na) lyo·ve·ra

Where can I	*¿Dónde puedo*	*don*·de *pwe*·do
buy ...?	*comprar ...?*	kom·*prar* ...
a rain	*un*	oon
jacket	*impermeable*	eem·per·me·a·ble
sunblock	*crema solar*	*kre*·ma so·*lar*
an umbrella	*un paraguas*	oon pa·*ra*·gwas
hail	*granizo* m	gra·*nee*·tho
storm	*tormenta* f	tor·*men*·ta
sun	*sol* m	sol

141

flora & fauna

What ... is that?	¿Qué ... es ése/ésa? m/f	ke ... es e·se/e·sa
animal	animal m	a·nee·mal
flower	flor f	flor
plant	planta f	plan·ta
tree	árbol m	ar·bol

What's it used for?
¿Para qué se usa?　　　　　pa·ra ke se oo·sa

Can you eat the fruit?
¿Se puede comer la fruta?　se pwe·de ko·mer la froo·ta

Is it endangered?
¿Está en peligro　　　　　es·ta en pe·lee·gro
de extinción?　　　　　　de eks·teen·thyon

Is it ...?	¿Es ...?	es ...
common	común	ko·moon
dangerous	peligroso/a m/f	pe·lee·gro·so/a
protected	protegido/a m/f	pro·te·khee·do/a

For geographical and agricultural terms, and names of animals and plants, see the **dictionary**.

SOCIAL

142

FOOD > eating out

saliendo a comer

key language

lenguaje clave

The main meal in Spain, 'lunchtime' is called *la hora de comer*, la o·ra de ko·*mer*. It's served between 1.30pm and 4.30pm.

63A	breakfast	*desayuno* m	de·sa·*yoo*·no
63B	lunch	*comida* f	ko·*mee*·da
63C	dinner	*cena* f	*the*·na
63D	snack	*tentempié* m	ten·tem·*pye*
63E	eat	*comer*	ko·*mer*
63F	drink	*beber*	be·*ber*

Please.	*Por favor.*	por fa·*vor*
Thank you.	*Gracias.*	*gra*·thyas
I'd like ...	*Quisiera ...*	kee·*sye*·ra ...
I'm starving!	*¡Estoy hambriento/a!* m/f	es·*toy* am·*bryen*·to/a

finding a place to eat

buscando un lugar para comer

64A Can you recommend a bar?
¿Puede recomendar un bar? pwe·de re·ko·men·*dar* oon bar

64B Can you recommend a cafe?
¿Puede recomendar un café? pwe·de re·ko·men·*dar* oon ka·*fe*

64C Can you recommend a restaurant?
¿Puede recomendar pwe·de re·ko·men·*dar*
un restaurante? oon res·tow·*ran*·te

Are you still serving food?
¿Siguen sirviendo comida? see·gen seer·*vyen*·do ko·*mee*·da

How long is the wait?
¿Cuánto hay que esperar? kwan·to ai ke es·pe·*rar*

eating out

143

Where would you go for (a) ...?	¿Adónde se va para ...?	a·*don*·de se va *pa*·ra ...
celebration	celebrar	sel·e·*brar*
cheap meal	comer barato	ko·*mer* ba·*ra*·to
local specialities	comer comida típica	ko·*mer* ko·*mee*·da *tee*·pee·ka

I'd like to reserve a table for ...	Quisiera reservar una mesa para ...	kee·*sye*·ra re·ser·*var* *oo*·na *me*·sa *pa*·ra ...
(two) people	(dos) personas	(dos) per·*so*·nas
(eight) o'clock	las (ocho)	las (*o*·cho)

listen for ...

lo *syen*·to e·*mos* the·*ra*·do
  Lo siento, hemos cerrado. **Sorry, we're closed.**
no te·*ne*·mos *me*·sa
  No tenemos mesa. **We have no tables.**
oon mo·*men*·to
  Un momento. **One moment.**

65A I'd like a table for (two), please.
Quisiera una mesa para (dos), por favor. kee·*sye*·ra *oo*·na *me*·sa *pa*·ra (dos) por fa·*vor*

65B I'd like the drink list, please.
Quisiera la lista de bebidas, por favor. kee·*sye*·ra la *lees*·ta de be·*bee*·das por fa·*vor*

65C I'd like the menu, please.
Quisiera el menú, por favor. kee·*sye*·ra el me·*noo* por fa·*vor*

I'd like the (non-)smoking section, please.
Quisiera (no) fumadores, por favor. kee·*sye*·ra (no) foo·ma·*do*·res por fa·*vor*

Do you have ... ?	¿Tienen ... ?	*tye*·nen ...
children's meals	comidas para niños	ko·*mee*·das *pa*·ra *nee*·nyos
a menu in English	un menú en inglés	oon me·*noo* en een·*gles*

at the restaurant

Is it self-serve?
¿Es de autoservicio? es de ow·to·ser·vee·thyo

Is service included in the bill?
¿La cuenta incluye la kwen·ta een·kloo·ye
servicio? ser·vee·thyo

66A **What would you recommend?**
¿Qué recomienda? ke re·ko·myen·da

I'll have what they're having.
Tomaré lo mismo que ellos. to·ma·re lo mees·mo ke e·lyos

Does it take long to prepare?
¿Tarda mucho en tar·da moo·cho en
prepararse? pre·pa·rar·se

What's in that dish?
¿Que lleva ese plato? ke lye·va e·se pla·to

For more on special diets, see **vegetarian & special meals**, page 159, and **health**, page 184.

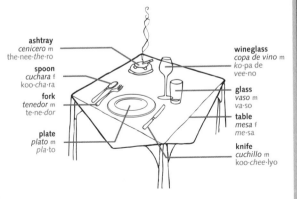

ashtray
cenicero m
the·nee·the·ro

spoon
cuchara f
koo·cha·ra

fork
tenedor m
te·ne·dor

plate
plato m
pla·to

wineglass
copa de vino m
ko·pa de
vee·no

glass
vaso m
va·so

table
mesa f
me·sa

knife
cuchillo m
koo·chee·lyo

Are these complimentary?
   ¿Éstos son gratis?   es·tos son gra·tees

We're just having drinks.
   Sólo queremos tomar algo.   so·lo ke·re·mos to·mar al·go

I'd like a local speciality.
   Quisiera un plato   kee·sye·ra oon pla·to
   típico.   tee·pee·ko

<table>
<tr><td colspan="3">signs</td></tr>
<tr><td>Reservado</td><td>re·ser·va·do</td><td>Reserved</td></tr>
</table>

at the table

a la mesa

65D **I'd like the bill, please.**
   Quisiera la cuenta, por favor.   kee·sye·ra la kwen·ta por fa·vor

Please bring ...	*Por favor nos trae ...*	por fa·vor nos tra·e ...
a glass	*un vaso*	oon va·so
a serviette	*una servilleta*	oo·na ser·vee·lye·ta
a wineglass	*una copa*	oo·na ko·pa
	de vino	de vee·no

For more words you might find on a menu, see the **culinary reader**, page 161.

<table>
<tr><td colspan="2">listen for ...</td></tr>
<tr><td>le goos·ta ...
¿Le gusta ...?</td><td>Do you like ...?</td></tr>
<tr><td>re·ko·myen·do ...
Recomiendo ...</td><td>I suggest the ...</td></tr>
<tr><td>ko·mo lo kye·re pre·pa·ra·do
¿Cómo lo quiere
preparado?</td><td>How would you like
that cooked?</td></tr>
</table>

Aperitivos	a·pe·ree·*tee*·vos	Appetisers
Caldos	*kal*·dos	Soups
Cervezas	ther·ve·thas	Beers
De Entrada	de en·*tra*·da	Entrees
Digestivos	dee·khes·*tee*·vos	Digestifs
Ensaladas	en·sa·*la*·das	Salads
Licores	lee·*ko*·res	Spirits
Postres	*pos*·tres	Desserts
Refrescos	re·*fres*·kos	Soft Drinks
Segundos Platos	se·*goon*·dos *pla*·tos	Main Courses
Vinos Blancos	vee·nos *blan*·kos	White Wines
Vinos Dulces	vee·no *dool*·thes	Dessert Wines
Vinos Espumosos	vee·nos es·poo·*mo*·sos	Sparkling Wines
Vinos Tintos	vee·nos *teen*·tos	Red Wines

talking food

hablando de comida

I love this dish.
Me encanta este plato.
me en·*kan*·ta es·te *pla*·to

We love the local cuisine.
Nos encanta la comida típica de la zona.
nos en·*kan*·ta la ko·*mee*·da *tee*·pee·ka de la *tho*·na

That was delicious!
¡Estaba buenísimo!
es·*ta*·ba bwe·*nee*·see·mo

My compliments to the chef.
Mi enhorabuena al cocinero.
mee en·o·ra·*bwe*·na al ko·thee·*ne*·ro

I'm full.
Estoy lleno/a. m/f
es·*toy* lye·no/a

This is ...	*Esto está ...*	es·to es·ta ...
burnt	*quemado*	ke·*ma*·do
(too) cold	*(muy) frío*	(mooy) *free*·o
superb	*exquisito*	eks·kee·*see*·to

meals

las comidas

> breakfast

What's a typical Spanish (breakfast)?

¿Cómo es un típico		ko·mo es oon tee·pee·ko
(desayuno) español?		(de·sa·yoo·no) es·pa·nyol

omelette	tortilla	tor·tee·lya
muesli	muesli	mwes·lee
toast	tostadas	tos·ta·das

For typical dishes, see the **culinary reader**, page 161, and for other food items see the **dictionary**.

> light meals

What's that called?

¿Cómo se llama eso?		ko·mo se lya·ma e·so

I'd like ..., please.	Quisiera ..., por favor.	kee·sye·ra ... por fa·vor
a piece	un trozo	oon tro·tho
a sandwich	un sándwich	oon san·weech
one slice	una loncha	oo·na lon·cha
that one	ése/a m/f	e·se/a
two	dos	dos

Is there any ...?	¿Hay ...?	ai ...
chilli sauce	salsa f de guindilla	sal·sa de geen·dee·lya
pepper	pimienta f	pee·myen·ta
salt	sal f	sal
tomato sauce/ketchup	salsa f de tomate	sal·sa de to·ma·te
vinegar	vinagre m	vee·na·gre

methods of preparation

los métodos de cocción

I'd like it ...	Lo quiero ...	lo kye·ro ...
I don't want it ...	No lo quiero ...	no lo kye·ro ...
deep-fried	frito en aceite abundante	free·to en a·they·te a·boon·dan·te
medium	no muy hecho	no mooy e·cho
rare	vuelta y vuelta	vwel·ta ee vwel·ta
re-heated	recalentado	re·ka·len·ta·do
steamed	al vapor	al va·por
well-done	muy hecho	mooy e·cho
with the dressing on the side	con el aliño aparte	kon el a·lee·nyo a·par·te
without ...	sin ...	seen ...

in the bar

Excuse me!	*¡Oiga!*	oy·ga
I'm next.	*Ahora voy yo.*	a·o·ra voy yo
I'll have ...	*Para mí ...*	pa·ra mee ...

Same again, please.
Otra de lo mismo.   o·tra de lo mees·mo

No ice, thanks.
Sin hielo, gracias.   seen ye·lo gra·thyas

66B I'll buy you a drink.
Te invito a una copa.   te een·vee·to a oo·na ko·pa

66C What would you like?
¿Qué desea tomar?   ke de·se·a to·mar

It's my round.
Es mi ronda.   es mee ron·da

You can get the next one.
La próxima la pagas tú.   la prok·see·ma la pa·gas too

How much is that?
¿Cuánto es eso?   kwan·to es e·so

Do you serve meals here?
¿Sirven comidas aquí?   seer·ven ko·mee·das a·kee

---

listen for ...

a·kee tye·ne
¡Aquí tiene! — **Here you go!**

don·de le gus·ta·ree·a sen·tar·se
¿Dónde le gustaría sentarse? — **Where would you like to sit?**

en ke le pwe·do ser·veer
¿En qué le puedo servir? — **What can I get for you?**

kye·re to·mar al·go myen·tras es·pe·ra
¿Quiere tomar algo mientras espera? — **Would you like a drink while you wait?**

tapas

Tapas are scrumptious cooked bar snacks, available pretty much around the clock at bars and some clubs. You'll find they're free in some places, laid out in the bar for you to choose from. This follows village tradition at the turn of the century in the whole of Andalusia, as well as in Extremadura, Low Castile, Murcia and the working-class districts of Madrid and Barcelona.

Other places will rotate the dishes. Listen for ...

da·me oo·na pree·*me*·ra
   ¡Dame una primera!   **Give me a starter!**

oo·na se·*goon*·da
   ¡Una segunda!   **Give me a main dish!**

... as the bar attendant orders a different speciality each time from the cook. See if you can stay on your stool long enough to get back to number one again.

• how hungry are you?

banderilla/	ban·de·*ree*·lya/	small tapa serving
moruno/	mo·*roo*·no/	on bread or a
pinchito	peen·*chee*·to	toothpick
ración	ra·*thyon*	large tapa serving

• common tapas:

montadito	mon·ta·*deet*·o	bread-topped tapa
pan tumaca	pan too·*ma*·ka	tapa of toasted bread rubbed with tomatoes & garlic, served with oil
queso en	*ke*·soh en	cheese in olive oil,
aceite	a·*say*·tay	served as a tapa

• regional tapas:

naveganta	na·ve·*gan*·ta	in Burgos
pintxo	*peen*·cho	in Basque Country

nonalcoholic drinks

I don't drink alcohol.
No bebo alcohol. no be·bo al·ko·hol

67A I'd like a cup of coffee.
Quisiera un café. kee·sye·ra oon ka·fe

67B I'd like a cup of tea.
Quisiera un té. kee·sye·ra oon te

67C with milk	*con leche*	kon le·che
67D without sugar	*sin azúcar*	seen a·thoo·kar
68A soft drink	*refrescos* m	re·fres·ko
68B (orange) juice	*zumo (de naranja)* m	thoo·mo (de na·ran·kha)
68C boiled water	*agua hervida* f	a·gwa er·vee·da
68D mineral water	*agua mineral* f	a·gwa mee·ne·ral
sparkling	*con gas*	kon gas

alcoholic drinks

beer	*cerveza* f	ther·ve·tha
brandy	*coñac* m	ko·nyak
champagne	*champán* m	cham·pan
cocktail	*combinado* m	kom·bee·na·do
sangria (red-wine punch)	*sangría* f	san·gree·a
69A a shot of (wisky)	*un chupito* m *de (güisqui)*	oon choo·pee·to de (gwees·kee)
a shot of ...	*un chupito* m *de ...*	oon choo·pee·to de ...
gin	*ginebra* f	khee·ne·bra
rum	*ron* m	ron
tequila	*tequila* m	te·kee·la
vodka	*vodka* m	vod·ka

a big fan of the mini

Many Spanish bars provide massive plastic beakers of beer to cater for young revellers. It's cut with water and average tasting – but cheap and free flowing! These fountains of froth are called *minis*. Here are some useful words for ordering a brew:

cerveza f ...	ther·*ve*·tha ...	... beer
de barril	de ba·*ril*	**draught**
negra	*neg*·ra	**dark**
rubia	*roo*·bee·a	**light**
sin alcohol	sin al·kol	**nonalcoholic**
botellín m	bo·tel·*yin*	**small bottle of beer (250 ml)**
jarra f	*kha*·ra	**jug**
litrona f	lee·*tro*·na	**litre bottle of beer**
mediana f	me·dee·*a*·na	**bottle of beer (300 ml)**
pinta f	*peen*·ta	**pint**

69B a bottle of red wine
una botella de vino tinto   oo·na bo·*te*·lya de *vee*·no *teen*·to

69C a glass of red wine
una copa de vino tinto   oo·na *ko*·pa de *vee*·no *teen*·to

69D a bottle of white wine
una botella de vino blanco oo·na bo·*te*·lya de *vee*·no *blan*·ko

69E a glass of white wine
una copa de vino blanco   oo·na *ko*·pa de *vee*·no *blan*·ko

... wine	*vino* ...	*vee*·no ...
dessert	*dulce*	*dool*·the
rose	*rosado*	ro·*sa*·do
sparkling	*espumoso*	es·poo·*mo*·so

69F a bottle of beer
una botella de cerveza   oo·na bo·*te*·lya de ther·*ve*·tha

69G a glass of beer
una caña de cerveza   oo·na *ka*·nya de ther·*ve*·tha

one too many?

66D Cheers!
¡Salud! — sa·*loo*

Thanks, but I don't feel like it.
Lo siento, pero no me apetece. — lo *syen*·to *pe*·ro no me a·pe·*te*·the

This is hitting the spot.
Me lo estoy pasando muy bien. — me lo es·*toy* pa·*san*·do mooy byen

I'm tired, I'd better go home.
Estoy cansado/a, mejor me voy a casa. m/f — es·*toy* kan·*sa*·do/a me·*khor* me voy a *ka*·sa

Where's the toilet?
¿Dónde está el lavabo? — *don*·de es·*ta* el la·*va*·bo

I'm feeling drunk.
Esto me está subiendo mucho. — *es*·to me es·*ta* soo·*byen*·do *moo*·cho

I feel fantastic!
¡Me siento fenomenal! — me *syen*·to fe·no·me·*nal*

I really, really love you.
Te quiero muchísimo. — te *kye*·ro moo·*chee*·see·mo

I think I've had one too many.
Creo que he tomado demasiado. — *kre*·o ke e to·*ma*·do de·ma·*sya*·do

Can you call a taxi for me?
¿Me puedes pedir un taxi? — me *pwe*·des pe·*deer* oon *tak*·see

I don't think you should drive.
No creo que deberías conducir. — no *kre*·o ke de·be·*ree*·as kon·doo·*theer*

I'm pissed.
Estoy borracho/a. m/f — es·*toy* bo·*ra*·cho/a

I feel ill.
Me siento mal. — me *syen*·to mal

key language

A piece.	Un trozo.	oon tro·tho
A slice.	Una loncha.	oo·na lon·cha
That one.	Ése.	e·se
This.	Esto.	es·to
A bit more.	Un poco más.	oon po·ko mas
Less.	Menos.	me·nos
Enough!	¡Basta!	ba·sta
cooked	cocido/a m/f	ko·thee·do/a
dried	seco/a m/f	se·ko/a
fresh	fresco/a m/f	fres·ko/a
frozen	congelado/a m/f	kon·khe·la·do/a
raw	crudo/a m/f	kroo·do/a

buying food

How much?
¿Cuánto? kwan·to

How many?
¿Cuántos? kwan·tos

How much is (a kilo of cheese)?
¿Cuánto vale (un kilo   kwan·to va·le (oon kee·lo
de queso)?   de ke·so)

70A What's the local speciality?
¿Cuál es la especialidad   kwal es la es·pe·thya·lee·da
de la zona?   de la tho·na

70B What's that?
¿Qué es eso?   ke es e·so

. en ke le pwe·do ser·veer	¿En qué le puedo servir?	Can I help you?
ke ke·ree·as	¿Qué querías?	What would you like?
no ten·go	No tengo.	I don't have any.

Can I taste it?
¿Puedo probarlo/a? m/f   pwe·do pro·bar·lo/a

Can I have a bag, please?
¿Me da una bolsa, por favor?   me da oo·na bol·sa por fa·vor

71A **I'd like ...**
Póngame ...   pon·ga·me ...

71B **I'd like (three) pieces.**
Póngame (tres) piezas.   pon·ga·me (tres) pye·thas

71C **I'd like(six) slices.**
Póngame (seis) pedazos.   pon·ga·me (seys) pe·da·thos

71D **I'd like(two) kilos.**
Póngame (dos) kilos.   pon·ga·me (dos) kee·los

71E **I'd like (200) grams.**
Póngame(doscientos)   pon·ga·me (dos·thyen·tos)
gramos.   gra·mos

Do you have ...?	¿Tiene ... ?	tye·ne ...
anything cheaper	algo más barato	al·go mas ba·ra·to
any other kinds	otros tipos	ot·ros tee·pos

Where can I find the ... section?	¿Dónde está la sección de ...?	don·de es·ta la sek·thyon de ...
dairy	productos lácteos	pro·dook·tos lak·te·os
frozen goods	productos congelados	pro·dook·tos kon·khe·la·dos
fruit and vegetable	frutas y verduras	froo·tas ee ver·doo·ras
meat	carne	kar·ne
poultry	aves	a·ves

FOOD

156

cooking utensils

Could I please borrow a/an ...?
¿Me puede prestar ...?   me *pwe*·de pres·*tar* ...

Where's a/an ...?
¿Dónde hay ...?   *don*·de ai ...

bottle opener	*abrebotellas* m	a·bre·bo·*te*·lyas
bowl	*bol* m	bol
can opener	*abrelatas* m	a·bre·*la*·tas
chopping board	*tabla* f *para cortar*	*tab*·la pa·ra kor·tar
cup	*taza* f	*ta*·tha
corkscrew	*sacacorchos* m	sa·ka·*kor*·chos
fork	*tenedor* m	ten·ne·*dor*
fridge	*nevera* m	ne·ve·ra
frying pan	*sartén* f	sar·*ten*
glass	*vaso* m	*va*·so
knife	*cuchillo* m	koo·*chee*·lyo
oven	*horno* m	*or*·no
plate	*plato* m	*pla*·to
saucepan	*cazo* m	*ka*·tho
spoon	*cuchara* f	koo·*cha*·ra
toaster	*tostadora* f	tos·ta·*do*·ra

listen for ...

e·so es (oon man·*che*·go) *Eso es (un manchego).*	That's (a manchego).
no *ke*·da mas *No queda más.*	There's none left.
e·so es (*theen*·ko e·oo·ros) *Eso es (cinco euros).*	That's (five euros).
al·go mas ¿Algo más?	Would you like anything else?

useful amounts

Please give me ...	Por favor, deme ...	por fa·vor de·me ...
(100) grams	(cien) gramos	(thyen) gra·mos
half a dozen	una media docena	oo·na me·dya do·the·na
half a kilo	un medio kilo	oon me·dyo kee·lo
a kilo	un kilo	oon kee·lo
a bottle (of ...)	una botella (de ...)	oo·na bo·te·lya (de ...)
a jar	una jarra	oo·na kha·ra
a packet	un paquete	oon pa·ke·te
a tin	una lata	oo·na la·ta
(just) a little	(sólo) un poquito	(so·lo) oon po·kee·to
many	muchos/as m/f	moo·chos/as
more	más	mas
some	algunos/as m/f	al·goo·nos/as
less	menos	me·nos

vegetarian & special meals
comidas vegetarianas & platos especiales

ordering food

pidiendo comida

I'm vegetarian.
Soy vegetariano/a. m/f
soy ve·khe·ta·rya·no/a

72A **Is there a (vegetarian) restaurant near here?**
¿Hay un restaurante (vegetariano) por aquí?
ai oon res·tow·ran·te (ve·khe·ta·rya·no) por a·kee

Do you have halal/kosher food?
¿Tienen comida halal/ kosher?
tye·nen ko·mee·da a·lal/ ko·sher

I don't eat red meat.
No como carne roja.
no ko·mo kar·ne ro·kha

Is it cooked in/with butter?
¿Esta cocinado en/con mantequilla?
es·ta ko·thee·na·do en/kon man·te·kee·lya

72B **Could you prepare a meal without eggs?**
¿Me puede preparar una comida sin huevo?
me pwe·de pre·pa·rar oo·na ko·mee·da seen we·vo

72C **Could you prepare a meal without meat stock?**
¿Me puede preparar una comida sin caldo de carne?
me pwe·de pre·pa·rar oo·na ko·mee·da seen kal·do de kar·ne

Is this ...?	*¿Esto es ...?*	es·to es ...
free of animal produce	*sin productos de animales*	seen pro·dook·tos de a·nee·ma·les
free-range	*de corral*	de ko·ral
genetically modified	*transgénico*	trans·khe·nee·ko
gluten-free	*sin gluten*	seen gloo·ten
low in sugar	*bajo en azúcar*	ba·kho en a·thoo·kar
low-fat	*bajo en grasas*	ba·kho en gra·sas
organic	*orgánico*	or·ga·nee·ko
salt-free	*sin sal*	seen sal

159

special diets & allergies

I'm on a special diet.
Estoy a régimen especial.   es·*toy* a re·khee·men es·pe·*thyal*

73A **I'm allergic to ...**
Soy alérgico a ... m   soy a·*ler*·khee·ko a ...

73B **I'm allergic to ...**
Soy alérgica a ... f   soy a·*ler*·khee·ka a ...

74A **I'm allergic to dairy produce.**
Soy alérgico a los   soy a·*ler*·khee·ko a los
productos lácteos. m   pro·*dook*·tos *lak*·te·os

74B **I'm allergic to dairy produce.**
Soy alérgica a los   soy a·*ler*·khee·ka a los
productos lácteos. f   pro·*dook*·tos *lak*·te·os

74C **I'm allergic to MSG.**
Soy alérgico al glutamato   soy a·*ler*·khee·ko al gloo·ta·*ma*·to
monosódico. m   mo·no·*so*·dee·ko

74D **I'm allergic to MSG.**
Soy alérgica al glutamato   soy a·*ler*·khee·ka al gloo·ta·*ma*·to
monosódico. f   mo·no·*so*·dee·ko

74E **I'm allergic to nuts.**
Soy alérgico a las nueces. m   soy a·*ler*·khee·ko a las *nwe*·thes

74F **I'm allergic to nuts.**
Soy alérgica a las nueces. f   soy a·*ler*·khee·ka a las *nwe*·thes

74G **I'm allergic to seafood .**
Soy alérgico a   soy a·*ler*·khee·ko a
los mariscos. m   los ma·*rees*·kos

74H **I'm allergic to seafood.**
Soy alérgica a   soy a·*ler*·khee·ka a
los mariscos. f   los ma·*rees*·kos

I'm allergic to shellfish .
Soy alérgico a   soy a·*ler*·khee·ko a
los crustáceos. m   los kroos·*ta*·thyos

I'm allergic to shellfish.
Soy alérgica a   soy a·*ler*·khee·ka a
los crustáceos. f   los kroos·*ta*·thyos

For a more detailed version of this glossary, see Lonely Planet's *World Food Spain*.

A

acebuche ⓜ a·the·*boo*·che *wild olive*
acedía ⓕ a·the·*dee*·a *plaice/flounder*
aceite ⓜ a·*they*·te *oil*
  — de girasol de khee·ra·*sol*
  sunflower oil
  — de oliva de o·*lee*·va *olive oil*
  — de oliva virgen extra de o·*lee*·va
  veer·khen eks·tra *extra virgin olive oil*
aceituna ⓕ a·they·*too*·na *olive*
  — negra ne·gra *black olive*
  — verde ver·de *green olive*
ácido/a ⓜ/ⓕ a·*thee*·do/a *tart (of fruit)*
adobo ⓜ a·*do*·bo *marinade*
agrios ⓜ pl a·gryos *citrus fruits*
aguacate ⓜ a·gwa·*ka*·te *avocado*
aguaturma ⓕ a·gwa·*toor*·ma *Jerusalem artichoke*
ajiaco ⓜ a·*khya*·ko *spicy potato dish*
ajoaceite ⓜ a·kho·a·*they*·te *garlic & oil sauce • garlic mayonnaise*
ajoharina ⓕ a·kho·a·*ree*·na *potatoes stewed in garlic sauce*
ajoarriero (al) a·kho·a·*rye*·ro (al) *'mule-driver's garlic' - anything cooked in a sauce of onions, garlic & chilli*
ala ⓕ a·la *(chicken) wing*
alajú ⓜ a·la·*khoo* *honey & almond cake*
albaricoque ⓜ al·ba·ree·*ko*·ke *apricot*
  — seco se·ko *dried apricot*
albóndigas ⓕ pl al·*bon*·dee·gas *meatballs*
  — de pescado de pes·*ka*·do *fish balls*
alcachofas ⓕ pl al·ka·*cho*·fas *artichokes*
  — guisadas a la española gee·sa·das a la es·pa·*nyo*·la *artichokes in wine*
  — rellenas re·*lye*·nas *stuffed artichokes*
alcaparra ⓕ al·ka·*pa*·ra *caper*

alioli ⓜ a·lee·o·lee *garlic mayonnaise*
almejas ⓕ pl al·*me*·khas *clams – superb eaten raw*
  — a la marinera a la ma·ree·*ne*·ra *clams in white wine*
  — al horno al or·no *baked clams*
almendrado ⓜ al·men·*dra*·do *almond cake or biscuit • chocolate covered ice cream bar*
almendras ⓕ pl al·*men*·dras *almonds*
alubia ⓕ a·*loo*·bya *haricot bean*
anacardo ⓜ a·na·*kar*·do *cashew nut*
anchoas ⓕ pl an·cho·as *anchovies – mostly eaten fresh, grilled or fried*
angelote ⓜ an·khe·*lo*·te *monkfish*
anguila ⓕ an·gee·la *adult eel*
angulas ⓕ pl an·*goo*·las *baby eels – prized as a delicacy, they resemble vermicelli*
  — en all i pebre en al ee pe·bre *baby eels with pepper & garlic*
apio ⓜ a·pyo *celery*
arándano ⓜ a·*ran*·da·no *blueberry*
arenque ⓜ a·*ren*·ke *herring*
  — ahumado a·oo·ma·do *kipper*
arroz ⓜ a·*roth* *rice*
  — a la Alcireña a la al·thee·re·nya *baked rice dish*
  — abanda (de València) a·*ban*·da (de va·*len*·thya) *fish paella*
  — con leche kon le·che *rice pudding*
  — con pollo kon po·lyo *chicken & rice*
  — integral een·te·*gral* *brown rice*
  — marinera ma·ree·*ne*·ra *seafood & rice*
  — salvaje sal·va·khe *wild rice*
asadillo ⓜ a·sa·*dee*·lyo *roasted red capsicums*

asados ⓜ pl a·*sa*·dos *roast meats*

atún ⓜ a·*toon* *tuna – often served marinated & raw*
— **al horno** al *or*·no *baked tuna*

avellana ⓕ a·ve·*lya*·na *hazelnut*

aves ⓕ pl *a*·ves *poultry*

azúcar ⓜ a·*thoo*·kar *sugar*

B

bacalao ⓜ ba·ka·*low* *cod – usually salted & dried*
— **a la vizcaína** a la veeth·ka·ee·na *cod with chillies & capsicums*
— **del convento** del kon·*ven*·to *cod with potatoes & spinach in broth*

bacón ⓜ ba·*kon* *bacon*

barbo ⓜ *bar*·bo *red mullet*

barra ⓕ *ba*·ra *long stick of bread*

batata ⓕ ba·*ta*·ta *sweet potato*

beicon ⓜ *bey*·kon *streaky bacon rashers*

berberechos ⓜ pl ber·be·*re*·chos *cockles*
— **en vinagre** en vee·*na*·gre *cockles in vinegar*

berenjenas ⓕ pl be·ren·*khe*·nas *eggplants*
— **a la mallorquina** a la ma·lyor·*kee*·na *eggplants with garlic mayonnaise*
— **con setas** kon *se*·tas *eggplants with mushrooms*

berza ⓕ *ber*·tha *cabbage*
— **a la andaluza** a la an·da·*loo*·tha *cabbage & meat hotpot*

besugo ⓜ be·*soo*·go *red bream*
— **a la Donostiarra** a la do·nos·*tya*·ra *barbecued red bream with garlic & paprika*
— **estilo San Sebastián** es·*tee*·lo san se·bas·*tyan* *barbecued red bream with garlic & paprika*

bienmesabe ⓜ byen·me·*sa*·be *sponge cake, egg & almond confection*

bisbe ⓜ *bees*·be *black & white blood sausage*

bistec ⓜ *bees*·tek *steak*
— **con patatas** kon pa·*ta*·tas *steak with chips*

bizcocha ⓕ **manchega** beeth·*ko*·cha man·*che*·ga *cake soaked in milk, sugar, vanilla & cinnamon*

bizcocho ⓜ beeth·*ko*·cho *sponge cake*
— **de almendra** de al·*men*·dra *almond cake*
— **de avellana** de a·ve·*lya*·na *hazelnut cake*

bizcochos ⓜ pl **borrachos** beeth·*ko*·chos bo·*ra*·chos *cake soaked in liqueur*

bocadillo ⓜ bo·ka·*dee*·lyo *bread roll with a filling*

bocas ⓕ pl **de la isla** *bo*·kas de la *ees*·la *large crab claws*

bogavante ⓜ bo·ga·*van*·te *lobster*

bollo ⓜ *bo*·lyo *crusty bread roll*

bonito ⓜ bo·*nee*·to *white fleshy tuna*

boquerón ⓜ bo·ke·*ron* *whitebait*

boquerones ⓜ pl bo·ke·*ro*·nes *anchovies marinated in wine vinegar*
— **fritos** *free*·tos *fried anchovies*

brama ⓕ *bra*·ma *sea bream*

bróculi ⓜ *bro*·ko·lee *broccoli*

budín ⓜ **de atún** boo·*deen* de a·*toon* *baked tuna pudding*

bull ⓜ **de atún** bool de a·*toon* *rabbit with garlic & tuna boiled with potatoes*

buñuelitos ⓜ pl boo·nywe·*lee*·tos *small cheese or ham fritters*
— **de San José** de san kho·*se* *lemon & vanilla crepes*

buñuelo ⓜ boo·*nywe*·lo *fried pastry*

burrida ⓕ **de ratjada** boo·*ree*·da de rat·*kha*·da *fish soup with almonds*

butifarra ⓕ **(blanca)** boo·tee·*fa*·ra (*blan*·ka) *cured pork sausage*
— **con setas** kon *se*·tas *Catalan sausage with mushrooms*

C

caballa ⓕ ka·*ba*·lya *mackerel*

cabra ⓕ *ka*·bra *goat*

cabracho ⓜ ka·*bra*·cho *scorpion fish • mullet*

cacahuete ⓜ ka·ka·*we*·te *peanut*

cachelos ⓜ pl ka·*che*·los *potatoes with spicy sausage & pork*

cádiz ⓜ *ka*·deeth *fresh goats' milk cheese*

calabacín ⓜ ka·la·ba·*theen* *zucchini*

calabaza ① ka·la·*ba*·tha *pumpkin*

calamares ⓜ pl ka·la·*ma*·res *calamari – popular fried or stuffed*
— **fritos a la romana** *free*·tos a la *ro*·ma·na *squid rings fried in batter*
— **rellenos** re·*lye*·nos *stuffed squid*

calçots ⓜ pl kal·*sots* *spring onion-like vegetables chargrilled and eaten with a romesco dipping sauce*

caldeirada ① kal·dey·*ra*·da *salted cod & potatoes in a paprika sauce • fish soup*

caldereta ① kal·de·*re*·ta *stew*
— **asturiana** as·too·*rya*·na *fish stew*
— **de cordero** de kor·*de*·ro *lamb stew*

caldillo ⓜ **de perro** kal·*dee*·lyo de *pe*·ro *'puppy dog soup' – stew of onions, fresh fish & orange juice*

caldo ⓜ *kal*·do *broth • clear soup • stock*
— **al estilo del Mar Menor** al es·*tee*·lo del mar me·*nor* *fish stew from the Mar Menor*
— **gallego** ga·*lye*·go *broth with haricot beans, ham & sausage*

callos ⓜ pl *ka*·lyos *tripe*

camarones fritos ⓜ pl ka·ma·*ro*·nes *free*·tos *deep-fried prawns*

canagroc ka·na·*grok* *mushroom*

cañaillas ① pl **de la Isla** ka·*nyay*·lyas de la *ees*·la *boiled sea snails*

canelones ⓜ pl ka·na·*lo*·nes *squares of pasta for making cannelloni*
— **con espinaca** kon es·pee·*na*·ka *cannelloni with spinach, anchovies & bechamel*
— **con pescado** kon pes·*ka*·do *cannelloni with cod, eggs & mushrooms*

canapés ⓜ pl **de fiambres** ka·na·*pes* de fee·*am*·bres *mini hors d'oeuvres with ham, anchovies or cheese*

cangrejo ⓜ kan·*gre*·kho *large-clawed crab usually eaten steamed or boiled*

cantalupo ⓜ kan·ta·*loo*·po *cantaloupe*

canutillos ⓜ pl ka·noo·*tee*·lyos *cream biscuits*

capones ⓜ pl **de Villalba** ka·*po*·nes de vee·*lyal*·ba *Christmas dish of chicken marinated in brandy*

caracoles ⓜ ka·ra·*ko*·les *snails*

caramelos ⓜ pl ka·ra·*me*·los *caramels • confection*

cardos ⓜ pl **fritos** *kar*·dos *free*·tos *fried thistles*

carne ① *kar*·ne *meat*
— **de membrillo** de mem·*bree*·lyo *quince 'cheese'*
— **molida** mo·*lee*·da *minced meat*

cassolada ① ka·so·*la*·da *potato & vegetable stew with bacon & ribs*

castaña ① kas·*ta*·nya *chestnut*

caviar ⓜ ka·*vyar* *caviar*

caza ① *ka*·tha *game*

cazón ⓜ ka·*thon* *dogfish or shark with a sweet scallop-like flavour*

cazuelitas ① pl **de langostinos San Rafael** ka·thwe·*lee*·tas de lan·gos·tee·nos san ra·fa·*el* *baked rice with seafood*

cebolla ① the·*bo*·lya *onion*

cecina ① the·*thee*·na *cured meat*

cerdo ⓜ *ther*·do *pork*

cereales ⓜ pl the·re·*a*·les *cereal*

cereza ① the·*re*·tha *cherry*
— **silvestre** seel·*ves*·tre *wild cherry*

ciervo ⓜ *thyer*·vo *deer*

cigala ① thee·*ga*·la *crayfish*

ciruela ① thee·*rwe*·la *plum*
— **pasa** *pa*·sa *prune*

civet ⓜ **de llebre** see·*vet* de *le*·bre *hare stew*

cochifrito ⓜ **de cordero** ko·chee·*free*·to de kor·*de*·ro *lamb fried with garlic & lemon*

cochinillo ⓜ ko·chee·nee·lyo *suckling pig*
— **asado** a·sa·do *roast suckling pig*
— **de pelotas** de pe·lo·tas *meatball stew*

coco ⓜ ko·ko *coconut*

codornices ⓕ pl **a la plancha** ko·dor·nee·thes a la *plan*·cha *grilled quail*

codorniz ⓕ ko·dor·neeth *quail*
— **con pimientos** kon pee·*myen*·tos *capsicums stuffed with quail*

col ⓕ kol *cabbage*
— **lombarda** lom·*bar*·da *red cabbage*

coles ⓕ pl **de bruselas** ko·les de broo·se·las *Brussels sprouts*

coliflor ⓕ ko·lee·*flor cauliflower*

conejo ⓜ ko·ne·kho *rabbit*
— **de monte** de mon·te *wild rabbit*

coquina ⓕ ko·kee·na *large clam*

corazón ⓜ ko·ra·*thon heart*

cordero ⓜ kor·de·ro *lamb*
— **al chilindrón** al chee·leen·*dron lamb in tomato & capsicum sauce*
— **con almendras** kon al·men·dras *lamb in almond sauce*

costillas ⓕ pl kos·tee·lyas *ribs*

crema ⓕ kre·ma *cream*
— **catalana** ka·ta·la·na *creme brulee*
— **de espinacas** de es·pee·na·kas *cream of spinach soup*
— **de naranja** de na·*ran*·kha *orange cream dessert*
— **de San José** de san kho·se *egg custard flavoured with cinnamon*
— **de verduras** de ver·doo·ras *cream of vegetable soup*

crocante ⓜ kro·kan·te *ice cream with chopped nuts & chocolate*

CH

chalote ⓜ cha·lo·te *shallot*

champiñones ⓜ pl cham·pee·*nyo*·nes *cultivated white mushrooms*

chanquetes ⓜ pl chan·ke·tes *whitebait • baby anchovies*

chilindrón (al) chee·leen·*dron* (al) *cooked in a tomato & red pepper sauce*

chipirón ⓜ chee·pee·ron *baby squid – very popular in the Basque Country*

chocolate ⓜ cho·ko·la·te *chocolate*
— **caliente** ka·lee·en·te *thick hot chocolate*

chocos ⓜ pl cho·kos *squid*

chorizo ⓜ cho·ree·tho *spicy red cooked sausage, similar to salami*
— **de Pamplona** de pam·*plo*·na *fine-textured, hard chorizo*
— **de Salamanca** de sa·la·man·ka *chunky chorizo from Salamanca*

chuletas ⓕ pl choo·le·tas *chops • cutlets*
— **al sarmiento** al sar·*myen*·to *chops prepared over wood from vines*
— **de buey** de bwey *ox chops*
— **de cerdo a la aragonesa** de ther·do a la a·ra·go·ne·sa *baked pork chops with wine & onion*

churros ⓜ choo·ros *fried doughnut strips bought from street-sellers or in cafes*

D

de soja de so·kha *with soya*

despojos ⓜ pl des·po·khos *offal*

dorada ⓕ **a la sal** do·ra·da a la sal *salted sea bream*

dulce ⓜ *dool*·the *sweet*
— **de batata** de ba·*ta*·ta *sweet potato pudding from Málaga*

dulces ⓜ pl *dool*·thes *sweets*
— **de las monjas** *dool*·thes de las mon·khas *confectionery made by nuns & sold in convents or cake shops*

E

embutidos ⓜ pl em·boo·tee·dos *generic name for cured sausages*

empanada ⓕ em·pa·na·da *savoury pie*
— **de carne** de kar·ne *spicy meat pie*
— **de espinaca** de es·pee·na·ka *spinach pie*

empanadilla ① em·pa·na·dee·lya *small pie, either sweet or savoury*

empanado ⓜ em·pa·na·do *coated in bread crumbs*

emparedado ⓜ em·pa·re·da·do *sandwich*
— **de jamón y espárragos** de kha·mon ee es·pa·ra·gos *fried ham & asparagus rolls*

empiñonado ⓜ em·pee·nyo·na·do *small marzipan-filled pastry with pinenuts*

en salsa verde en sal·sa ver·de *in a parsley & garlic sauce*

encurtidos ⓜ pl en·koor·tee·dos *pickles*

ensaimada ① **mallorquina** en·sai·ma·da ma·lyor·kee·na *spiral-shaped bun made with lard*

ensalada ① en·sa·la·da *salad*
— **de frutas** de froo·tas *fruit salad*
— **de patatas** de pa·ta·tas *potato salad*
— **del tiempo** del tyem·po *seasonal salad*
— **mixta** meeks·ta *mixed salad*

escaldadillas ① pl es·kal·da·dee·lyas *dough soaked in orange juice & fried*

escalivada ① es·ka·lee·va·da *roasted red capsicums in olive oil*

escalopes ⓜ pl **de ternera rellenos** es·ka·lo·pes de ter·ne·ra re·lye·nos *deep fried veal cutlets stuffed with egg & cheese*

espaguetis ⓜ pl es·pa·ge·tees *spaghetti*

espárragos ⓜ pl es·pa·ra·gos *asparagus*
— **con dos salsas** kon dos sal·sas *asparagus & tomato or paprika mayonnaise*
— **en vinagreta** en vee·na·gre·ta *asparagus in vinaigrette*

espinacas ① pl es·pee·na·kas *spinach*
— **a la catalana** a la ka·ta·la·na *spinach with pinenuts & raisins*

esqueixada ① es·kee·sha·da *cod dressed with olives, tomato & onion*

etxeko kopa e·che·ko ko·pa *ice cream dessert*

F

fabada ① **asturiana** fa·ba·da as·too·rya·na *stew made with pork, blood sausage & white beans*

faisán ⓜ fai·san *pheasant*

faves ① pl **a la catalana** fa·ves a la ka·ta·la·na *broad beans with ham*

fiambres ⓜ pl *free·am·bres cold meats*
— **surtidos** soor·tee·dos *selection of cold meats*

fideos ⓜ pl fee·de·os *pasta noodles*

fideua ① fee·de·wa *rice or noodles with fish & shellfish*

fideus ⓜ pl **a la cassola** fee·de·oos a la ka·so·la *Catalan noodle dish*

filete ⓜ fee·le·te *steak • any boneless slice of meat*
— **a la parrilla** a la pa·ree·lya *grilled beef steak*
— **de ternera** de ter·ne·ra *veal steak*

filloas ① pl fee·lyo·as *Galician pancakes filled with cream*

flan ⓜ flan *creme caramel*

flaó ① fla·o *sweet cheese flan*

flor manchega ① flor man·che·ga *deep-fried sweet wafers*

frambuesa ① fram·bwe·sa *raspberry*

frangellos ⓜ pl fran·khe·lyos *sweet made from cornmeal, milk & honey*

fresa ① fre·sa *strawberry*

fricandó ⓜ **de langostinos** free·kan·do de lan·gos·tee·nos *shrimp in almond sauce*

frite ⓜ free·te *lamb stew, served on festive occasions*

fritos ⓜ pl free·tos *fritters*
— **con miel** kon myel *honey-roasted fritters*

fritura ① free·too·ra *mixed fried fish*

fruta ① froo·ta *fruit*
— **variada** va·ree·a·da *a selection of fresh fruit*

frutas ① pl **en almibar** froo·tas en al·mee·bar *fruit in syrup*

frutos ⓜ pl **secos** froo·tos se·kos *nuts & dried fruit*

fuet ① foo·et *thin pork sausage*

G

gachas ① pl **manchegas** ga·chas man·che·gas *flavoured porridge*

galleta ① ga·lye·ta *biscuit*

gambas ① pl gam·bas *prawns*
— **a la plancha** a la plan·cha *grilled prawns*
— **en gabardina** en ga·bar·dee·na *prawns in batter*

Gamonedo ⑩ ga·mo·ne·do *sharp-tasting cheese, smoked & cured*

garbanzos ⑩ pl gar·ban·thos *chickpeas*
— **con cebolla** kon the·bo·lya *chickpeas in onion sauce*
— **tostados** tos·ta·dos *roasted chickpeas (sold as a snack)*

garbure ① gar·boo·re *green vegetable soup • pork & ham dish*

garúm ⑩ ga·room *olive & anchovy dip*

Gata-Hurdes ga·ta·oor·des *cheese*

gazpacho ⑩ gath·pa·cho *cold tomato soup*
— **andaluz** an·da·looth *cold tomato soup with chopped salad vegetables*
— **pastoril** pas·to·reel *rabbit stew with tomato & garlic*

gazpachos ⑩ pl **manchegos** gath·pa·chos man·che·gos *game & vegetable hotpot*

Gaztazarra ⑩ gath·ta·tha·ra *cheese*

gitano ⑩ khee·ta·no *Andalusian chickpea & tripe stew*

gofio ⑩ go·fyo *toasted cornmeal or barley*

granadilla ① gra·na·dee·lya *passion fruit*

grano ⑩ gra·no *grain*
— **largo** lar·go *long-grain (rice)*

gratinado ⑩ **de berenjenas** gra·tee·na·do de be·ren·khe·nas *eggplant gratin*

Grazalema ① gra·tha·le·ma *semi-cured sheep's milk cheese*

guindilla ① geen·dee·lya *mild green chilli*

guisado ⑩ gee·sa·do *stew*
— **de cordero** de kor·de·ro *lamb ragout*
— **de ternera** de ter·ne·ra *veal ragout*

guisante ⑩ gee·san·te *pea*
— **seco** se·ko *split pea*
— **mollar** mo·lyar *snow pea*

guisantes ⑩ pl **con jamón a la española** gee·san·tes kon kha·mon a la es·pa·nyo·la *pea & ham dish*

guisat ⑩ **de marisco** gee·sat de ma·rees·ko *stew made with seafood*

guiso ⑩ **de conejo estilo canario** gee·so de ko·ne·kho es·tee·lo ka·na·ryo *rabbit stew*

guiso ⑩ **de rabo de toro** gee·so de ra·bo de to·ro *stewed bull's tail with potatoes*

H

habas ① pl a·bas *broad beans*
— **a la granadina** a la gra·na·dee·na *broad beans with eggs & ham*
— **fritas** free·tas *fried broad beans (sold as a snack)*

habichuela ① a·bee·chwe·la *white bean*

hamburguesa ① am·boor·ge·sa *hamburger*

harina ① a·ree·na *flour*
— **integral** een·te·gral *wholemeal flour*

helado ⑩ e·la·do *ice cream*

hígado ⑩ ee·ga·do *liver*

higo ⑩ ee·go *fig*
— **seco** se·ko *dried fig*

hogaza ① o·ga·tha *dense, thick-crusted bread*

hoja ① **de parra** o·kha de pa·ra *vine leaf*

hojaldres ⑩ pl o·khal·dres *small flaky pastries covered in sugar*

hojas ① pl **verdes** o·khas ver·des *green vegetables*

hornazo ⑩ or·na·tho *bread stuffed with sausage*

hortalizas ① pl or·ta·lee·thas *vegetables*

huevo ⓜ *we·vo* egg
 — **cocido** *ko-thee·do* boiled egg
 — **de chocolate** *de cho·ko·la·te* chocolate egg
 — **frito** *free·to* fried egg
huevos ⓜ pl *we·vos* egg dishes
 — **a la flamenca** *a la fla·men·ka* baked vegetables with egg & ham
 — **al estilo Sóller** *al es·tee·lo so·lyer* fried eggs served with a milk & vegetable sauce
 — **en salsa agria** *en sal·sa a·grya* boiled eggs in wine & vinegar
 — **escalfados** *es·kal·fa·dos* poached eggs
 — **revueltos** *re·vwel·tos* scrambled eggs

J

jabalí ⓜ *kha·ba·lee* wild boar
 — **con salsa de castaños** *kon sal·sa de kas·ta·nyos* wild boar in chestnut sauce
jamón ⓜ *kha·mon* ham
 — **cocido** *ko·thee·do* cooked ham
 — **ibérico** *ee·ber·ik·o* ham from the Iberian pig, said to be the best in Spain
 — **serrano** *se·ra·no* cured mountain ham
jengibre ⓜ *khen·gee·bre* ginger
jerez (al) *khe·reth* (al) in a sherry sauce
judía ⓕ *khoo·dee·a* fresh green bean • dried kidney bean
judías ⓕ pl **del tío Lucas** *khoo·dee·as del tee·o loo·kas* bean stew with garlic & bacon
judías ⓕ pl **verdes a la castellana** *khoo·dee·as ver·des a la kas·te·lya·na* fried capsicums, garlic & green beans
judiones ⓜ pl **de la granja** *kho·dee·o·nes de la gran·kha* pork & bean stew

K

kiskilla *kees·kee·lya* shrimp (also spelled quisquilla)

L

langosta ⓕ *lan·gos·ta* lobster
 — **a la ibicenca** *a la ee·bee·then·ka* lobster with stuffed squid
langostinos ⓜ pl *lan·gos·tee·nos* king prawns
 — **a la plancha** *a la plan·cha* grilled king prawns
lavanco ⓜ *la·van·ko* wild duck
lechuga ⓕ *le·choo·ga* lettuce
legumbres ⓕ pl *le·goom·bres* pulses • vegetables • vegetable dishes
 — **secas** *se·kas* dried pulses
leguminosas ⓕ pl *le·goo·mee·no·sas* legumes
lengua ⓕ *len·gwa* tongue
 — **a la aragonesa** *a la a·ra·go·ne·sa* tongue in tomato & capsicum sauce
lenguado ⓜ *len·gwa·do* sole
 — **al chacolí con hongos** *al cha·ko·lee kon on·gos* sole with white wine & mushrooms
lenguados ⓜ pl **al plato** *len·gwa·dos al pla·to* sole & mushroom casserole
lenguas ⓕ pl **con salsa de almendras** *len·gwas kon sal·sa de al·men·dras* tongue in almond sauce
lentejas ⓕ pl *len·te·khas* lentils
liebre ⓕ *lye·bre* hare
 — **con castañas** *kon kas·ta·nyas* hare with chestnuts
 — **estofada** *es·to·fa·da* stewed hare
lima ⓕ *lee·ma* lime
limón ⓜ *lee·mon* lemon
lomo ⓜ *lo·mo* fillet • loin • sirloin
 — **curado** *koo·ra·do* cured pork sausage
 — **de cerdo** *de ther·do* loin of pork
longaniza ⓕ *lon·ga·nee·tha* chorizo, long & skinny sausage
lubina ⓕ *loo·bee·na* sea bass
 — **a la marinera** *a la ma·ree·ne·ra* sea bass in parsley sauce
lucio ⓜ *loo·thyo* pike

LL

llagostí ⓜ **a l'allioli** lyan·gos·*tee* a la·*lyee*·o·lee *grilled prawns in garlic mayonnaise*

llenguado ⓜ **a la nyoca** lyen·*gwa*·do a la *nyo*·ka *sole with pine nuts & raisins*

M

macedonia ⓕ **de frutas** ma·the·*do*·nya de *froo*·tas *fruit salad*

macedonia ⓕ **de verduras** ma·the·*do*·nya de ver·*doo*·ras *mixed vegetables*

magdalena ⓕ ma·da·*le*·na *small fairy cake to dunk in coffee*

magras ⓕ pl *ma*·gras *fried eggs, ham, cheese & tomato*

maíz ⓜ ma·*eeth* maize • *corn*
— **tierno** *tyer*·no *sweetcorn*

mandarina ⓕ man·da·*ree*·na *tangerine* • *mandarin*

mango ⓜ *man*·go *mango*

manitas ⓕ pl **de cerdo** ma·*nee*·tas de *ther*·do *pig's trotters*

manitas ⓕ pl **de cordero** ma·*nee*·tas de kor·*de*·ro *leg of lamb*

manteca ⓕ man·*te*·ka *lard*

mantecado ⓜ man·te·*ka*·do *a soft lard biscuit* • *dairy ice cream*

mantequilla ⓕ man·te·*kee*·lya *butter*
— **sin sal** seen sal *unsalted butter*

manzana ⓕ man·*tha*·na *apple*

manzanas ⓕ **asadas** man·*tha*·nas a·sa·das *baked apples*

margarina ⓕ mar·ga·*ree*·na *margarine*

marinera (a la) ma·ree·*ne*·ra (a la) *cooked or served in a white wine sauce*

mariscos ⓜ ma·*rees*·kos *shellfish* • *seafood*

marmitako mar·mee·*ta*·ko *fresh tuna & potato casserole*

marrano ⓜ ma·*ra*·no *pork*

mar y cel ⓜ mar es el *dish of sausages, rabbit, shrimp & angler fish*

masa ⓕ *ma*·sa *pastry (dough)*

mayonesa ⓕ ma·yo·*ne*·sa *mayonnaise*

medallones ⓜ pl **de merluza** me·da·*lyo*·nes de mer·*loo*·tha *hake steaks*

mejillones ⓜ pl me·khee·*lyo*·nes *mussels*
— **al vino blanco** al *vee*·no *blan*·ko *mussels in white wine*
— **con salsa** kon *sal*·sa *mussels with tomato sauce*

mel ⓜ **i mató** mel ee ma·*to* *a dessert of curd cheese with honey*

melocotón ⓜ me·lo·ko·*ton* *peach*

melocotones ⓜ pl **al vino** me·lo·ko·*to*·nes al *vee*·no *peaches in red wine*

melón ⓜ me·*lon* *melon*

membrillo ⓜ mem·*bree*·lyo *quince*

menestra ⓕ me·*nes*·tra *mixed vegetable stew*
— **de pollo** de *po*·lyo *chicken & vegetable stew*

merengue ⓜ me·*ren*·ge *meringue*

merluza ⓕ mer·*loo*·tha *hake*

mermelada ⓕ mer·me·*la*·da *marmalade*

mero ⓜ *me*·ro *halibut* • *grouper* • *sea bass*

miel ⓕ myel *honey*
— **de azahar** de a·tha·*ar* *orange blossom honey*
— **de caña** de *ka*·nya *treacle*

migas ⓕ pl *mee*·gas *fried cubes of bread with capsicums*
— **a la aragonesa** a la a·ra·go·*ne*·sa *fried bread with bacon rashers in tomato sauce*
— **mulatas** moo·*la*·tas *cubes of bread soaked in chocolate & fried*

mojarra ⓕ mo·*kha*·ra *type of sea bream*

moje ⓜ **manchego** mo·*khe* man·*che*·go *cold broth with black olives*

mojete ⓜ mo·*khe*·te *dipping sauce for bread, made from potatoes, garlic, tomatoes & paprika*
— **murciano** moor·*thya*·no *fish & capsicum dish*

mojo ⓜ *mo*·kho *spicy capsicum sauce*

mollejas ⓕ pl mo·*lye*·khas *sweetbreads*

mollete m mo·lye·te *soft round bap roll*

monas f pl **de pascua** mo·nas de pas·kwa *Easter cakes • figures made of chocolate*

mongetes f pl **seques i butifarra** mon·zhe·tes se·kes ee boo·tee·fa·ra *haricot beans with roasted pork sausage*

mora f mo·ra *blackberry*

moraga f **de sardina** mo·ra·ga de sar·dee·na *fresh anchovies on a spit*

morcilla f mor·thee·lya *black pudding, often stewed with beans & vegetables*

mortadela f mor·ta·de·la *mortadella sausage*

morteruelo m mor·te·rwe·lo *pate dish containing offal, game & spices*

mostachones m pl mos·ta·cho·nes *small cakes for dipping in coffee or hot chocolate (also spelled mostatxones)*

mostaza f mos·ta·tha *mustard*

— **en grano** en gra·no *mustard seed*

múgil m moo·kheel *grey mullet*

mujol m **guisado** moo·khol gee·sa·do *red mullet*

mus m **de chocolate** moos de cho·ko·la·te *chocolate mousse*

muslo m moos·lo *(chicken) leg & thigh*

N

nabo m na·bo *root vegetable • turnip*

naranja f na·ran·kha *orange*

nata f na·ta *cream*

— **agria** a·grya *sour cream*

— **montada** mon·ta·da *whipped cream*

natillas f pl na·tee·lyas *creamy custard dessert*

— **de chocolate** de cho·ko·la·te *chocolate custard*

navaja f na·va·kha *razor clam*

nécora f ne·ko·ra *small crab*

nueces f pl nwe·thes *nuts*

nuez f nweth *nut*

— **de América** de a·me·ree·ka *pecan nut*

— **de nogal** de no·gal *walnut*

Ñ

ñora f nyo·ra *sweet red capsicum (usually dried)*

O

oca f o·ka *goose*

olla f o·lya *meat & vegetable stew • cooking pot*

oreja f **de mar** o·re·kha de mar *abalone*

ostiones m pl **a la gaditana** os·tyo·nes a la ga·dee·ta·na *Cádiz oysters with garlic, parsley & bread crumbs*

ostra f os·tra *oyster*

oveja f o·ve·kha *mutton*

P

pá m **amb oli** pa amb o·lee *toasted bread with garlic & olive oil*

pacana f pa·ka·na *pecan*

paella f pa·e·lya *rice dish which has many regional variations*

— **marinera** ma·ree·ne·ra *paella with fish & seafood*

— **zamorana** tha·mo·ra·na *paella with meat*

palitos m pl **de queso** pa·lee·tos de ke·so *cheese straws*

palmera f pal·me·ra *leaf-shaped flaky pastry, often coated in chocolate*

palomitas f pl pa·lo·mee·tas *popcorn*

pan m pan *bread*

— **aceite** a·they·te *flat round bread*

— **árabe** a·ra·be *pita bread*

— **de Alá** de a·la *'Allah's Bread' – dessert*

— **de boda** de bo·da *sculpted bread traditionally made for weddings*

— **de centeno** de then·te·no *rye bread*

— **duro** doo·ro *stale bread, used for toasting & eating with olive oil*

— **integral** een·te·gral *wholemeal bread*

panaché ⓜ pa·na·*che* mixed vegetable stew

panallets ⓟⓛ pa·na·*lyets* marzipan sweets

panceta ⓕ pan·*the*·ta salt-cured, streaky bacon

panchineta ⓕ pan·chee·*ne*·ta almond tart

panecillo ⓜ pa·ne·*thee*·lyo small bread roll

panojas ⓟⓛ **malagueñas** pa·*no*·khas ma·la·ge·*nyas* sardine dish

papas ⓕ ⓟⓛ **arrugadas** *pa*·pas a·roo·*ga*·das potatoes boiled in their jackets

pargo ⓜ *par*·go sea bream

parrillada ⓕ pa·ree·*lya*·da grilled meat
— **de mariscos** de ma·*rees*·kos seafood grill

pastel ⓜ pas·*tel* cake
— **de boda** de *bo*·da wedding cake
— **de chocolate** de cho·ko·*la*·te chocolate cake
— **de cierva** de *thyer*·va meat pie
— **de cumpleaños** de koom·ple·a·*nyos* birthday cake

pastelitos ⓟⓛ **de miel** pas·te·*lee*·tos de myel honey fritters

pataco ⓜ pa·*ta*·ko tuna & potato stew

patatas ⓕ ⓟⓛ pa·*ta*·tas potatoes
— **a la riojana** a la ree·o·*kha*·na potatoes with chorizo & paprika
— **alioli** a·lee·o·*lee* potatoes in garlic mayonnaise
— **bravas** *bra*·vas potatoes in spicy tomato sauce
— **con chorizo** kon cho·*ree*·tho potatoes with chorizo
— **estofadas** es·to·*fa*·das boiled potatoes

pato ⓜ *pa*·to duck
— **a la sevillana** a la se·vee·*lya*·na duck with orange sauce
— **alcaparrada** al·ka·pa·*ra*·da duck with capers & almonds

pavo ⓜ *pa*·vo turkey

pececillos ⓜ ⓟⓛ pe·the·*thee*·lyos small fish

pechina ⓕ pe·*chee*·na scallop

pecho ⓜ *pe*·cho breast of lamb

pechuga ⓕ pe·*choo*·ga breast of poultry

pepinillo ⓜ pe·pee·*nee*·lyo gherkin

pepino ⓜ pe·*pee*·no cucumber

pepitoria ⓕ pe·pee·*to*·rya sauce made with egg & almond

pepitos ⓜ ⓟⓛ pe·*pee*·tos chocolate eclair cakes filled with custard

pera ⓕ *pe*·ra pear

La Peral ⓕ la pe·*ral* soft cheese

perca ⓕ *per*·ka perch

perdices ⓕ ⓟⓛ per·*dee*·thes partridges
— **a la manchega** a la man·*che*·ga partridge in red wine & capsicums
— **con chocolate** kon cho·ko·*la*·te partridge with chocolate

perdiz ⓕ per·*deeth* partridge

peregrina ⓕ pe·re·*gree*·na scallop

pericana ⓕ pe·ree·*ka*·na dish of olives, cod oil, capsicums & garlic

perrito ⓜ **caliente** pe·*ree*·to ka·lee·*en*·te hot dog

pescada ⓕ **á galega** pes·*ka*·da a ga·*le*·ga hake fried in olive oil & served with garlic & paprika sauce

pescadilla ⓕ pes·ka·*dee*·lya whiting • young hake

pescaditos ⓜ ⓟⓛ **rebozados** pes·ka·*dee*·tos re·bo·*tha*·dos small fish fried in batter

pescado ⓜ pes·*ka*·do fish
— **a l'all cremat** a lal kre·*mat* fish in burnt garlic

pescaíto ⓜ **frito** pes·ka·ee·to *free*·to tiny fried fish

pestiños ⓜ ⓟⓛ pes·*tee*·nyos honey-coated aniseed pastries, fried with filling

pez ⓕ **espada** peth es·*pa*·da swordfish
— **frito** *free*·to fried swordfish steaks on a skewer

picada ① pee·ka·da *mixture of garlic, parsley, toasted almonds & nuts, often used to thicken sauces*

picadillo ⓜ pee·ka·dee·lyo *salad consisting of diced vegetables*
— **de atún** de a·toon *salad made with diced tuna & capsicums*
— **de ternera** de ter·ne·ra *minced veal*

pichón ⓜ pee·chon *pigeon*

pichones ⓜ pl **asados** pee·cho·nes a·sa·dos *roast pigeons*

pilotes ⓜ pl pee·lo·tes *Catalan meatballs*

pimiento ⓜ pee·myen·to *capsicum*
— **amarillo** a·ma·ree·lyo *yellow capsicum*
— **rojo** ro·kho *red capsicum*
— **verde** ver·de *green capsicum*

pimientos ⓜ pl pee·myen·tos *capsicums (the ones from El Bierzo are especially good)*
— **a la riojana** a la ree·o·kha·na *roast red capsicum fried in oil & garlic*
— **al chilindrón** al chee·leen·dron *capsicum casserole*

piña ① pee·nya *pineapple*

pinchito ⓜ **moruno** peen·chee·to mo·roo·no *lamb & chicken kebabs*

piñón ⓜ pee·nyon *pinenut*

pinta ① peen·ta *pinto bean*

pintada ① peen·ta·da *guinea fowl*

piquillo ⓜ pee·kee·lyo *sweet & spicy capsicums*

pistacho ⓜ pees·ta·cho *pistachio nut*

pisto ⓜ **manchego** pees·to man·che·go *zucchini with capsicum & tomato, fried or stewed*

plátano ⓜ pla·ta·no *banana*

pochas ① pl po·chas *beans*
— **a la riojana** a la ree·o·kha·na *beans with chorizo in spicy paprika sauce*
— **con almejas** kon al·me·khas *beans with clams*

pollo ⓜ po·lyo *chicken*
— **asado** a·sa·do *roast chicken*
— **con samfaina** kon sam·fai·na *chicken with mixed vegetables*
— **en escabeche** en es·ka·be·che *marinated chicken*
— **en salsa de ajo** en sal·sa de a·kho *chicken in garlic sauce*
— **granadina** gra·na·dee·na *chicken with wine & ham*
— **y langosta** ee lan·gos·ta *chicken with crayfish*

pulpo ⓜ **a feira** pool·po a fey·ra *spicy boiled octopus*

polvorón ⓜ pol·vo·ron *almond shortbread, often eaten at Christmas*

pomelo ⓜ po·me·lo *grapefruit*

postre ⓜ pos·tre *dessert*
— **de naranja** de na·ran·kha *cream-filled oranges*

potaje ⓜ po·ta·khe *broth*
— **castellano** kas·te·lya·no *broth with beans & sausages*
— **de garbanzos** de gar·ban·thos *broth with chickpeas*
— **de lentejas** de len·te·khas *lentil broth*

pote ⓜ **gallego** po·te ga·lye·go *stew*

potito ⓜ po·tee·to *jar of baby food*

pringada ① preen·ga·da *bread dipped in sauce • a marinated sandwich*

productos ⓜ pl **biológicos** pro·dook·tos bee·o·lo·khee·kos *organic produce*

productos ⓜ pl **del mar** pro·dook·tos del mar *seafood products*

productos ⓜ pl **lácteos** pro·dook·tos lak·te·os *dairy products*

puchero ⓜ poo·che·ro *casserole*

pudin ⓜ poo·din *pudding*

puerco ⓜ pwer·ko *pork*

puerro ⓜ pwe·ro *leek*

pulpo ⓜ pool·po *octopus*

punta ① **de diamante** poon·ta de dya·man·te *confection from Valencia*

porrusalda ① po·roo·sal·da *cod & potato stew*

Q

queso ⓜ *ke·so* cheese
— **azul** *a·thool* blue cheese
— **crema** *kre·ma* cream cheese
quisquilla ⓕ *kees·kee·lya* shrimp (also spelled kiskilla)

R

rábano ⓜ *ra·ba·no* radish
rabas ⓕ **en salsa verde** *ra·bas* en *sal·sa ver·de* squid in green sauce
rabassola ⓕ *ra·ba·so·la* mushroom
rape ⓜ *ra·pe* monkfish
— **a la gallega** a la *ga·lye·ga* monkfish with potatoes & garlic sauce
— **a la Monistrol** a la mo·nees·trol monkfish with bechamel sauce
redondo ⓜ *re·don·do* round (of beef)
— **al horno** al or·no roast beef
regañaos ⓜ pl *re·ga·nya·os* pastry stuffed with sardines & red capsicum
relleno ⓜ *re·lye·no* stuffing
remolacha ⓕ *re·mo·la·cha* beetroot
reo ⓜ *re·o* sea trout
repollo ⓜ *re·po·lyo* cabbage
repostería ⓕ *re·pos·te·ree·a* confectionery
requesón ⓜ *re·ke·son* cottage cheese
riñón ⓜ *ree·nyon* kidney
róbalo ⓜ *ro·ba·lo* haddock • sea bass
rodaballo ⓜ *ro·da·ba·lyo* turbot • brill
romero ⓜ *ro·me·ro* rosemary
romesco ⓜ *ro·mes·ko* sweet red capsicum, almond & garlic sauce
rosca ⓕ **de carne** *ros·ka* de *kar·ne* meatloaf wrapped in bacon
rosco ⓜ *ros·ko* small sweet bun
rossejat ⓜ *ro·se·dyat* rice with fish & shellfish
rovellons ⓜ pl **a la plancha** *ro·ve·lyons* a la *plan·cha* garlic mushrooms
ruibarbo ⓜ *roo·ee·bar·bo* rhubarb

S

salchicha ⓕ *sal·chee·cha* pork sausage
salchichón ⓜ *sal·chee·chon* cured & peppery white sausage
salmón ⓜ *sal·mon* salmon
— **a la ribereña** a la *ree·be·re·nya* salmon in a cider sauce
— **ahumado** *a·oo·ma·do* smoked salmon
salmonete ⓜ *sal·mo·ne·te* red mullet
salmorejo ⓜ *sal·mo·re·kho* thick gazpacho soup made from tomato, bread, olive oil, vinegar, garlic & green capsicum
— **de Córdoba** de *kor·do·ba* gazpacho soup made with more vinegar than usual
salpicón ⓜ *sal·pee·kon* fish or meat salad
salsa ⓕ *sal·sa* sauce
— **alioli** *a·lee·o·lee* garlic & olive oil vinaigrette • garlic mayonnaise
— **de holandesa** de *o·lan·de·sa* hollandaise sauce
— **de mayonesa** de *ma·yo·ne·sa* mayonnaise sauce
— **de tomate** de *to·ma·te* tomato sauce
— **inglesa** *een·gle·sa* Worcestershire sauce
— **tártara** *tar·ta·ra* tartar sauce
— **verde** *ver·de* parsley & garlic sauce
samfaina ⓕ *sam·fai·na* grilled vegetable sauce
sancocho ⓜ *san·ko·cho* fish dish served with potatoes
sandía ⓕ *san·dee·a* watermelon
sándwich ⓜ *san·weech* sandwich
— **mixto** *meeks·*to toasted ham & cheese sandwich
sanocho ⓜ **canario** *sa·no·*cho ka·na·ryo baked monkfish with potatoes
sardinas ⓕ *sar·dee·nas* sardines
— **a la parrilla** a la pa·ree·lya sardines grilled
— **en cazuela** en ka·thwe·la sardines served in a clay pot

sargo ⓜ *sar*·go *bream*

sepia ⓕ *se*·pya *cuttlefish*

sesos ⓜ pl *se*·sos *brains*

setas ⓕ pl *se*·tas *wild mushrooms*
— **a la kashera** a la ka·*she*·ra *sauteed wild mushrooms*
— **rellenas** re·*lye*·nas *mushrooms stuffed*

sofrit pagés ⓜ so·*freet* pa·*zhes vegetable stew*

sofrito ⓜ so·*free*·to *fried tomato sauce*

soja ⓕ so·*kha* soya bean*

soldaditos ⓜ pl **de Pavia** sol·da·*dee*·tos de pa·*vee*·a *cod fritters*

solomillo ⓜ so·lo·*mee*·lyo *fillet*

sopa ⓕ so·pa *soup*
— **del día** del *dee*·a *a soup of the day*

sopas ⓕ pl **de leche** so·pas de *le*·che *pieces of bread soaked in milk & cinnamon*

sopas ⓕ pl **engañadas** so·pas en·ga·*nya*·das *soup made from capsicum, onion shoots, vinegar, figs & grapes*

sorbete ⓜ sor·*be*·te *sorbet*

sorroputún ⓜ so·ro·poo·*toon* *tuna casserole*

suizo ⓜ *swee*·tho *sugared bun*

sukaldi soo·*kal*·dee *beef stew*

suquet ⓜ soo·*ket* *clams in almond sauce*

suquet de peix ⓜ soo·*ket* de peysh *fish stew*

suspiros ⓜ pl **de monja** soos·*pee*·ros de mon·kha *'nun's sighs' – custard sweets*

T

tallarines ⓜ pl ta·lya·*ree*·nes *pasta noodles*

tarta ⓕ *tar*·ta *cake • tart*
— **de almendra** de al·*men*·dra *almond tart*
— **de manzana** de man·*tha*·na *apple tart*

tartaleta ⓕ tar·ta·*le*·ta *tartlet*

tartaletas ⓕ pl **de huevos revueltos** tar·ta·*le*·tas de we·vos re·*vwel*·tos *scrambled egg tartlets*

ternera ⓕ ter·*ne*·ra *veal*
— **a la sevillana** a la se·vee·*lya*·na *veal served with wine & olives*
— **en cazuela con berenjenas** en ka·*thwe*·la kon be·ren·*khe*·nas *veal & eggplant casserole*

tocino ⓜ to·*thee*·no *salted pork • bacon*
— **del cielo** del *thye*·lo *creamy dessert made with egg yolk & sugar, with a caramel topping*

tocrudo ⓜ to·*kroo*·do *'everything raw'– salad of meat, garlic, onion & green capsicum*

tomate ⓜ to·*ma*·te *tomatoes*
— **(de) pera** (de) *pe*·ra *plum tomato*
— **frito** *free*·to *tinned tomato sauce*

tomates ⓜ pl to·*ma*·tes
— **enteros y pelados** en·*te*·ros ee pe·*la*·dos *tinned whole tomatoes*
— **rellenos de atún** re·*lye*·nos de a·*toon* *tomatoes stuffed with tuna*

toro ⓜ to·ro *bull meat*

torrefacto ⓜ to·re·*fak*·to *dark-roasted coffee beans*

torrija ⓕ to·*ree*·kha *French toast*

torta ⓕ *tor*·ta *pie • tart • flat bread*
— **de aceite** de a·*they*·te *sweet, flat cake or biscuit made with oil*
— **pascualina** pas·kwa·*lee*·na *spinach & egg pie, eaten at Easter*

tortilla ⓕ tor·*tee*·lya *omelette*
— **española** es·pa·*nyo*·la *potato & onion omelette*
— **francesa** fran·*the*·sa *plain omelette*

tortillas ⓕ pl **de camarones** tor·*tee*·lyas de ka·ma·*ro*·nes *shrimp fritters*

tortita ⓕ tor·*tee*·ta *waffle*

tostada ⓕ tos·*ta*·da *toasted bread*

tocino ⓜ to·*thee*·no *bacon*

tripas ⓕ pl *tree*·pas *intestines • guts*

trucha ⓕ *troo*·cha *trout*
— **a la marinera** a la ma·ree·*ne*·ra *trout in a white wine sauce*

truchas ① pl *troo*·chas *trout*
— **a la navarra** a la na·*va*·ra *trout with ham*
— **con vino y romero** kon *vee*·no ee ro·*me*·ro *trout with red wine & rosemary*
trufa ① *troo*·fa *truffle*
— **tarta** *tar*·ta *chocolate truffle cake*
tumbet (de peix) ⑩ toom·*bet* (de peysh) *vegetable souffle, sometimes containing fish*
turrón ⑩ too·*ron* *Spanish nougat*

U

uva ① *oo*·va *grape*
— **de corinto** de ko·*reen*·to *currant*
— **pasa** *pa*·sa *raisin*
— **sultana** sool·*ta*·na *sultana*

V

vacuno ⑩ va·*koo*·no *beef*
venado ⑩ ve·*na*·do *venison*

verduras ① ver·*doo*·ras *vegetables*
vieira ① vee·*ey*·ra *scallop*
villagodio ⑩ vee·lya·go·*dyo* *large steak*
vinagre ⑩ vee·*na*·gre *vinegar*
visita ① vee·*see*·ta *almond cake*

Y

yemas ① pl *ye*·mas *small round cakes*
yogur ⑩ yo·*goor* *yogurt*

Z

zanahoria ① tha·na·o·*rya* *carrot*
zarangollo ⑩ tha·ran·go·*lyo* *fried zucchini*
zarzamora ① thar·tha·*mo*·ra *blackberry*
zarzuela ① **de mariscos** thar·*thwe*·la de ma·*rees*·kos *spicy shellfish stew*
zarzuela ① **de pescado** thar·*thwe*·la de pes·*ka*·do *fish in almond sauce*
zurrukutano thoo·roo·koo·*ta*·no *cod & green capsicum soup*

emergencies

emergencias

	English	Spanish	Pronunciation
75A	Help!	¡Socorro!	so·ko·ro
75B	Stop!	¡Pare!	pa·re
75C	Go away!	¡Váyase!	va·ya·se
75D	Thief!	¡Ladrón!	lad·ron
75E	Fire!	¡Fuego!	fwe·go
75F	Watch out!	¡Cuidado!	kwee·da·do

76A It's an emergency.
Es una emergencia.　es oo·na e·mer·khen·thya

76B Call the police!
¡Llame a la policía!　lya·me a la po·lee·thee·a

76C Call a doctor!
¡Llame a un médico!　lya·me a oon me·dee·ko

76D Call an ambulance!
*¡Llame a una
ambulancia!*　lya·me a oo·na
am·boo·lan·thya

I'm ill.
Estoy enfermo/a. m/f　es·toy en·fer·mo/a

My friend is ill.
*Mi amigo/a está
enfermo/a.* m/f　mee a·mee·go/a es·ta
en·fer·mo/a

77A Could you help me, please?
*¿Me puede ayudar,
por favor?*　me pwe·de a·yoo·dar
por fa·vor

essentials

175

77B I have to use the telephone.
Necesito usar el   ne·the·*see*·to oo·*sar* el
teléfono.   te·*le*·fo·no

77C I'm lost.
Estoy perdido. m   es·*toy* per·*dee*·do

77D I'm lost.
Estoy perdida. f   es·*toy* per·*dee*·da

77E Where are the toilets?
¿Dónde están los   *don*·de es·*tan* los
servicios?   ser·*vee*·thyos

the underground

Petty crime is common in Madrid and Barcelona. Try not to stand near the train doors and keep money out of sight. If someone attempts to rob you, try screaming these phrases at the top of your lungs:

Leave me alone!	*¡Déjame en paz!*	de·kha·me en path
Help, thief!	*¡Socorro, al ladron!*	so·ko·ro al lad·ron

police

la policia

In an emergency, call the police, who will then put you through to other emergency services (fire brigade and ambulance). For more on making a call, see **communications**, page 72.

78A Where's the police station?
¿Dónde está la   *don*·de es·*ta* la
comisaría?   ko·mee·sa·*ree*·a

78B I want to report an offence.
Quiero denunciar un   *kye*·ro de·noon·*thyar* oon
delito.   de·*lee*·to

78C I have insurance.
Tengo seguro.   *ten*·go se·*goo*·ro

He/She tried to assault me.
Él/Ella intentó asaltarme.   el/e·lya een·ten·to a·sal·tar·me

He/She tried to rob me.
Él/Ella intentó robarme.   el/e·lya een·ten·to ro·bar·me

79A I've been robbed.
Me han robado.   me an ro·ba·do

79B I've been raped.
He sido violado. m   e see·do vee·o·la·do

79C I've been raped.
He sido violada. f   e see·do vee·o·la·da

My ... was stolen.
Mi ... fue robado/a. m/f   mee ... fwe ro·ba·do/a

My ... were stolen.
*Mis ... fueron
robados/as.* m/f   mee ... fwe·ron
ro·ba·dos/as

80A I've lost my bags.
He perdido mis maletas.   e per·dee·do mees ma·le·tas

80B I've lost my money.
He perdido mi dinero.   e per·dee·do mee dee·ne·ro

80C I've lost my passport.
He perdido mi pasaporte.   e per·dee·do mee pa·sa·por·te

I apologise.
Lo siento.   lo syen·to

I didn't realise I was doing anything wrong.
*No sabía que estaba
haciendo algo mal.*   no sa·bee·a ke es·ta·ba
a·thyen·do al·go mal

I'm innocent.
Soy inocente.   soy ee·no·then·te

81A I want to contact my consulate.
*Quiero ponerme en
contacto con mi
consulado.*   kye·ro po·ner·me en
kon·tak·to kon mee
kon·soo·la·do

81B I want to contact my embassy.
*Quiero ponerme en
contacto con mi
embajada.*   kye·ro po·ner·me en
kon·tak·to kon mee
em·ba·kha·da

Can I call a lawyer?

¿Puedo llamar a un abogado?	pwe·do lya·mar a oon a·bo·ga·do

I need a lawyer who speaks English.

Necesito un abogado que hable inglés.	ne·the·see·to oon a·bo·ga·do ke a·ble een·gles

Can I pay an on-the-spot fine?

¿Podemos pagar una multa al contado?	po·de·mos pa·gar oo·na mool·ta al kon·ta·do

This drug is for personal use.

Esta droga es para uso personal.	es·ta dro·ga es pa·ra oo·so per·so·nal

I have a prescription for this drug.

Tengo receta para esta droga.	ten·go re·the·ta pa·ra es·ta dro·ga

What am I accused of?

¿De qué me acusan?	de ke me a·ku·san

the police may say ...

You have overstayed your visa.

El plazo de tu visado se ha pasado.	el pla·tho de too vee·sa·do se a pa·sa·do

You'll be charged with ...

Será acusado/a de ... m/f	se·ra a·koo·sa·do/a de ...

He'll/She'll be charged with ...

Él/Ella será acusado/a de ...	el/e·lya se·ra a·koo·sa·do/a de ...

assault	asalto	a·sal·to
possession (of illegal substances)	posesión (de sustancias ilegales)	po·se·syon (de soos·tan·thyas ee·le·ga·les)
shoplifting	ratería	ra·te·ree·a
speeding	exceso de velocidad	eks·the·so de ve·lo·thee·da

doctor

el médico

82A Where's the nearest (night) pharmacist?
¿Dónde está la farmacia   don·de es·ta la far·ma·thya
(de guardía) más cercana?   (de gwar·dee·a) mas ther·ka·na

82B Where's the nearest dentist?
¿Dónde está el dentista   don·de es·ta el den·tees·ta
más cercano?   mas ther·ka·no

82C Where's the nearest doctor?
¿Dónde está el médico   don·de es·ta el me·dee·ko
más cercano?   mas ther·ka·no

82D Where's the nearest hospital?
¿Dónde está el hospital   don·de es·ta el os·pee·tal
más cercano?   mas ther·ka·no

82D Where's the nearest optometrist?
¿Dónde está el oculista   don·de es·ta el o·koo·lees·ta
más cercano?   mas ther·ka·no

I've been vaccinated for ...	*Estoy vacunado/a contra ...* m/f	es·toy va·koo·na·do/a kon·tra ...
tetanus	*el tétano*	el te·ta·no
typhoid	*la tifus*	la tee·foos
hepatitis A/B/C	*la hepatitis A/B/C*	la e·pa·tee·tees a/be/the

84A I'm sick.   *Estoy enfermo.* m   es·toy en·fer·mo
84B I'm sick.   *Estoy enferma.* f   es·toy en·fer·ma

83A I need a doctor (who speaks English).
Necesito un doctor   ne·the·see·to oon dok·tor
(que hable inglés).   (ke a·ble een·gles)

83B Could I see a female doctor?
¿Puede examinarme   pwe·de ek·sa·mee·nar·me
una doctora?   oo·na dok·to·ra

the doctor may say ...

What's the problem?
¿Qué le pasa?   ke le *pa*·sa

Where does it hurt?
¿Dónde le duele?   *don*·de le *dwe*·le

Do you have a temperature?
¿Tiene fiebre?   *tye*·ne *fye*·bre

How long have you been like this?
¿Desde cuándo se   *des*·de *kwan*·do se
siente así?   *syen*·te a·*see*

Have you had this before?
¿Ha tenido esto antes?   a te·*nee*·do *es*·to *an*·tes

Have you had unprotected sex?
¿Ha tenido relaciones   a te·*nee*·do re·la·*thyo*·nes
sexuales sin   sek·*swa*·les seen
protección?   pro·tek·*thyon*

Are you allergic?
¿Tiene usted alergias?   *tye*·ne oos·*te* a·*ler*·khyas

Are you on medication?
¿Se encuentra   se en·*kwen*·tra
bajo medicación?   *ba*·kho me·dee·ka·*thyon*

You need to be admitted to hospital.
Necesita ingresar   ne·the·*see*·ta een·gre·*sar*
en un hospital.   en oon os·pee·*tal*

How long are you travelling for?
Por cuánto tiempo   por *kwan*·to *tyem*·po
está viajando.   es·*ta* vya·*khan*·do

**You should have it checked when
you go home.**
Debería revisarlo   de·be·*ree*·a re·vee·*sar*·lo
cuando vuelva a casa.   *kwan*·do *vwel*·va a *ka*·sa

Do you ...?	¿Usted ...?	oos·te ...
drink	bebe	*be*·be
smoke	fuma	*foo*·ma
take drugs	toma drogas	*to*·ma *dro*·gas

83C I've run out of my medication.
Se me terminaron los medicamentos.
se me ter·mee·*na*·ron los me·dee·ka·*men*·tos

This is my usual medicine.
Éste es mi medicamento habitual.
es·te es mee me·dee·ka·*men*·to a·bee·too·*al*

My prescription is ...
Mi receta es ...
mee re·*the*·ta es ...

I don't want a blood transfusion.
No quiero que me hagan una transfusión de sangre.
no *kye*·ro ke me a·gan oo·na trans·foo·*syon* de *san*·gre

Please use a new syringe.
Por favor, use una jeringa nueva.
por fa·*vor* oo·se oo·na khe·*reen*·ga *nwe*·va

I need new ...	*Necesito ... nuevas.*	ne·the·*see*·to ... *nwe*·vas
glasses	*gafas*	ga·fas
contact lenses	*lentes de contacto*	*len*·tes de kon·*tak*·to

For cost & receipts, see **shopping**, page 64.

symptoms & conditions

los síntomas & las condiciones

I have ...
Tengo ...
ten·go ...

I've recently had ...
Hace poco he tenido ...
a·the po·ko e te·*nee*·do ...

There's a history of ...
Hay antecedentes de ...
ai an·te·the·*den*·tes de ...

I'm on regular medication for ...
Estoy bajo medicación para ...
es·*toy* ba·kho me·dee·ka·*thyon* pa·ra ...

asthma	*asma* m	*as*·ma
diarrhoea	*diarrea* f	dee·a·*re*·a
fever	*fiebre* f	*fye*·bre
infection	*infección* f	in·fek·*thyon*
sprain	*torcedura* f	tor·the·*doo*·ra

84C It hurts here.

Me duele aquí.   me *dwe*·le a·*kee*

I've been injured.
He sido herido/a. m/f   e *see*·do e·*ree*·do/a

I've been vomiting.
He estado vomitando.   e es·*ta*·do vo·mee·*tan*·do

I'm dehydrated.
Estoy deshidratado/a. m/f   es·*toy* de·seed·ra·*ta*·do/a

I can't sleep.
No puedo dormir.   no *pwe*·do dor·*meer*

I think it's the medication I'm on.
Me parece que son los   me pa·*re*·the ke son los
medicamentos que   me·dee·ka·*men*·tos ke
estoy tomando.   es·*toy* to·*man*·do

I feel ...	*Me siento ...*	me *syen*·to ...
better	*mejor*	me·*khor*
depressed	*deprimido/a* m/f	de·pree·*mee*·do
dizzy	*mareado/a* m/f	ma·re·a·do
shivery	*destemplado/a* m/f	des·tem·*pla*·do
strange	*raro/a* m/f	*ra*·ro
weak	*débil*	*de*·beel
worse	*peor*	pe·*or*

For more symptoms & conditions, see the **dictionary**.

women's health

la salud femenina

I think I'm pregnant.
Creo que estoy embarazada. kre·o ke es·toy em·ba·ra·tha·da

I haven't had my period for … weeks.
Hace … semanas que no a·the … se·ma·nas ke no
me viene la regla. me vye·ne la reg·la

I need a pregnancy test.
Necesito una prueba ne·the·see·to oo·na prwe·ba
de embarazo. de em·ba·ra·tho

I'm on the Pill.
Tomo la píldora. to·mo la peel·do·ra

I've noticed a lump here.
He notado que tengo e no·ta·do ke ten·go
un bulto aquí. oon bool·to a·kee

I need …	*Quisiera …*	kee·sye·ra …
contraception	*usar algún*	oo·sar al·goon
	método anti-	me·to·do an·tee·
	conceptivo	kon·thep·tee·vo
the morning-	*tomar la*	to·mar la
after pill	*píldora del*	peel·do·ra del
	día siguiente	dee·a see·gyen·te

the doctor may say …

Are you pregnant?
¿Está embarazada? es·ta em·ba·ra·tha·da

You're pregnant.
Está embarazada. es·ta em·ba·ra·tha·da

When did you last have your period?
¿Cuándo le vino la kwan·do le vee·no la
regla por última vez? reg·la por ool·tee·ma veth

Are you using contraception?
¿Usa anticonceptivos? oo·sa an·tee·kon·thep·tee·vos

Do you have your period?
¿Tiene la regla? tye·ne la reg·la

health

183

allergies

85A I'm allergic to antibiotics.
Soy alérgico a los   soy a·*ler*·khee·ko a los
antibióticos. m   an·tee·*byo*·tee·kos

85B I'm allergic to antibiotics.
Soy alérgica a los   soy a·*ler*·khee·ka a los
antibióticos. f   an·tee·*byo*·tee·kos

86A I'm allergic to anti-inflammatories.
Soy alérgico a los anti-   soy a·*ler*·khee·ko a los an·tee·
inflamatorios. m   een·fla·ma·*to*·ryos

86B I'm allergic to anti-inflammatories.
Soy alérgica a los anti-   soy a·*ler*·khee·ka a los an·tee·
inflamatorios. f   een·fla·ma·*to*·ryos

87A I'm allergic to aspirin.
Soy alérgico a la aspirina. m   soy a·*ler*·khee·ko a la as·pee·*ree*·na

87B I'm allergic to aspirin.
Soy alérgica a la aspirina. f   soy a·*ler*·khee·ka a la as·pee·*ree*·na

88A I'm allergic to bees.
Soy alérgico a las abejas. m   soy a·*ler*·khee·ko a las a·*be*·khas

88B I'm allergic to bees.
Soy alérgica a las abejas. f   soy a·*ler*·khee·ka a las a·*be*·khas

89A I'm allergic to codeine.
Soy alérgico a la codeina. m   soy a·*ler*·khee·ko a la ko·de·e·*ee*·na

89B I'm allergic to codeine.
Soy alérgica a la codeina. f   soy a·*ler*·khee·ka a la ko·de·e·*ee*·na

90A I'm allergic to penicillin.
Soy alérgico a la   soy a·*ler*·khee·ko a la
penicilina. m   pe·nee·thee·*lee*·na

90B I'm allergic to penicillin.
Soy alérgica a la   soy a·*ler*·khee·ka a la
penicilina. f   pe·nee·thee·*lee*·na

For more food-related allergies, see **vegetarian & special meals** page 160.

I have a skin allergy.
Tengo una alergia en la piel.
ten·go oo·na a·ler·khya en la pyel

alternative treatments

tratamientos alternativos

I don't use Western medicine.
No uso la medicina occidental.
no oo·so la me·dee·thee·na ok·thee·den·tal

I prefer ...
Prefiero ...
pre·fye·ro ...

Can I see someone who practises ...?
¿Puedo ver a alguien que practique ...?
pwe·do ver al·gyen ke prak·tee·ke ...

---

waiting room

Here are some tips on Spanish etiquette in public places.
• Men usually wait for women to be seated before they take a seat themselves, and when they finally do it's the guys who cross their legs at the knees, not the ladies.
• Yawning and stretching when you have an audience, no matter how small, is considered inappropriate.

---

parts of the body

las partes del cuerpo

My ... hurts.
Me duele ...
me dwe·le ...

I can't move my ...
No puedo mover ...
no pwe·do mo·ver ...

I have a cramp in my ...
Tengo calambres en ...
ten·go ka·lam·bres en ...

My ... is swollen.
Mi ... está hinchado.
mee ... es·ta een·cha·do

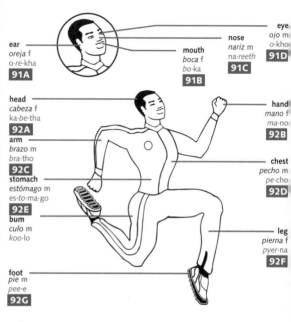

ear
oreja f
o·re·kha
91A

eye
ojo m
o·kho
91D

nose
nariz m
na·reeth
91C

mouth
boca f
bo·ka
91B

head
cabeza f
ka·be·tha
92A

hand
mano f
ma·no
92B

arm
brazo m
bra·tho
92C

chest
pecho m
pe·cho
92D

stomach
estómago m
es·to·ma·go
92E

bum
culo m
koo·lo

leg
pierna f
pyer·na
92F

foot
pie m
pee·e
92G

chemist

la farmacia

Is there a (night) chemist nearby?
¿Hay una farmacia (de   ai oo·na far·ma·thya (de
guardía) por aquí?   gwar·dee·a) por a·kee

I need something for ...
Necesito algo para ...   ne·the·see·to al·go pa·ra ...

Do I need a prescription for ...?
¿Necesito receta   ne·the·see·to re·the·ta
para ...?   pa·ra ...

I have a prescription.
   Tengo receta médica.   ten·go re·*the*·ta me·dee·ka

How many times a day?
   ¿Cuántas veces al día?   kwan·tas ve·thes al dee·a

listen for ...

a to·*ma*·do es·to *an*·tes
  ¿Ha tomado esto   **Have you taken this**
  antes?   **before?**

de·be ter·mee·*nar* el tra·ta·*myen*·to
  Debe terminar el   **You must complete the**
  tratamiento.   **course.**

dos ve·thes al *dee*·a (kon la ko·*mee*·da)
  Dos veces al día   **Twice a day**
  (con la comida).   **(with food).**

es·ta·*ra lees*·to en (*veyn*·te mee·*noo*·tos)
  Estará listo en   **It'll be ready to pick up**
  (veinte minutos).   **in (20 minutes).**

dentist

el dentista

I have a broken tooth.
   Se me ha roto un diente.   se me a *ro*·to oon *dyen*·te

I have a toothache.
   Me duele una muela.   me *dwe*·le *oo*·na *mwe*·la

listen for ...

a·bra	*Abra.*	**Open wide.**
no se *mwe*·va	*No se mueva.*	**Don't move.**
en·*khwa*·ge	*¡Enjuague!*	**Rinse!**

I've lost a filling.
Se me ha caído un empaste.
se me a ka·ee·do oon em·pas·te

My gums hurt.
Me duelen las encías.
me dwe·len las en·thee·as

I don't want it extracted.
No quiero que me lo saquen.
no kye·ro ke me lo sa·ken

I need a/an ...	*Necesito ...*	ne·the·see·to ...
anaesthetic	*una anestesia*	oo·ne a·nes·te·sya
filling	*un empaste*	oon em·pas·te

signs

Asistencia Sanitaria	a·see·sten·thee·a sa·nee·ta·ree·a	First Aid
Farmacia	far·ma·thee·a	Pharmacy/ Drug Store
Horas de Visita	o·ras de vee·see·ta	Visiting Hours
Hospital	o·spee·tal	Hospital
Médico	me·dee·ko	Doctor
Planta	plan·ta	Ward
Urgencias	ur·khen·thee·as	Casualty/ Emergency

SUSTAINABLE TRAVEL

As the climate change debate heats up, the matter of sustainability becomes an important part of the travel vernacular. In practical terms, this means assessing our impact on the environment and local cultures and economies – and acting to make that impact as positive as possible. Here are some basic phrases to get you on your way …

communication & cultural differences

Would you like me to teach you some English?
¿Quieres que te enseñe   kye·res ke te en·se·nye
algo de inglés?   al·go de een·gles

Is this a local or national custom?
¿Esto es una costumbre   es·to es oo·na kos·toom·bre
local o nacional?   lo·kal o na·thyo·nal

I respect your customs.
Respeto sus costumbres.   res·pe·to soos kos·toom·bres

community benefit & involvement

What sorts of issues is this community facing?
¿A qué tipo de problemas se a ke tee·po de pro·ble·mas se
enfrenta esta comunidad?   en·fren·ta es·ta ko·moo·nee·da

climate change	*cambio*	*kam*·byo
	climático m	klee·*ma*·tee·ko
freedom of	*libertad de*	lee·ber·*ta* de
religion	*religión* f	re·lee·*khyon*
interregional	*tirantez*	tee·ran·*teth*
tension	*interregional* f	een·ter·re·khyo·*nal*
racism	*racismo* m	ra·*thees*·mo
unemployment	*desempleo* m	des·em·*ple*·o

I'd like to volunteer my skills.

Me gustaría ofrecer mis conocimientos.

me goos·ta·*ree*·a o·fre·*ther* mees ko·no·thee·*myen*·tos

Are there any volunteer programs available in the area?

¿Hay programas de voluntariado en la zona?

ai pro·*gra*·mas de vo·loon·ta·*rya*·do en la *tho*·na

environment

Where can I recycle this?

¿Dónde se puede reciclar esto?

don·de se *pwe*·de re·thee·*klar es*·to

transport

Can we get there by public transport?

¿Se puede ir en transporte público?

se *pwe*·de eer en trans·*por*·te *poo*·blee·ko

Can we get there by bike?

¿Se puede ir en bici?

se *pwe*·de eer en *bee*·thee

I'd prefer to walk there.

Prefiero ir a pie.

pre·*fye*·ro eer a pye

accommodation

I'd like to stay at a locally-run hotel.

Me gustaría alojarme en un hotel del barrio.

me goos·ta·*ree*·a a·lo·*khar*·me en oon o·*tel* del *ba*·ryo

Are there any ecolodges here?

¿Hay algún ecolodge por aquí?

ai al·*goon* e·ko·loch por a·*kee*

Can I turn the air conditioning off and open the window?

¿Puedo apagar el aire acondicionado y abrir la ventana?

pwe·do a·pa·*gar* el *ai*·re a·kon·dee·thyo·*na*·do ee a·*breer* la ven·*ta*·na

There's no need to change my sheets.

No hace falta cambiar   no a·the *fal*·ta kam·*byar*
las sábanas.   las sa·ba·nas

shopping

Where can I buy locally produced goods/souvenirs?

¿Dónde puedo comprar   *don*·de *pwe*·do kom·*prar*
recuerdos de la zona?   re·*kwer*·dos de la *tho*·na

Do you sell Fair Trade products?

¿Se venden productos de   se *ven*·den pro·*dook*·tos de
comercio equitativo?   ko·*mer*·thyo e·kee·ta·*tee*·vo

food

Do you sell ...?	*¿Se venden ...?*	se *ven*·den ...
locally produced food	*comestibles de la zona*	ko·mes·*tee*·bles de la *tho*·na
organic produce	*productos agrícolas biológicos*	pro·*dook*·tos a·*gree*·ko·las bee·o·*lo*·khee·kos

Can you tell me which traditional foods I should try?

¿Que platos típicos   ke *pla*·tos *tee*·pee·kos
debería probar?   de·be·*ree*·a pro·*bar*

sightseeing

Are cultural tours available?

¿Se pueden hacer   se *pwe*·den a·*ther*
recorridos culturales?   re·ko·*ree*·dos kool·too·*ra*·les

Does the guide speak any of the regional languages?

¿El guía habla alguna   el *gee*·a *a*·bla al·*goo*·na
lengua regional?   *len*·gwa re·khyo·*nal*

Basque	euskera m	e·oos·ke·ra
Catalan	catalán m	ka·ta·lan
Galician	gallego m	ga·lye·go
Does your company …?	Su empresa …?	soo em·pre·sa …
donate	hace	a·the
money	donativos a	do·na·ti·vos a
to charity	organizaciones benéficas	or·ga·nee·tha·thyo·nes be·ne·fee·kas
hire local	contrata a	kon·tra·ta a
guides	guías de la zona	gee·as de la tho·na
visit local	visita a	vee·see·ta a
businesses	negocios locales	ne·go·thyos lo·ka·les

Nouns in the dictionary have their gender indicated by ⓜ or ⓕ. If it's a plural noun, you'll also see pl. Where a word that could be either a noun or a verb has no gender indicated, it's a verb.

A

(to be) able *poder* po·*der*
aboard *a bordo* a bor·do
abortion *aborto* ⓜ a·bor·to
about *sobre* so·bre
above *arriba* a·ree·ba
abroad *en el extranjero* en el eks·tran·khe·ro
accept *aceptar* a·thep·tar
accident *accidente* ⓜ ak·thee·*den*·te
accommodation *alojamiento* ⓜ a·lo·kha·*myen*·to
across *a través* a tra·ves
activist *activista* ⓜ&ⓕ ak·tee·vees·ta
acupuncture *acupuntura* ⓕ a·koo·poon·too·ra
adaptor *adaptador* ⓜ a·dap·ta·dor
address *dirección* ⓕ dee·rek·thyon
administration *administración* ⓕ ad·mee·nees·tra·thyon
admission price *precio* ⓜ *de entrada* pre·thyo de en·tra·da
admit *admitir* ad·mee·teer
adult *adulto* ⓜ a·*dool*·to
advertisement *anuncio* ⓜ a·*noon*·thyo
advice *consejo* ⓜ kon·se·kho
aerobics *aeróbic* ⓜ ai·ro·beek
Africa *África* ⓕ a·free·ka
after *después de* des·pwes de
aftershave *bálsamo de aftershave* bal·sa·mo de ahf·ter·sha·eev
again *otra vez* o·tra veth
age *edad* ⓕ e·da
aggressive *agresivo/a* ⓜ/ⓕ a·gre·see·vo/a

agree *estar de acuerdo* es·tar de a·kwer·do
agriculture *agricultura* ⓕ a·gree·kul·too·ra
AIDS *SIDA* ⓜ see·da
air *aire* ⓜ ai·re
air mail *por vía aérea* por vee·a a·e·re·a
air-conditioned *con aire acondicionado* kon ai·re a·kon·dee·thyo·na·do
air-conditioning *aire* ⓜ *acondicionado* ai·re a·kon·dee·thyo·na·do
airline *aerolínea* ⓕ ay·ro·lee·nya
airport *aeropuerto* ⓜ ay·ro·pwer·to
airport tax *tasa* ⓕ *del aeropuerto* ta·sa del ay·ro·pwer·to
alarm clock *despertador* ⓜ des·per·ta·dor
alcohol *alcohol* ⓜ al·col
all *todo* to·do
allergy *alergia* ⓕ a·ler·khya
allow *permitir* per·mee·teer
almonds *almendras* ⓕ pl al·men·dras
almost *casi* ka·see
alone *solo/a* ⓜ/ⓕ so·lo/a
already *ya* ya
also *también* tam·byen
altar *altar* ⓜ al·tar
altitude *altura* ⓕ al·too·ra
always *siempre* syem·pre
amateur *amateur* ⓜ&ⓕ a·ma·ter
ambassador *embajador/ embajadora* ⓜ/ⓕ em·ba·kha·dor/ em·ba·kha·do·ra
among *entre* en·tre
anarchist *anarquista* ⓜ&ⓕ a·nar·kees·ta
ancient *antiguo/a* ⓜ/ⓕ an·tee·gwo/a
and *y* ee
angry *enfadado/a* ⓜ/ⓕ en·fa·da·do/a

animal *animal* ⓜ a·nee·*mal*
ankle *tobillo* ⓜ to·*bee*·lyo
answer *respuesta* ⓕ res·*pwes*·ta
answering machine *contestador* ⓜ *automático* kon·tes·ta·*dor* ow·to·ma·*tee*·ko
ant *hormiga* ⓕ or·*mee*·ga
anthology *antología* ⓕ an·to·lo·*khee*·a
antibiotics *antibióticos* ⓜ pl an·tee·byo·*tee*·kos
antinuclear *antinuclear* an·tee·noo·kle·*ar*
antique *antigüedad* ⓕ an·tee·gwe·*da*
antiseptic *antiséptico* ⓜ an·tee·*sep*·tee·ko
any *alguno/a* ⓜ/ⓕ al·*goo*·no/a
appendix *apéndice* ⓜ a·*pen*·dee·the
apple *manzana* ⓕ man·*tha*·na
appointment *cita* ⓕ *thee*·ta
apricot *albaricoque* ⓜ al·ba·ree·*ko*·ke
archaeological *arqueológico/a* ⓜ/ⓕ ar·keo·*lo*·khee·ko/a
architect *arquitecto/a* ⓜ/ⓕ ar·kee·*tek*·to/a
architecture *arquitectura* ⓕ ar·kee·tek·*too*·ra
argue *discutir* dees·koo·*teer*
arm *brazo* ⓜ *bra*·tho
army *ejército* ⓜ e·*kher*·thee·to
arrest *detener* de·te·*ner*
arrivals *llegadas* ⓕ pl lye·*ga*·das
arrive *llegar* lye·*gar*
art *arte* ⓜ *ar*·te
art gallery *museo* ⓜ *de arte* moo·*se*·o de *ar*·te
artichoke *alcachofa* ⓕ al·ka·*cho*·fa
artist *artista* ⓜ&ⓕ ar·*tees*·ta
ashtray *cenicero* ⓜ the·nee·*the*·ro
Asia *Asia* ⓕ *a*·sya
ask (a question) *preguntar* pre·goon·*tar*
ask (for something) *pedir* pe·*deer*
aspirin *aspirina* ⓕ as·pee·*ree*·na
assault *asalto* ⓜ a·*sal*·to
asthma *asma* ⓜ *as*·ma
athletics *atletismo* ⓜ at·le·*tees*·mo
atmosphere *atmósfera* ⓕ at·*mos*·fe·ra
aubergine *berenjena* ⓕ be·ren·*khe*·na
aunt *tía* ⓕ *tee*·a

Australia *Australia* ⓕ ow·*stra*·lya
Australian Rules football *fútbol* ⓜ *australiano* foot·bol ow·stra·*lya*·no
automatic teller machine *cajero* ⓜ *automático* ka·*khe*·ro ow·to·ma·*tee*·ko
autumn *otoño* ⓜ o·*to*·nyo
avenue *avenida* ⓕ a·ve·*nee*·da
avocado *aguacate* ⓜ a·gwa·*ka*·te

B

B&W (film) *blanco y negro* blan·ko ee *ne*·gro
baby *bebé* ⓜ be·*be*
baby food *comida* ⓕ *de bebé* ko·*mee*·da de be·*be*
baby powder *talco* ⓜ *tal*·ko
babysitter *canguros* ⓜ kan·*goo*·ros
back (of body) *espalda* ⓕ es·*pal*·da
back (of chair) *respaldo* ⓜ res·*pal*·do
backpack *mochila* ⓕ mo·*chee*·la
bacon *tocino* ⓜ to·*thee*·no
bad *malo/a* ⓜ/ⓕ *ma*·lo/a
bag *bolso* ⓜ *bol*·so
baggage *equipaje* ⓜ e·kee·*pa*·khe
baggage allowance *límite de equipaje* lee·*mee*·te de e·kee·*pa*·khe
baggage claim *recogida* ⓕ *de equipajes* re·ko·*khee*·da de e·kee·*pa*·khes
bakery *panadería* ⓕ pa·na·de·*ree*·a
balance (account) *saldo* ⓜ *sal*·do
balcony *balcón* ⓜ bal·*kon*
ball *pelota* ⓕ pe·*lo*·ta
ballet *ballet* ⓜ ba·*le*
banana *plátano* ⓜ *pla*·ta·no
band *grupo* ⓜ *groo*·po
bandage *vendaje* ⓜ ven·*da*·khe
band-aids *tiritas* ⓕ pl tee·*ree*·tas
bank *banco* ⓜ *ban*·ko
bank account *cuenta* ⓕ *bancaria* *kwen*·ta ban·*ka*·rya
banknotes *billetes* ⓜ pl *(de banco)* bee·*lye*·tes (de *ban*·ko)
baptism *bautizo* ⓜ bow·*tee*·tho

bar *bar* ⓜ bar
bar (with music) *pub* ⓜ poob
bar work *trabajo* ⓜ *de camarero/a* ⓜ/ⓕ
  tra·ba·kho de ka·ma·re·ro/a
baseball *béisbol* ⓜ beys·bol
basket *canasta* ⓕ ka·nas·ta
basketball *baloncesto* ⓜ ba·lon·thes·to
bath *bañera* ⓕ ba·nye·ra
bathing suit *bañador* ⓜ ba·nya·dor
bathroom *baño* ⓜ ba·nyo
battery (car) *batería* ⓕ ba·te·ree·a
battery (small) *pila* ⓕ pee·la
be *ser* ser • *estar* es·tar
beach *playa* ⓕ pla·ya
bean sprouts *brotes* ⓜ pl *de soja*
  bro·tes de so·kha
beans *judías* khoo·dee·as
beautiful *hermoso/a* ⓜ/ⓕ er·mo·so/a
beauty salon *salón* ⓜ *de belleza* sa·lon
  de be·lye·tha
because *porque* por·ke
bed *cama* ⓕ ka·ma
bedding *ropa* ⓕ *de cama* ro·pa de ka·ma
bedroom *habitación* ⓕ a·bee·ta·thyon
bee *abeja* ⓕ a·be·kha
beef *carne* ⓕ *de vaca* kar·ne de va·ka
beer *cerveza* ⓕ ther·ve·tha
beetroot *remolacha* ⓕ re·mo·la·cha
before *antes* an·tes
beggar *mendigo/a* ⓜ/ⓕ men·dee·go/a
begin *comenzar* ko·men·thar
behind *detrás de* de·tras de
below *abajo* a·ba·kho
best *lo mejor* lo me·khor
bet *apuesta* ⓕ a·pwes·ta
better *mejor* me·khor
between *entre* en·tre
bible *biblia* ⓕ bee·blya
bicycle *bicicleta* ⓕ bee·thee·kle·ta
big *grande* gran·de
bike *bici* ⓕ bee·thee
bike chain *cadena* ⓕ *de bici* ka·de·na
  de bee·thee
bike path *camino* ⓜ *de bici* ka·mee·no
  de bee·thee
bill *cuenta* ⓕ kwen·ta

biodegradable *biodegradable*
  bee·o·de·gra·da·ble
biography *biografía* ⓕ bee·o·gra·fee·a
bird *pájaro* ⓜ pa·kha·ro
birth certificate *partida* ⓕ *de*
  nacimiento par·tee·da de
  na·thee·myen·to
birthday *cumpleaños* ⓜ koom·ple·a·nyos
birthday cake *pastel* ⓜ *de cumpleaños*
  pas·tel de koom·ple·a·nyos
biscuit *galleta* ga·lye·ta
bite (dog) *mordedura* ⓕ mor·de·doo·ra
bite (food) *bocado* ⓜ bo·ka·do
bite (insect) *picadura* ⓕ pee·ka·doo·ra
black *negro/a* ⓜ/ⓕ ne·gro/a
blanket *manta* ⓕ man·ta
bleed *sangrar* san·grar
blind *ciego/a* ⓜ/ⓕ thye·go/a
blister *ampolla* ⓕ am·po·lya
blocked *atascado/a* ⓜ/ⓕ a·tas·ka·do/a
blood *sangre* ⓕ san·gre
blood group *grupo* ⓜ *sanguíneo*
  groo·po san·gee·neo
blood pressure *presión* ⓕ *arterial*
  pre·syon ar·te·ryal
blood test *análisis* ⓜ *de sangre*
  a·na·lee·sees de san·gre
blue *azul* a·thool
board (ship, etc) *embarcarse*
  em·bar·kar·se
boarding house *pensión* ⓕ pen·syon
boarding pass *tarjeta* ⓕ *de embarque*
  tar·khe·ta de em·bar·ke
bone *hueso* ⓜ we·so
book *libro* ⓜ lee·bro
book (make a reservation) *reservar*
  re·ser·var
booked out *lleno/a* ⓜ/ⓕ lye·no/a
bookshop *librería* ⓕ lee·bre·ree·a
boots *botas* ⓕ pl bo·tas
border *frontera* ⓕ fron·te·ra
boring *aburrido/a* ⓜ/ⓕ a·boo·ree·do/a
borrow *tomar prestado* to·mar
  pres·ta·do
botanic garden *jardín* ⓜ *botánico*
  khar·deen bo·ta·nee·ko
both *dos* ⓜ/ⓕ pl dos

bottle *botella* ⓕ bo·te·lya
bottle opener *abrebotellas* ⓜ a·bre·bo·te·lyas
bowl *bol* ⓜ bol
box *caja* ⓕ ka·kha
boxer shorts *calzones* ⓜ pl kal·*tho*·nes
boxing *boxeo* ⓜ bo·se·o
boy *chico* ⓜ chee·ko
boyfriend *novio* ⓜ no·vyo
bra *sujetador* ⓜ soo·khe·ta·*dor*
Braille *Braille* ⓜ brai·lye
brakes *frenos* ⓜ pl fre·nos
branch office *sucursal* ⓕ soo·koor·*sal*
brandy *coñac* ⓜ ko·*nyak*
brave *valiente* va·*lyen*·te
bread *pan* ⓜ pan
 brown bread *pan moreno* pan mo·re·no
 bread rolls *bollos* bo·lyos
 rye *pan de centeno* pan de then·te·no
 sourdough *pan de masa fermentada* pan de *ma*·sa fer·men·*ta*·da
 white bread *pan blanco* pan blan·ko
 wholemeal *integral* een·te·*gral*
break *romper* rom·per
break down *descomponerse* des·kom·po·*ner*·se
breakfast *desayuno* ⓜ des·a·yoo·no
breasts *senos* ⓜ pl se·nos
breathe *respirar* res·pee·*rar*
bribe *soborno* ⓜ so·*bor*·no
bribe *sobornar* so·bor·*nar*
bridge *puente* ⓜ pwen·te
briefcase *maletín* ⓜ ma·le·*teen*
brilliant *cojonudo/a* ⓜ/ⓕ ko·kho·noo·do/a
bring *traer* tra·*er*
brochure *folleto* ⓜ fo·lye·to
broken *roto/a* ⓜ/ⓕ ro·to/a
bronchitis *bronquitis* ⓕ bron·kee·tees
brother *hermano* ⓜ er·ma·no
brown *marrón* ma·*rron*
bruise *cardenal* ⓜ kar·de·*nal*
brussels sprouts *coles* ⓜ pl *de Bruselas* ko·les de broo·se·las

bucket *cubo* ⓜ koo·bo
Buddhist *budista* ⓜ&ⓕ boo·dees·ta
buffet *buffet* ⓜ boo·fe
bug *bicho* ⓜ bee·cho
build *construir* kons·troo·*eer*
building *edificio* ⓜ e·dee·fee·thyo
bull *toro* ⓜ to·ro
bullfight *corrida* ⓕ ko·ree·da
bullring *plaza* ⓕ *de toros* pla·tha de to·ros
bum (of body) *culo* ⓜ koo·lo
burn *quemadura* ⓕ ke·ma·doo·ra
bus *autobús* ⓜ ow·to·boos
bus (intercity) *autocar* ⓜ ow·to·*kar*
bus station *estación de autobuses/ autocares* ⓕ es·ta·*thyon* de ow·to·boo·ses/ow·to·ka·res
bus stop *parada* ⓕ *de autobús* pa·ra·da de ow·to·boos
business *negocios* ⓜ pl ne·go·thyos
business class *clase* ⓕ *preferente* kla·se pre·fe·*ren*·te
business person *comerciante* ⓜ&ⓕ ko·mer·*thyan*·te
busker *artista callejero/a* ⓜ/ⓕ ar·tees·ta ka·lye·khe·ro/a
busy *ocupado/a* ⓜ/ⓕ o·koo·pa·do/a
but *pero* pe·ro
butcher's shop *carnicería* ⓕ kar·nee·the·ree·a
butter *mantequilla* ⓕ man·te·kee·lya
butterfly *mariposa* ⓕ ma·ree·po·sa
buttons *botónes* ⓜ pl bo·to·nes
buy *comprar* kom·*prar*

C

cabbage *col* kol
cable *cable* ⓜ ka·ble
cable car *teleférico* ⓜ te·le·fe·ree·ko
café *café* ⓜ ka·fe
cake *pastel* ⓜ pas·*tel*
cake shop *pastelería* ⓕ pas·te·le·ree·a
calculator *calculadora* ⓕ kal·koo·la·do·ra
calendar *calendario* ⓜ ka·len·da·ryo

calf *ternero* ⓜ ter·ne·ro
camera *cámara* ⓕ *(fotográfica)* ka·ma·ra (fo·to·gra·fee·ka)
camera shop *tienda* ⓕ *de fotografía* tyen·da de fo·to·gra·fee·a
camp *acampar* a·kam·par
camping store *tienda* ⓕ *de provisiones de cámping* tyen·da de pro·vee·syo·nes de kam·peen
campsite *cámping* ⓜ kam·peen
can *lata* ⓕ la·ta
can (be able) *poder* po·der
can opener *abrelatas* ⓜ a·bre·la·tas
Canada *Canadá* ⓕ ka·na·da
cancel *cancelar* kan·the·lar
cancer *cáncer* ⓜ kan·ther
candle *vela* ⓕ ve·la
cantaloupe *cantalupo* ⓜ kan·ta·loo·po
capsicum (red/green) *pimiento* ⓜ *rojo/verde* pee·myen·to ro·kho/ ver·de
car *coche* ⓜ ko·che
car hire *alquiler* ⓜ *de coche* al·kee·ler de ko·che
car owner's title *papeles* ⓜ pl *del coche* pa·pe·les del ko·che
car registration *matrícula* ⓕ ma·tree·koo·la
caravan *caravana* ⓕ ka·ra·va·na
cards *cartas* ⓕ pl kar·tas
care (about something) *preocuparse por* pre·o·koo·par·se por
care (for someone) *cuidar de* kwee·dar de
caring *bondadoso/a* ⓜ/ⓕ bon·da·do·so/a
carpark *aparcamiento* ⓜ a·par·ka·myen·to
carpenter *carpintero/a* ⓜ/ⓕ kar·peen·te·ro/a
carrot *zanahoria* ⓕ tha·na·o·rya
carry *llevar* lye·var
carton *cartón* ⓜ kar·ton
cash *dinero* ⓜ *en efectivo* dee·ne·ro en e·fek·tee·vo
cash (a cheque) *cambiar (un cheque)* kam·byar (oon che·ke)

cash register *caja* ⓕ *registradora* ka·kha re·khees·tra·do·ra
cashew nut *anacardo* ⓜ a·na·kar·do
cashier *caja* ⓕ ka·kha
casino *casino* ⓜ ka·see·no
cassette *casete* ⓜ ka·se·te
castle *castillo* ⓜ kas·tee·lyo
casual work *trabajo* ⓜ *eventual* tra·ba·kho e·ven·twal
cat *gato/a* ⓜ/ⓕ ga·to/a
cathedral *catedral* ⓕ ka·te·dral
Catholic *católico/a* ⓜ/ⓕ ka·to·lee·ko/a
cauliflower *coliflor* ⓕ ko·lee·flor
caves *cuevas* ⓕ pl kwe·vas
CD *cómpact* ⓜ kom·pakt
celebrate (an event) *celebrar* the·le·brar
celebration *celebración* ⓕ the·le·bra·thyon
cemetery *cementerio* ⓜ the·men·te·ryo
cent *centavo* ⓜ then·ta·vo
centimetre *centímetro* ⓜ then·tee·me·tro
central heating *calefacción* ⓕ *central* ka·le·fak·thyon then·tral
centre *centro* ⓜ then·tro
ceramic *cerámica* ⓕ the·ra·mee·ka
cereal *cereales* ⓜ pl the·re·a·les
certificate *certificado* ⓜ ther·tee·fee·ka·do
chair *silla* ⓕ see·lya
champagne *champán* ⓜ cham·pan
chance *oportunidad* ⓕ o·por·too·nee·da
change (money) *cambio* ⓜ kam·byo
change *cambiar* kam·byar
changing rooms *vestuarios* ⓜ pl ves·twa·ryos
charming *encantador/encantadora* ⓜ/ⓕ en·kan·ta·dor/en·kan·ta·do·ra
chat up *ligar* lee·gar
cheap *barato/a* ⓜ/ⓕ ba·ra·to/a
cheat *tramposo/a* ⓜ/ⓕ tram·po·so/a
check *revisar* re·vee·sar
check (bank) *cheque* ⓜ che·ke
check-in *facturación* ⓕ *de equipajes* fak·too·ra·thyon de e·kee·pa·khes

checkpoint *control* ⓜ kon·*trol*

cheese *queso* ⓜ *ke*·so

chef *cocinero* ⓜ ko·thee·*ne*·ro

chemist (person) *farmacéutico/a* ⓜ/①
far·ma·*the*·oo·ti·ko/a

chemist (shop) *farmacia* ① far·*ma*·thya

chess *ajedrez* ⓜ a·khe·*dreth*

chess board *tablero* ⓜ *de ajedrez*
ta·*ble*·ro de a·khe·*dreth*

chest *pecho* ⓜ *pe*·cho

chewing gum *chicle* ⓜ *chee*·kle

chicken *pollo* ⓜ *po*·lyo

chicken breast *pechuga* ① pe·*choo*·ga

chickpeas *garbanzos* ⓜ pl gar·*ban*·thos

child *niño/a* ⓜ/① *nee*·nyo/a

child seat *asiento* ⓜ *de seguridad para
bebés* a·*syen*·to de se·goo·ree·*da*
pa·ra be·*bes*

childminding service *guardería* ①
gwar·de·*ree*·a

children *hijos* ⓜ pl *ee*·khos

chilli *guindilla* ① geen·*dee*·lya

chilli sauce *salsa* ① *de guindilla* *sal*·sa
de geen·*dee*·lya

chocolate *chocolate* ⓜ cho·ko·*la*·te

choose *escoger* es·ko·*kher*

Christian *cristiano/a* ⓜ/①
krees·*tya*·no/a

Christian name *nombre* ⓜ *de pila*
nom·bre de *pee*·la

Christmas *Navidad* ① na·vee·*da*

Christmas Eve *Nochebuena* ①
no·che·*bwe*·na

church *iglesia* ① ee·*gle*·sya

cider *sidra* ① *see*·dra

cigar *cigarro* ⓜ thee·*ga*·ro

cigarette *cigarillo* ⓜ thee·ga·*ree*·lyo

cigarette lighter *mechero* ⓜ me·*che*·ro

cigarette machine *máquina* ① *de
tabaco* *ma*·kee·na de ta·*ba*·ko

cigarette paper *papel* ⓜ *de fumar*
pa·*pel* de foo·*mar*

cinema *cine* ⓜ *thee*·ne

circus *circo* ⓜ *theer*·ko

citizenship *ciudadanía* ①
theew·da·da·*nee*·a

city *ciudad* ① theew·*da*

city centre *centro* ⓜ *de la ciudad*
then·tro de la theew·*da*

city walls *murallas* ① pl moo·*ra*·lyas

civil rights *derechos civiles* ⓜ pl
de·*re*·chos thee·*vee*·les

classical *clásico/a* ⓜ/① *kla*·see·ko/a

clean *limpio/a* ⓜ/① *leem*·pyo/a

cleaning *limpieza* ① leem·*pye*·tha

client *clienta/e* ⓜ/① klee·*en*·ta/e

cliff *acantilado* ⓜ a·kan·tee·*la*·do

climb *subir* soo·*beer*

cloak *capote* ⓜ ka·*po*·te

cloakroom *guardarropa* ⓜ gwar·da·*ro*·pa

clock *reloj* ⓜ re·*lokh*

close *cerrar* the·*rar*

closed *cerrado/a* ⓜ/① the·*ra*·do/a

clothes line *cuerda* ① *para tender la
ropa* *kwer*·da *pa*·ra ten·*der* la *ro*·pa

clothing *ropa* ① *ro*·pa

clothing store *tienda* ① *de ropa*
tyen·da de *ro*·pa

cloud *nube* ① *noo*·be

cloudy *nublado* noo·*bla*·do

clove (garlic) *diente* ⓜ *(de ajo)* *dyen*·te
(de *a*·kho)

cloves *clavos* ⓜ pl *kla*·vos

clutch *embrague* ① em·*bra*·ge

coach *entrenador/entrenadora* ⓜ/①
en·tre·na·*dor*/en·tre·na·*do*·ra

coast *costa* ① *kos*·ta

cocaine *cocaína* ① ko·ka·ee·*na*

cockroach *cucaracha* ① koo·ka·*ra*·cha

cocoa *cacao* ⓜ ka·*kow*

coconut *coco* ⓜ *ko*·ko

codeine *codeína* ① ko·de·ee·*na*

coffee *café* ⓜ ka·*fe*

coins *monedas* ① pl mo·*ne*·das

cold *frío/a* ⓜ/① *free*·o/a

cold (illness) *resfriado* ⓜ res·free·*a*·do

colleague *colega* ⓜ&① ko·*le*·ga

collect call *llamada* ① *a cobro revertido* lya·ma·da a ko·bro re·ver·tee·do
college *residencia* ① *de estudiantes* re·see·den·thya de es·too·dyan·tes
colour *color* ⑩ ko·lor
colour (film) *película* ① *en color* pe·lee·koo·la en ko·lor
comb *peine* ⑩ pey·ne
come *venir* ve·neer
come (arrive) *llegar* lye·gar
comedy *comedia* ① ko·me·dya
comfortable *cómodo/a* ⑩/① ko·mo·do/a
communion *comunión* ① ko·moo·nyon
communist *comunista* ⑩&① ko·moo·nees·ta
companion *compañero/a* ⑩/① kom·pa·nye·ro/a
company *compañía* ① kom·pa·nyee·a
compass *brújula* ① broo·khoo·la
complain *quejarse* ke·khar·se
computer *ordenador* ⑩ or·de·na·dor
computer game *juegos* ⑩ pl *de ordenador* khwe·gos de or·de·na·dor
concert *concierto* ⑩ kon·thyer·to
conditioner *acondicionador* ⑩ a·kon·dee·thyo·na·dor
condoms *condones* ⑩ pl kon·do·nes
confession *confesión* ① kon·fe·syon
confirm *confirmar* kon·feer·mar
connection *conexión* ① ko·ne·ksyon
conservative *conservador/conservadora* ⑩/① kon·ser·va·dor/kon·ser·va·do·ra
constipation *estreñimiento* ⑩ es·tre·nyee·myen·to
consulate *consulado* ⑩ kon·soo·la·do
contact lenses *lentes* ⑩ pl *de contacto* len·tes de kon·tak·to
contraceptives *anticonceptivos* ⑩ pl an·tee·kon·thep·tee·vos
contract *contrato* ⑩ kon·tra·to
convenience store *negocio* ⑩ *de artículos básicos* ne·go·thyo de ar·tee·koo·los ba·see·kos

convent *convento* ⑩ kon·ven·to
cook *cocinero* ⑩ ko·thee·ne·ro
cook *cocinar* ko·thee·nar
cookie *galleta* ① ga·lye·ta
corn *maíz* ⑩ ma·eeth
corn flakes *copos* ⑩ pl *de maíz* ko·pos de ma·eeth
corner *esquina* ① es·kee·na
corrupt *corrupto/a* ⑩/① ko·roop·to/a
cost *costar* kos·tar
cottage cheese *requesón* ⑩ re·ke·son
cotton *algodón* ⑩ al·go·don
cotton balls *bolas* ① pl *de algodón* bo·las de al·go·don
cough *tos* ① tos
cough medicine *jarabe* ⑩ kha·ra·be
count *contar* kon·tar
counter *mostrador* ⑩ mos·tra·dor
country *país* ⑩ pa·ees
countryside *campo* ⑩ kam·po
coupon *cupón* ⑩ koo·pon
courgette *calabacín* ⑩ ka·la·ba·theen
court (tennis) *pista* ① pees·ta
cous cous *cus cus* ⑩ koos koos
cover charge *precio* ⑩ *del cubierto* pre·thyo del koo·byer·to
cow *vaca* ① va·ka
crab *cangrejo* ⑩ kan·gre·kho
crackers *galletas* ① pl *saladas* ga·lye·tas sa·la·das
crafts *artesanía* ① ar·te·sa·nee·a
crash *choque* ⑩ cho·ke
crazy *loco/a* ⑩/① lo·ko/a
cream (food) *crema* kre·ma
cream (moisturising) *crema* ① *hidratante* kre·ma ee·dra·tan·te
cream cheese *queso* ⑩ *crema* ke·so kre·ma
creche *guardería* ① gwar·de·ree·a
credit card *tarjeta* ① *de crédito* tar·khe·ta de kre·dee·to
cricket *críquet* ⑩ kree·ket
crop *cosecha* ① ko·se·cha
crowded *abarrotado/a* ⑩/① a·ba·ro·ta·do/a

cucumber *pepino* ⑩ pe·pee·no
cuddle *abrazo* ⑩ a·bra·tho
cup *taza* ① ta·tha
cupboard *armario* ⑩ ar·ma·ryo
currency exchange *cambio* ⑩ *(de dinero)* kam·byo (de dee·ne·ro)
current (electricity) *corriente* ① ko·ryen·te
current affairs *informativo* ⑩ een·for·ma·tee·vo
curry *curry* ⑩ koo·ree
curry powder *curry* ⑩ *en polvo* koo·ree en pol·vo
customs *aduana* ① a·dwa·na
cut *cortar* kor·tar
cutlery *cubiertos* ⑩ pl koo·byer·tos
CV *historial* ⑩ *profesional* ees·to·ryal pro·fe·syo·nal
cycle *andar en bicicleta* an·dar en bee·thee·kle·ta
cycling *ciclismo* ⑩ thee·klees·mo
cyclist *ciclista* ⑩&① thee·klees·ta
cystitis *cistitis* ① thees·tee·tees

D

dad *papá* ⑩ pa·pa
daily *diariamente* dya·rya·men·te
dance *bailar* bai·lar
dancing *bailar* bai·lar
dangerous *peligroso/a* ⑩/① pe·lee·gro·so/a
dark *oscuro/a* ⑩/① os·koo·ro/a
date *citarse* thee·tar·se
date (a person) *salir con* sa·leer kon
date (time) *fecha* ① fe·cha
date of birth *fecha* ① *de nacimiento* fe·cha de na·thee·myen·to
daughter *hija* ① ee·kha
dawn *alba* ① al·ba
day *día* ⑩ dee·a
day after tomorrow *pasado mañana* pa·sa·do ma·nya·na
day before yesterday *anteayer* an·te·a·yer
dead *muerto/a* ⑩/① mwer·to/a

deaf *sordo/a* ⑩/① sor·do/a
deal (cards) *repartir* re·par·teer
decide *decidir* de·thee·deer
deep *profundo/a* ⑩/① pro·foon·do/a
deforestation *deforestación* ① de·fo·res·ta·thyon
degree *título* ⑩ tee·too·lo
delay *demora* ① de·mo·ra
delirious *delirante* de·lee·ran·te
deliver *entregar* en·tre·gar
democracy *democracia* ① de·mo·kra·thya
demonstration *manifestación* ① ma·nee·fes·ta·thyon
dental floss *hilo* ⑩ *dental* ee·lo den·tal
dentist *dentista* ⑩&① den·tees·ta
deny *negar* ne·gar
deodorant *desodorante* ⑩ de·so·do·ran·te
depart *salir de* sa·leer de
department store *grande almacen* ⑩ gran·de al·ma·then
departure *salida* ① sa·lee·da
deposit *depósito* ⑩ de·po·see·to
descendant *descendiente* ⑩ des·then·dyen·te
desert *desierto* ⑩ de·syer·to
design *diseño* ⑩ dee·se·nyo
destination *destino* ⑩ des·tee·no
destroy *destruir* des·troo·eer
detail *detalle* ⑩ de·ta·lye
diabetes *diabetes* ① dee·a·be·tes
diaper *pañal* ⑩ pa·nyal
diaphragm *diafragma* ⑩ dee·a·frag·ma
diarrhoea *diarrea* ① dee·a·re·a
diary *agenda* ① a·khen·da
dice (die) *dados* ⑩ pl da·dos
dictionary *diccionario* ⑩ deek·thyo·na·ryo
die *morir* mo·reer
diet *régimen* ⑩ re·khee·men
different *diferente* ⑩/① dee·fe·ren·te
difficult *difícil* ⑩/① dee·fee·theel
dining car *vagón* ⑩ *restaurante* va·gon res·tow·ran·te

dinner *cena* ① the·na
direct *directo/a* ⑩/① dee·rek·to/a
direct-dial *marcar directo* mar·kar
  dee·rek·to
director *director/directora* ⑩/①
  dee·rek·tor/dee·rek·to·ra
dirty *sucio/a* ⑩/① soo·thyo/a
disabled *minusválido/a* ⑩/①
  mee·noos·va·lee·do/a
disco *discoteca* ① dees·ko·te·ka
discount *descuento* ⑩ des·kwen·to
discover *descubrir* des·koo·breer
discrimination *discriminación* ①
  dees·kree·mee·na·thyon
disease *enfermedad* ① en·fer·me·da
disk *disco* ⑩ dees·ko
dive *bucear* boo·the·ar
diving *submarinismo* ⑩
  soob·ma·ree·nees·mo
diving equipment *equipo* ⑩
  de inmersión e·kee·po de
  ee·mer·syon
dizzy *mareado/a* ⑩/① ma·re·a·do/a
do *hacer* a·ther
doctor *doctor/doctora* ⑩/① dok·tor/
  dok·to·ra
documentary *documental* ⑩
  do·koo·men·tal
dog *perro/a* ⑩/① pe·ro/a
dole *paro* ⑩ pa·ro
doll *muñeca* ① moo·nye·ka
dollar *dólar* ⑩ do·lar
domestic flight *vuelo* ⑩ *doméstico*
  vwe·lo do·mes·tee·ko
donkey *burro* ⑩ boo·ro
door *puerta* ① pwer·ta
dope *droga* ① dro·ga
double *doble* ⑩/① do·ble
double bed *cama* ① *de matrimonio*
  ka·ma de ma·tree·mo·nyo
double room *habitación* ① *doble*
  a·bee·ta·thyon do·ble
down *abajo* a·ba·kho
downhill *cuesta abajo* kwes·ta a·ba·kho
dozen *docena* ① do·the·na

drama *drama* ⑩ dra·ma
draw *dibujar* dee·boo·khar
dream *soñar* so·nyar
dress *vestido* ⑩ ves·tee·do
dried fruit *fruto* ⑩ *seco* froo·to se·ko
drink *bebida* ① be·bee·da
drink *beber* be·ber
drive *conducir* kon·doo·theer
drivers licence *carnet* ⑩ *de conducir*
  kar·ne de kon·doo·theer
drug *droga* ① dro·ga
drug addiction *drogadicción* ①
  dro·ga·deek·thyon
drug dealer *traficante* ⑩ *de drogas*
  tra·fee·kan·te de dro·gas
drums *batería* ① ba·te·ree·a
drumstick (chicken) *muslo* moos·lo
drunk *borracho/a* ⑩/① bo·ra·cho/a
dry *secar* se·kar
duck *pato* ⑩ pa·to
dummy (pacifier) *chupete* ⑩ choo·pe·te

E

each *cada* ka·da
ear *oreja* ① o·re·kha
early *temprano* tem·pra·no
earn *ganar* ga·nar
earplugs *tapones* ⑩ pl *para los oídos*
  ta·po·nes pa·ra los o·ee·dos
earrings *pendientes* ⑩ pl pen·dyen·tes
Earth *Tierra* ① tye·ra
earthquake *terremoto* ⑩ te·re·mo·to
east *este* es·te
Easter *Pascua* ① pas·kwa
easy *fácil* fa·theel
eat *comer* ko·mer
economy class *clase* ① *turística* kla·se
  too·rees·tee·ka
eczema *eczema* ① ek·the·ma
editor *editor/editora* ⑩/① e·dee·tor/
  e·dee·to·ra
education *educación* ① e·doo·ka·thyon
eggplant *berenjenas* ① pl
  be·ren·khe·nas

egg *huevo* ⓜ *we·vo*
elections *elecciones* ⓕ pl
e·lek·*thyo*·nes
electrical store *tienda* ⓕ *de productos*
*eléctricos tyen·*da de pro·*dook*·tos
e·*lek*·tree·kos
electricity *electricidad* ⓕ
e·lek·tree·thee·*da*
elevator *ascensor* ⓜ as·then·*sor*
embarrassed *avergonzado/a* ⓜ/ⓕ
a·ver·gon·*tha*·do/a
embassy *embajada* ⓕ em·ba·*kha*·da
emergency *emergencia* ⓕ
e·mer·*khen*·thya
emotional *emocional* e·mo·thyo·*nal*
employee *empleado/a* ⓜ/ⓕ
em·ple·a·do/a
employer *jefe/a* ⓜ/ⓕ *khe*·fe/a
empty *vacío/a* ⓜ/ⓕ va·*thee*·o/a
end *fin* ⓜ feen
end *acabar* a·ka·*bar*
endangered species *especies* ⓕ pl *en*
peligro de extinción es·pe·thyes en
pe·*lee*·gro de eks·teen·*thyon*
engagement *compromiso* ⓜ
kom·pro·*mee*·so
engine *motor* ⓜ mo·*tor*
engineer *ingeniero/a* ⓜ/ⓕ
een·khe·*nye*·ro/a
engineering *ingeniería* ⓕ
een·khe·nye·*ree*·a
England *Inglaterra* ⓕ een·gla·*te*·ra
English *inglés* ⓜ een·*gles*
enjoy (oneself) *divertirse* dee·ver·*teer*·se
enough *suficiente* ⓜ/ⓕ
soo·fee·*thyen*·te
enter *entrar* en·*trar*
entertainment guide *guía* ⓕ *del ocio*
gee·a del o·*thyo*
envelope *sobre* ⓜ *so*·bre
environment *medio* ⓜ *ambiente*
me·dyo am·*byen*·te
epilepsy *epilepsia* ⓕ e·pee·*lep*·sya
equal opportunity *igualdad* ⓕ *de*
oportunidades ee·gwal·*da* de
o·por·too·nee·*da*·des

equality *igualdad* ⓕ ee·gwal·*da*
equipment *equipo* ⓜ e·*kee*·po
escalator *escaleras* ⓕ pl *mecánicas*
es·ka·*le*·ras me·ka·nee·kas
euro *euro* ⓜ e·oo·ro
Europe *Europa* ⓕ e·oo·ro·pa
euthanasia *eutanasia* ⓕ e·oo·ta·*na*·sya
evening *noche* ⓕ *no*·che
everything *todo* to·do
example *ejemplo* ⓜ e·*khem*·plo
excellent *excelente* ⓜ/ⓕ eks·the·*len*·te
exchange *cambio* ⓜ *kam*·byo
exchange (money) *cambiar* kam·*byar*
exchange rate *tipo* ⓜ *de cambio*
tee·po de kam·byo
exchange (give gifts) *regalar* re·ga·*lar*
excluded *no incluido* no een·kloo·ee·do
exhaust *tubo* ⓜ *de escape* too·bo de
es·ka·pe
exhibit *exponer* eks·po·*ner*
exhibition *exposición* ⓕ
eks·po·see·thyon
exit *salida* ⓕ sa·*lee*·da
expensive *caro/a* ⓜ/ⓕ ka·ro/a
experience *experiencia* ⓕ
eks·pe·*ryen*·thya
express *expreso/a* ⓜ/ⓕ eks·*pre*·so/a
express mail *correo* ⓜ *urgente* ko·re·o
oor·*khen*·te
extension (visa) *prolongación* ⓕ
pro·lon·ga·thyon
eye *ojo* ⓜ o·kho
eye drops *gotas* ⓕ pl *para los ojos*
go·tas *pa*·ra los o·khos

F

fabric *tela* ⓕ *te*·la
face *cara* ⓕ *ka*·ra
face cloth *toallita* ⓕ to·a·*lyee*·ta
factory *fábrica* ⓕ *fa*·bree·ka
factory worker *obrero/a* ⓜ/ⓕ o·bre·ro/a
fall *caída* ⓕ ka·ee·da
family *familia* ⓕ fa·*mee*·lya
family name *apellido* ⓜ a·pe·*lyee*·do
famous *famoso/a* ⓜ/ⓕ fa·*mo*·so/a

fan (hand held) *abanico* ⓜ a·ba·nee·ko
fan (electric) *ventilador* ⓜ
    ven·tee·la·dor
fanbelt *correa* ⓕ del ventilador ko·re·a
    del ven·tee·la·dor
far *lejos* le·khos
farm *granja* ⓕ gran·kha
farmer *agricultor/agricultora* ⓜ/ⓕ
    a·gree·kool·tor/a·gree·kool·to·ra
fast *rápido/a* ⓜ/ⓕ ra·pee·do/a
fat *gordo/a* ⓜ/ⓕ gor·do/a
father *padre* ⓜ pa·dre
father-in-law *suegro* ⓜ swe·gro
fault *falta* ⓕ fal·ta
faulty *defectuoso/a* ⓜ/ⓕ
    de·fek·too·o·so/a
feed *dar de comer* dar de ko·mer
feel *sentir* sen·teer
feelings *sentimientos* ⓜ pl
    sen·tee·myen·tos
fence *cerca* ⓕ ther·ka
fencing *esgrima* ⓕ es·gree·ma
festival *festival* ⓜ fes·tee·val
fever *fiebre* ⓕ fye·bre
few *pocos* po·kos
fiance *prometido* ⓜ pro·me·tee·do
fiancee *prometida* ⓕ pro·me·tee·da
fiction *ficción* ⓕ feek·thyon
field *campo* ⓜ kam·po
fig *higo* ⓜ ee·go
fight *pelea* ⓕ pe·le·a
fight against *luchar contra* loo·char
    kon·tra
fill *llenar* lye·nar
fillet *filete* ⓜ fee·le·te
film *película* ⓕ pe·lee·koo·la
film speed *sensibilidad* ⓕ
    sen·see·bee·lee·da
filtered *con filtro* kon feel·tro
find *encontrar* en·kon·trar
fine *multa* ⓕ mool·ta
finger *dedo* ⓜ de·do
finish *terminar* ter·mee·nar
fire *fuego* ⓜ fwe·go
firewood *leña* ⓕ le·nya
first *primero/a* ⓜ/ⓕ pree·me·ro/a

first-class *de primera clase* de
    pree·me·ra kla·se
first-aid kit *maletín* ⓜ de primeros
    auxilios ma·le·teen de pree·me·ros
    ow·ksee·lyos
fish *pez* ⓜ peth
fish (as food) *pescado* ⓜ pes·ka·do
fish shop *pescadería* ⓕ pes·ka·de·ree·a
fishing *pesca* ⓕ pes·ka
flag *bandera* ⓕ ban·de·ra
flannel *franela* ⓕ fra·ne·la
flashlight *linterna* ⓕ leen·ter·na
flat *llano/a* ⓜ/ⓕ lya·no/a
flea *pulga* ⓕ pool·ga
flooding *inundación* ⓕ ee·noon·da·thyon
floor *suelo* ⓜ swe·lo
florist *florista* ⓜ&ⓕ flo·rees·ta
flour *harina* ⓕ a·ree·na
flower *flor* ⓕ flor
flower seller *vendedor/vendedora* ⓜ/ⓕ
    de flores ⓜ/ⓕ ven·de·dor/
    ven·de·do·ra de flo·res
fly *volar* vo·lar
foggy *brumoso/a* ⓜ/ⓕ broo·mo·so
follow *seguir* se·geer
food *comida* ⓕ ko·mee·da
food supplies *víveres* ⓜ pl vee·ve·res
foot *pie* ⓜ pye
football *fútbol* ⓜ foot·bol
footpath *acera* ⓕ a·the·ra
foreign *extranjero/a* ⓜ/ⓕ
    eks·tran·khe·ro/a
forest *bosque* ⓜ bos·ke
forever *para siempre* pa·ra syem·pre
forget *olvidar* ol·vee·dar
forgive *perdonar* per·do·nar
fork *tenedor* ⓜ te·ne·dor
fortnight *quincena* ⓕ keen·the·na
foul *sucio/a* ⓜ/ⓕ soo·thee·o/a
foyer *vestíbulo* ⓜ ves·tee·boo·lo
fragile *frágil* fra·kheel
free (not bound) *libre* lee·bre
free (of charge) *gratis* gra·tees
freeze *helarse* e·lar·se
friend *amigo/a* ⓜ/ⓕ a·mee·go/a

frost *escarcha* ① es·kar·cha
frozen foods *productos congelados* ⓜ pl pro·dook·tos kon·khe·*la*·dos
fruit *fruta* ① froo·ta
fruit picking *recolección* ① de fruta re·ko·lek·thyon de froo·ta
fry *freír* fre·eer
frying pan *sartén* ① sar·ten
fuck *follar* fo·lyar
full *lleno/a* ⓜ/① lye·no/a
full-time *a tiempo completo* a tyem·po kom·ple·to
fun *diversión* ① dee·ver·syon
funeral *funeral* ⓜ foo·ne·ral
funny *gracioso/a* ⓜ/① gra·thyo·so/a
furniture *muebles* ⓜ pl mwe·bles
future *futuro* ⓜ foo·too·ro

G

gay *gay* gai
general *general* khe·ne·ral
Germany *Alemania* ① a·le·ma·nya
gift *regalo* ⓜ re·ga·lo
gig *bolo* ⓜ bo·lo
gin *ginebra* ① khee·ne·bra
ginger *jengibre* ⓜ khen·khee·bre
girl *chica* ① chee·ka
girlfriend *novia* ① no·vya
give *dar* dar
glandular fever *fiebre* ① *glandular* fye·bre glan·doo·lar
glass (material) *vidrio* ⓜ vee·dryo
glass (drinking) *vaso* ⓜ va·so
glasses *gafas* ① pl ga·fas
gloves *guantes* ⓜ pl gwan·tes
go *ir* eer
go out with *salir con* sa·leer kon
go shopping *ir de compras* eer de kom·pras
goal *gol* ⓜ gol
goalkeeper *portero/a* ⓜ/① por·te·ro/a
goat *cabra* ① ka·bra
goat's cheese *queso* ⓜ de cabra ke·so de ka·bra
god *Dios* ⓜ dyos

goggles *gafas* ① pl de submarinismo ga·fas de soob·ma·ree·*nees*·mo
golf ball *pelota* ① de golf pe·lo·ta de golf
golf course *campo* ⓜ de golf kam·po de golf
good *bueno/a* ⓜ/① bwe·no/a
government *gobierno* ⓜ go·byer·no
gram *gramo* ⓜ gra·mo
grandchild *nieto/a* ⓜ/① nye·to/a
grandfather *abuelo* ⓜ a·bwe·lo
grandmother *abuela* ① a·bwe·la
grapefruit *pomelo* ⓜ po·me·lo
grapes *uvas* ① pl oo·vas
graphic art *arte* ⓜ *gráfico* ar·te gra·fee·ko
grass *hierba* ① yer·ba
grave *tumba* ① toom·ba
gray *gris* grees
great *fantástico/a* ⓜ/① fan·tas·tee·ko/a
green *verde* ver·de
greengrocery (shop) *verdulería* ① ver·doo·le·ree·a
grocer (shopkeeper) *verdulero/a* ⓜ/① ver·doo·le·ro/a
grey *gris* grees
grocery *tienda* ① de comestibles tyen·da de ko·mes·tee·bles
grow *crecer* kre·ther
g-string *tanga* ① tan·ga
guess *adivinar* a·dee·vee·nar
guide (audio) *guía* ① *audio* gee·a ow·dyo
guide (person) *guía* ⓜ&① gee·a
guide dog *perro lazarillo* ⓜ pe·ro la·tha·ree·lyo
guidebook *guía* ① gee·a
guided tour *recorrido* ⓜ *guiado* re·ko·ree·do gee·a·do
guilty *culpable* kool·pa·ble
guitar *guitarra* ① gee·ta·ra
gum *chicle* ⓜ chee·kle
gymnastics *gimnasia* ① *rítmica* kheem·na·sya reet·mee·ka
gynaecologist *ginecólogo* ⓜ khee·ne·ko·lo·go

H

hair *pelo* ⓜ *pe·*lo
hairbrush *cepillo* ⓜ the·*pee·*lyo
hairdresser *peluquero/a* ⓜ/①
    pe·loo·*ke·*ro/a
halal *halal* a·*lal*
half *medio/a* ⓜ/① *me·*dyo/a
half a litre *medio litro* ⓜ *me·*dyo *lee·*tro
hallucinate *alucinar* a·loo·thee·*nar*
ham *jamón* ⓜ kha·*mon*
hammer *martillo* ⓜ mar·*tee·*lyo
hammock *hamaca* ① a·*ma·*ka
hand *mano* ① *ma·*no
handbag *bolso* ⓜ *bol·*so
handicrafts *artesanía* ① ar·te·sa·*nee·*a
handlebar *manillar* ⓜ ma·nee·*lyar*
handmade *hecho a mano* e·cho a *ma·*no
handsome *hermoso* ⓜ er·*mo·*so
happy *feliz* fe·*leeth*
harassment *acoso* ⓜ a·*ko·*so
harbour *puerto* ⓜ *pwer·*to
hard *duro/a* ⓜ/① *doo·*ro/a
hardware store *ferretería* ① fe·re·te·*ree·*a
hash *hachís* ⓜ a·*chees*
hat *sombrero* ⓜ som·*bre·*ro
have *tener* te·*ner*
have a cold *estar constipado/a* ⓜ/①
    es·*tar* kons·tee·*pa·*do
have fun *divertirse* dee·ver·*teer·*se
hay fever *alergia* ① *al polen* a·*ler·*khya
    al *po·*len
he *él* el
head *cabeza* ① ka·*be·*tha
headache *dolor* ⓜ *de cabeza* do·*lor* de
    ka·*be·*tha
headlights *faros* ⓜ pl *fa·*ros
health *salud* ① sa·*loo*
hear *oír* o·*eer*
hearing aid *audífono* ⓜ ow·*dee·*fo·no
heart *corazón* ⓜ ko·ra·*thon*
heart condition *condición* ① *cardíaca*
    kon·dee·*thyon* kar·*dee·*a·ka
heat *calor* ⓜ ka·*lor*
heater *estufa* ① es·*too·*fa
heavy *pesado/a* ⓜ/① pe·*sa·*do/a

helmet *casco* ⓜ *kas·*ko
help *ayudar* a·yoo·*dar*
hepatitis *hepatitis* ① e·pa·*tee·*tees
her *su* soo
herbalist *herbolario/a* ⓜ/①
    er·bo·la·*ree·*o/a
herbs *hierbas* ① pl *yer·*bas
here *aquí* a·*kee*
heroin *heroína* ① e·ro·*ee·*na
herring *arenque* ⓜ a·*ren·*ke
high *alto/a* ⓜ/① *al·*to/a
high school *instituto* ⓜ eens·tee·*too·*to
hike *ir de excursión*
    eer de eks·koor·*syon*
hiking *excursionismo* ⓜ
    eks·koor·syo·*nees·*mo
hiking boots *botas* ① pl *de montaña*
    *bo·*tas de mon·*ta·*nya
hiking routes *caminos* ⓜ pl *rurales*
    ka·*mee·*nos roo·*ra·*les
hill *colina* ① ko·*lee·*na
Hindu *hindú* een·*doo*
hire *alquilar* al·kee·*lar*
his *su* soo
historical *histórico/a* ⓜ/①
    ees·*to·*ree·ko/a
hitchhike *hacer dedo* a·*ther* de·do
HIV positive *seropositivo/a* ⓜ/①
    se·ro·po·see·*tee·*vo/a
hockey *hockey* ⓜ *kho·*kee
holiday *día festivo* ⓜ *dee·*a fes·*tee·*vo
holidays *vacaciones* ① pl
    va·ka·*thyo·*nes
Holy Week *Semana* ① *Santa* se·*ma·*na
    *san·*ta
homeless *sin hogar* seen o·*gar*
homemaker *ama* ① *de casa*
    *a·*ma de *ka·*sa
homosexual *homosexual* ⓜ&①
    o·mo·se·*kswal*
honey *miel* ① myel
honeymoon *luna* ① *de miel* *loo·*na
    de myel
horoscope *horóscopo* ⓜ o·*ros·*ko·po
horse *caballo* ⓜ ka·*ba·*lyo

horse riding *equitación* ① e·kee·ta·thyon
horseradish *rábano* ⑩ *picante* ra·ba·no pee·kan·te
hospital *hospital* ⑩ os·pee·tal
hospitality *hosteleria* ① os·te·le·ree·a
hot *caliente* ka·lyen·te
hot water *agua caliente* ⑩ a·gwa ka·lyen·te
hotel *hotel* ⑩ o·tel
house *casa* ① ka·sa
housework *trabajo* ⑩ *de casa* tra·ba·kho de ka·sa
how *cómo* ko·mo
how much *cuánto* kwan·to
hug *abrazo* ⑩ a·bra·tho
huge *enorme* e·nor·me
human rights *derechos* ⑩ pl *humanos* de·re·chos oo·ma·nos
humanities *humanidades* ① pl oo·ma·nee·da·des
hungry *hambriento/a* ⑩/① am·bryen·to/a
hungry *tener hambre* te·ner am·bre
hunting *caza* ① ka·tha
hurt *dañar* da·nyar
husband *marido* ⑩ ma·ree·do

I

I *yo* yo
ice *hielo* ⑩ ye·lo
ice axe *piolet* ⑩ pyo·le
ice cream *helado* ⑩ e·la·do
ice cream parlour *heladería* ① e·la·de·ree·a
ice hockey *hockey* ⑩ *sobre hielo* kho·kee so·bre ye·lo
identification *identificación* ① ee·den·tee·fee·ka·thyon
identification card *carnet* ⑩ *de identidad* kar·net de ee·den·tee·da
idiot *idiota* ⑩&① ee·dyo·ta
if *si* see
ill *enfermo/a* ⑩/① en·fer·mo/a
immigration *inmigración* ① een·mee·gra·thyon

important *importante* eem·por·tan·te
in a hurry *de prisa* de pree·sa
in front of *enfrente de* en·fren·te de
included *incluido* een·kloo·ee·do
income tax *impuesto* ⑩ *sobre la renta* eem·pwes·to so·bre la ren·ta
India *India* ① een·dya
indicator *indicador* ⑩ een·dee·ka·dor
indigestion *indigestion* ① een·dee·khes·tyon
industry *industria* ① een·doos·trya
infection *infección* ① een·fek·thyon
inflammation *inflamación* ① een·fla·ma·thyon
influenza *gripe* ① gree·pe
ingredient *ingrediente* ⑩ een·gre·dyen·te
inject *inyectarse* een·yek·tar·se
injection *inyección* ① een·yek·thyon
injury *herida* ① e·ree·da
innocent *inocente* ee·no·then·te
inside *adentro* a·den·tro
instructor *profesor/profesora* ⑩/① pro·fe·sor/pro·fe·sor·ra
insurance *seguro* ⑩ se·goo·ro
interesting *interesante* een·te·re·san·te
intermission *descanso* ⑩ des·kan·so
international *internacional* een·ter·na·thyo·nal
Internet *Internet* ⑩ een·ter·net
Internet cafe *cibercafé* ⑩ thee·ber·ka·fe
interpreter *intérprete* ⑩&① een·ter·pre·te
interview *entrevista* ① en·tre·vees·ta
invite *invitar* een·vee·tar
Ireland *Irlanda* ① plan·cha
iron *plancha* ① plan·cha
island *isla* ① ees·la
IT *informática* ① een·for·ma·tee·ka
itch *picazón* ① pee·ka·thon
itemised *detallado/a* ⑩/① de·ta·lya·do/a
itinerary *itinerario* ⑩ ee·tee·ne·ra·ryo
IUD *DIU* ⑩ de ee oo

J

jacket *chaqueta* ① cha·ke·ta
jail *cárcel* ① kar·thel
jam *mermelada* ① mer·me·la·da
Japan *Japón* ⑩ kha·pon
jar *jarra* ① kha·ra
jaw *mandíbula* ① man·dee·boo·la
jealous *celoso/a* ⑩/① the·lo·so/a
jeans *vaqueros* ⑩ pl va·ke·ros
jeep *yip* ⑩ yeep
jet lag *jet lag* ① dyet lag
jewellery shop *joyería* ① kho·ye·ree·a
Jewish *judío/a* ⑩/① khoo·dee·o/a
job *trabajo* ⑩ tra·ba·kho
jockey *jockey* ⑩ dyo·kee
jogging *footing* ⑩ foo·teen
joke *broma* ① bro·ma
joke *bromear* bro·me·ar
journalist *periodista* ⑩&①
  pe·ryo·dees·ta
judge *juez* ⑩&① khweth
juice *jugo* ⑩ khoo·go • *zumo* ⑩
  thoo·mo
jump *saltar* sal·tar
jumper (sweater) *jersey* ⑩ kher·say
jumper leads *cables* ⑩ pl *de arranque*
  ka·bles de a·ran·ke

K

ketchup *salsa* ① *de tomate* sal·sa de
  to·ma·te
key *llave* ① lya·ve
keyboard *teclado* ⑩ te·kla·do
kick *dar una patada* dar oo·na pa·ta·da
kick (a goal) *meter (un gol)* me·ter
  (oon gol)
kill *matar* ma·tar
kilogram *kilogramo* ⑩ kee·lo·gram·o
kilometre *kilómetro* ⑩ kee·lo·me·tro
kind *amable* a·ma·ble
kindergarten *escuela* ① *de párvulos*
  es·kwe·la de par·voo·los
king *rey* ⑩ rey

kiss *beso* ⑩ be·so
kiss *besar* be·sar
kitchen *cocina* ① ko·thee·na
kitten *gatito/a* ⑩/① ga·tee·to/a
kiwifruit *kiwi* ⑩ kee·wee
knapsack *mochila* ① mo·chee·la
knee *rodilla* ① ro·dee·lya
knife *cuchillo* ⑩ koo·chee·lyo
know (someone) *conocer* ko·no·ther
know (something) *saber* sa·ber
Kosher *kosher* ko·sher

L

labourer *obrero/a* ⑩/① o·bre·ro/a
lace *encaje* ⑩ en·ka·khe
lager *cerveza* ① *rubia* ther·ve·tha
  roo·bya
lake *lago* ⑩ la·go
lamb *cordero* ⑩ kor·de·ro
land *tierra* ① tye·ra
landlady *propietaria* ① pro·pye·ta·rya
landlord *propietario* ⑩ pro·pye·ta·ryo
languages *idiomas* ⑩ pl ee·dyo·mas
laptop *ordenador* ⑩ *portátil*
  or·de·na·dor por·ta·teel
lard *manteca* ① man·te·ka
large *grande* gran·de
late *tarde* tar·de
laugh *reírse* re·eer·se
laundrette *lavandería* ① la·van·de·ree·a
laundry *lavadero* ⑩ la·va·de·ro
law *ley* ① ley
lawyer *abogado/a* ⑩/① a·bo·ga·do/a
leader *líder* ⑩&① lee·der
leaf *hoja* ① o·kha
learn *aprender* a·pren·der
leather *cuero* ⑩ kwe·ro
leave *dejar* de·khar
lecturer *profesor/profesora* ⑩/①
  pro·fe·sor/pro·fe·so·ra
ledge *saliente* ⑩ sa·lyen·te
leek *puerro* ⑩ pwe·ro
left *izquierda* ① eeth·kyer·da

left (behind/over) *quedar* ke·dar
left luggage *consigna* ① kon·seeg·na
left-wing *de izquierda* de eeth·kyer·da
leg *pierna* ① pyer·na
legal *legal* le·gal
legislation *legislación* ①
le·khees·la·thyon
lemon *limón* ⑩ lee·mon
lemonade *limonada* ① lee·mo·na·da
lens *objetivo* ⑩ ob·khe·tee·vo
Lent *Cuaresma* ① kwa·res·ma
lentils *lentejas* ① pl len·te·khas
lesbian *lesbiana* ① les·bee·a·na
less *menos* me·nos
letter *carta* ① kar·ta
lettuce *lechuga* ① le·choo·ga
liar *mentiroso/a* ⑩/① men·tee·ro·so/a
library *biblioteca* ① bee·blyo·te·ka
lice *piojos* ⑩ pl pyo·khos
license plate number *matrícula* ①
ma·tree·koo·la
lie (not stand) *tumbarse* toom·bar·se
life *vida* ① vee·da
lifejacket *chaleco* ⑩ *salvavidas*
cha·le·ko sal·va·vee·das
lift *ascensor* ⑩ as·then·sor
light (weight) *leve* le·ve
light *luz* ① looth
light bulb *bombilla* ① bom·bee·lya
light meter *fotómetro* ⑩ fo·to·me·tro
lighter *encendedor* ⑩ en·then·de·dor
like *gustar(le)* goos·tar(le)
lime *lima* ① lee·ma
line *línea* ① lee·ne·a
lip balm *bálsamo* ⑩ *de labios*
bal·sa·mo de la·byos
lips *labios* ⑩ pl la·byos
lipstick *pintalabios* ⑩ peen·ta la·byos
liquor store *bodega* ① bo·de·ga
listen *escuchar* es·koo·char
live (life) *vivir* vee·veer
live (somewhere) *ocupar* o·koo·par
liver *hígado* ⑩ ee·ga·do
lizard *lagartija* ① la·gar·tee·kha

local *de cercanías* de ther·ka·nee·as
lock *cerradura* ① the·ra·doo·ra
lock *cerrar* the·rar
locked *cerrado/a* ⑩/① *con llave*
the·ra·do/a kon lya·ve
lollies *caramelos* ⑩ pl ka·ra·me·los
long *largo/a* ⑩/① lar·go/a
long-distance *a larga distancia* a lar·ga
dees·tan·thya
look *mirar* mee·rar
look after *cuidar* kwee·dar
look for *buscar* boos·kar
lookout *mirador* ⑩ mee·ra·dor
lose *perder* per·der
lost *perdido/a* ⑩/① per·dee·do/a
lost property office *oficina* ① *de*
objetos perdidos o·fee·thee·na de
ob·khe·tos per·dee·dos
loud *ruidoso/a* ⑩/① rwee·do·so/a
love *querer* ke·rer
lover *amante* ⑩&① a·man·te
low *bajo/a* ⑩/① ba·kho/a
lubricant *lubricante* ⑩ loo·bree·kan·te
luck *suerte* ① swer·te
lucky *afortunado/a* ⑩/①
a·for·too·na·do/a
luggage *equipaje* ⑩ e·kee·pa·khe
luggage lockers *consigna* ①
automática kon·seeg·na
ow·to·ma·tee·ka
luggage tag *etiqueta* ① *de equipaje*
e·tee·ke·ta de e·kee·pa·khe
lump *bulto* ⑩ bool·to
lunch *almuerzo* ⑩ al·mwer·tho
lungs *pulmones* ⑩ pl pool·mo·nes
luxury *lujo* ⑩ loo·kho

M

machine *máquina* ① ma·kee·na
made of (cotton) *hecho a de (algodón)*
e·cho a de (al·go·don)
magazine *revista* ① re·vees·ta
magician *mago/a* ⑩/① ma·go/a
mail *correo* ⑩ ko·re·o

mailbox *buzón* ⓜ boo·*thon*
main *principal* preen·thee·*pal*
make *hacer* a·*ther*
make fun of *burlarse de* boor·*lar*·se de
make-up *maquillaje* ⓜ ma·kee·*lya*·khe
mammogram *mamograma* ⓜ
   ma·mo·*gra*·ma
man *hombre* ⓜ *om*·bre
manager *gerente* ⓜ&ⓕ khe·*ren*·te
mandarin *mandarina* ⓕ man·da·*ree*·na
mango *mango* ⓜ *man*·go
manual worker *obrero/a* ⓜ/ⓕ o·*bre*·ro/a
many *muchas/os* ⓜ/ⓕ pl *moo*·chas/os
map *mapa* ⓜ *ma*·pa
margarine *margarina* ⓕ mar·ga·*ree*·na
marijuana *marihuana* ⓕ ma·ree·*wa*·na
marital status *estado* ⓜ *civil* es·*ta*·do
   thee·*veel*
market *mercado* ⓜ mer·*ka*·do
marmalade *mermelada* ⓕ
   mer·me·*la*·da
marriage *matrimonio* ⓜ ma·tree·*mo*·nyo
marry *casarse* ka·*sar*·se
martial arts *artes* ⓕ pl *marciales* ar·tes
   mar·*thya*·les
mass *misa* ⓕ *mee*·sa
massage *masaje* ⓜ ma·*sa*·khe
masseur/masseuse *masajista* ⓜ&ⓕ
   ma·sa·*khees*·ta
mat *esterilla* ⓕ es·te·*ree*·lya
match *partido* ⓜ par·*tee*·do
matches *cerillas* ⓕ pl the·*ree*·lyas
mattress *colchón* ⓜ kol·*chon*
maybe *quizás* kee·*thas*
mayonnaise *mayonesa* ⓕ ma·yo·*ne*·sa
mayor *alcalde* ⓜ&ⓕ al·*kal*·de
measles *sarampión* ⓜ sa·ram·*pyon*
meat *carne* ⓕ *kar*·ne
mechanic *mecánico/a* ⓜ/ⓕ
   me·*ka*·nee·ko
media *medios* ⓜ pl *de comunicación*
   me·dyos de ko·moo·nee·ka·*thyon*
medicine *medicina* ⓕ me·dee·*thee*·na
meet *encontrar* en·kon·*trar*

melon *melón* ⓜ me·*lon*
member *miembro* ⓜ *myem*·bro
menstruation *menstruación* ⓕ
   mens·trwa·*thyon*
menu *menú* ⓜ me·*noo*
message *mensaje* ⓜ men·*sa*·khe
metal *metal* ⓜ me·*tal*
metre *metro* ⓜ *me*·tro
metro station *estación* ⓕ *de metro*
   es·ta·*thyon* de *me*·tro
microwave *microondas* ⓜ
   mee·kro·on·das
midnight *medianoche* ⓕ me·dya·*no*·che
migraine *migraña* ⓕ mee·*gra*·nya
military service *servicio* ⓜ *militar*
   ser·*vee*·thyo mee·lee·*tar*
milk *leche* ⓕ *le*·che
millimetre *milímetro* ⓜ mee·*lee*·me·tro
million *millón* ⓜ mee·*lyon*
mince (meat) *carne* ⓕ *molida* kar·ne
   mo·*lee*·da
mind (object) *cuidar* kwee·*dar*
mineral water *agua* ⓜ *mineral* a·gwa
   mee·ne·*ral*
mints *pastillas* ⓕ pl *de menta*
   pas·*tee*·lyas de *men*·ta
minute *minuto* ⓜ mee·*noo*·to
mirror *espejo* ⓜ es·*pe*·kho
miscarriage *aborto* ⓜ *natural* a·*bor*·to
   na·too·*ral*
miss (feel sad) *echar de menos* e·*char*
   de *me*·nos
mistake *error* ⓜ e·*ror*
mix *mezclar* meth·*klar*
mobile phone *teléfono* ⓜ *móvil*
   te·*le*·fo·no *mo*·veel
modem *módem* ⓜ *mo*·dem
moisturiser *crema* ⓕ *hidratante* kre·ma
   ee·dra·*tan*·te
monastery *monasterio* ⓜ mo·nas·*te*·ryo
money *dinero* ⓜ dee·*ne*·ro
month *mes* ⓜ mes
monument *monumento* ⓜ
   mo·noo·*men*·to

(full) moon *luna* ① *(llena)* loo·na
(*lye*·na)

morning (6am - 1pm) *mañana* ①
ma·*nya*·na

morning sickness *náuseas* ① pl *del
embarazo* now·se·as del em·ba·*ra*·tho

mosque *mezquita* ① meth·*kee*·ta

mosquito *mosquito* ⓜ mos·*kee*·to

mosquito coil *rollo* ⓜ *repelente contra
mosquitos* ro·lyo re·pe·*len*·te kon·tra
mos·*kee*·tos

mosquito net *mosquitera* ①
mos·kee·*te*·ra

mother *madre* ① *ma*·dre

mother-in-law *suegra* ① *swe*·gra

motorboat *motora* ① mo·*to*·ra

motorcycle *motocicleta* ①
mo·to·thee·*kle*·ta

motorway *autovia* ① ow·to·*vee*·a

mountain *montaña* ① mon·*ta*·nya

mountain bike *bicicleta* ① *de montaña*
bee·thee·*kle*·ta de mon·*ta*·nya

mountain path *sendero* ⓜ sen·*de*·ro

mountain range *cordillera* ①
kor·dee·*lye*·ra

mountaineering *alpinismo* ⓜ
al·pee·*nees*·mo

mouse *ratón* ⓜ ra·*ton*

mouth *boca* ① *bo*·ka

movie *película* ① pe·*lee*·koo·la

mud *lodo* ⓜ *lo*·do

muesli *muesli* ⓜ *mwes*·lee

mum *mamá* ① ma·*ma*

muscle *músculo* ⓜ *moos*·koo·lo

museum *museo* ⓜ moo·*se*·o

mushroom *champiñón* ⓜ
cham·pee·*nyon*

music *música* ① *moo*·see·ka

musician *músico/a* ⓜ/① *moo*·see·ko/a

Muslim *musulmán/musulmána* ⓜ/①
moo·sool·*man*/moo·sool·*ma*·na

mussels *mejillones* ⓜ pl
me·khee·*lyo*·nes

mustard *mostaza* ① mos·*ta*·tha

mute *mudo/a* ⓜ/① *moo*·do/a

my *mi* mee

N

nail clippers *cortauñas* ⓜ pl
kor·ta·*oo*·nyas

name *nombre* ⓜ *nom*·bre

napkin *servilleta* ① ser·vee·*lye*·ta

nappy *pañal* ⓜ pa·*nyal*

nappy rash *irritación* ① *de pañal*
ee·ree·ta·*thyon* de pa·*nyal*

national park *parque* ⓜ *nacional*
par·ke na·thyo·*nal*

nationality *nacionalidad* ①
na·thyo·na·lee·*da*

nature *naturaleza* ① na·too·ra·*le*·tha

naturopathy *naturopatia* ①
na·too·ro·pa·*tya*

nausea *náusea* ① *now*·se·a

near *cerca* *ther*·ka

nearby *cerca* *ther*·ka

nearest *más cercano/a* ⓜ/①
mas ther·*ka*·no/a

necessary *necesario/a* ⓜ/①
ne·the·*sa*·ryo/a

neck *cuello* ⓜ *kwe*·lyo

necklace *collar* ⓜ ko·*lyar*

need *necesitar* ne·the·see·*tar*

needle (sewing) *aguja* ① a·*goo*·kha

needle (syringe) *jeringa* ① khe·*reen*·ga

neither *tampoco* tam·*po*·ko

net *red* ① red

Netherlands *Holanda* ① o·*lan*·da

never *nunca* *noon*·ka

new *nuevo/a* ⓜ/① *nwe*·vo/a

New Year *Año Nuevo* ⓜ a·nyo *nwe*·vo

New Year's Eve *Nochevieja* ①
no·che·*vye*·kha

New Zealand *Nueva Zelanda* ①
nwe·va the·*lan*·da

news *noticias* ① pl no·*tee*·thyas

news stand *quiosco* ⓜ *kyos*·ko

newsagency *quiosco* ⓜ *kyos*·ko

newspaper *periódico* ⓜ pe·*ryo*·dee·ko

next (month) *el próximo (mes)* el
prok·see·mo (mes)

next to *al lado de* al *la*·do de

nice *simpático/a* ⓜ/ⓕ seem·pa·tee·ko/a
nickname *apodo* ⓜ a·po·do
night *noche* ⓕ no·che
no *no* no
noisy *ruidoso/a* ⓜ/ⓕ rwee·do·so/a
none *nada* na·da
non-smoking *no fumadores* no
  foo·ma·do·res
noodles *fideos* ⓜ pl fee·de·os
noon *mediodía* ⓜ me·dyo·dee·a
north *norte* ⓜ nor·te
nose *nariz* ⓕ na·reeth
notebook *cuaderno* ⓜ kwa·der·no
nothing *nada* na·da
now *ahora* a·o·ra
nuclear energy *energía* ⓕ *nuclear*
  e·ner·khee·a noo·kle·ar
nuclear testing *pruebas* ⓕ pl *nucleares*
  prwe·bas noo·kle·a·res
nuclear waste *desperdicios* ⓜ pl
  nucleares des·per·dee·thyos
  noo·kle·a·res
number *número* ⓜ noo·me·ro
nun *monja* ⓕ mon·kha
nurse *enfermero/a* ⓜ/ⓕ en·fer·me·ro/a
nuts *nueces* ⓕ pl nwe·thes
nuts (raw) *nueces* ⓕ pl *(crudas)*
  nwe·thes (kroo·das)
nuts (roasted) *nueces* ⓕ pl *(tostadas)*
  nwe·thes (tos·ta·das)

O

oats *avena* ⓕ a·ve·na
ocean *océano* ⓜ o·the·a·no
off (food) *pasado/a* ⓜ/ⓕ pa·sa·do/a
office *oficina* ⓕ o·fee·thee·na
office worker *oficinista* ⓜ&ⓕ
  o·fee·thee·nees·ta
offside *fuera de juego* fwe·ra de khwe·go
often *a menudo* a me·noo·do
oil *aceite* ⓜ a·they·te
old *viejo/a* ⓜ/ⓕ vye·kho/a
olive oil *aceite* ⓜ *de oliva* a·they·te
  de o·lee·va

Olympic Games *juegos* ⓜ pl *olímpicos*
  khwe·gos o·leem·pee·kos
on *en* en
once *vez* ⓕ veth
one-way ticket *billete* ⓜ *sencillo*
  bee·lye·te sen·thee·lyo
onion *cebolla* ⓕ the·bo·lya
only *sólo* so·lo
open *abierto/a* ⓜ/ⓕ a·byer·to/a
open *abrir* a·breer
opening hours *horas* ⓕ pl *de abrir*
  o·ras de a·breer
opera *ópera* ⓕ o·pe·ra
opera house *teatro* ⓜ *de la ópera*
  te·a·tro de la o·pe·ra
operation *operación* ⓕ o·pe·ra·thyon
operator *operador/operadora* ⓜ/ⓕ
  o·pe·ra·dor/o·pe·ra·do·ra
opinion *opinión* ⓕ o·pee·nyon
opposite *frente a* fren·te a
or *o* o
orange (fruit) *naranja* ⓕ na·ran·kha
orange (colour) *naranja* na·ran·kha
orange juice *zumo* ⓜ *de naranja*
  thoo·mo de na·ran·kha
orchestra *orquesta* ⓕ or·kes·ta
order *orden* ⓜ or·den
order *ordenar* or·de·nar
ordinary *corriente* ko·ryen·te
orgasm *orgasmo* ⓜ or·gas·mo
original *original* o·ree·khee·nal
other *otro/a* ⓜ/ⓕ o·tro/a
our *nuestro/a* ⓜ/ⓕ nwes·tro/a
outside *exterior* ⓜ eks·te·ryor
ovarian cyst *quiste* ⓜ *ovárico* kees·te
  o·va·ree·ko
oven *horno* ⓜ or·no
overcoat *abrigo* ⓜ a·bree·go
overdose *sobredosis* ⓕ so·bre·do·sees
owe *deber* de·ver
owner *dueño/a* ⓜ/ⓕ dwe·nyo/a
oxygen *oxígeno* ⓜ o·ksee·khe·no
oyster *ostra* ⓕ os·tra
ozone layer *capa* ⓕ *de ozono* ka·pa
  de o·tho·no

P

pacemaker *marcapasos* ⓜ mar·ka·*pa*·sos
pacifier *chupete* ⓜ choo·*pe*·te
package *paquete* ⓜ pa·*ke*·te
packet *paquete* ⓜ pa·*ke*·te
padlock *candado* ⓜ kan·*da*·do
page *página* ⓕ *pa*·khee·na
pain *dolor* ⓜ do·*lor*
painful *doloroso/a* ⓜ/ⓕ do·lo·*ro*·so/a
painkillers *analgésicos* ⓜ pl
a·nal·*khe*·see·kos
paint *pintar* peen·*tar*
painter *pintor/pintora* ⓜ/ⓕ peen·*tor*/
peen·*to*·ra
painting *pintura* ⓕ peen·*too*·ra
pair (couple) *pareja* ⓕ pa·*re*·kha
palace *palacio* ⓜ pa·*la*·thyo
pan *cazuela* ⓕ ka·*thwe*·la
pants *pantalones* ⓜ pl pan·ta·*lo*·nes
panty liners *salvaeslips* ⓜ pl
sal·va·e·*sleeps*
pantyhose *medias* ⓕ pl *me*·dyas
pap smear *citología* ⓕ thee·to·lo·*khee*·a
paper *papel* ⓜ pa·*pel*
paperwork *trabajo* ⓜ *administrativo*
tra·*ba*·kho ad·mee·nees·tra·*tee*·vo
paraplegic *parapléjico/a* ⓜ/ⓕ
pa·ra·*ple*·khee·ko/a
parasailing *esquí* ⓜ *acuático con
paracaídas* es·*kee* a·*kwa*·tee·ko kon
pa·ra·ka·*ee*·das
parcel *paquete* ⓜ pa·*ke*·te
parents *padres* ⓜ pl *pa*·dres
park *parque* ⓜ *par*·ke
park (car) *estacionar* es·ta·thyo·*nar*
parliament *parlamento* ⓜ
par·la·*men*·to
parsley *perejil* ⓜ pe·re·*kheel*
part *parte* ⓕ *par*·te
part-time *a tiempo parcial* a *tyem*·po
par·*thyal*
party *fiesta* ⓕ *fyes*·ta
party (political) *partido* ⓜ par·*tee*·do
pass *pase* ⓜ *pa*·se

passenger *pasajero/a* ⓜ/ⓕ
pa·sa·*khe*·ro
passport *pasaporte* ⓜ pa·sa·*por*·te
passport number *número* ⓜ *de pasaporte*
noo·me·ro de pa·sa·*por*·te
past *pasado* ⓜ pa·*sa*·do
pasta *pasta* ⓕ *pas*·ta
pate (food) *paté* ⓜ pa·*te*
path *sendero* ⓜ sen·*de*·ro
pay *pagar* pa·*gar*
payment *pago* ⓜ *pa*·go
peace *paz* ⓕ *path*
peach *melocotón* ⓜ me·lo·ko·*ton*
peak *cumbre* ⓕ *koom*·bre
peanuts *cacahuetes* ⓜ pl ka·ka·*we*·tes
pear *pera* ⓕ *pe*·ra
peas *guisantes* ⓜ pl gee·*san*·tes
pedal *pedal* ⓜ pe·*dal*
pedestrian *peatón* ⓜ&ⓕ pe·a·*ton*
pedestrian crossing *paso* ⓜ *de cebra*
pa·so de *the*·bra
pen *bolígrafo* ⓜ bo·lee·gra·fo
pencil *lápiz* ⓜ *la*·peeth
penis *pene* ⓜ *pe*·ne
penknife *navaja* ⓕ na·va·kha
pensioner *pensionista* ⓜ&ⓕ
pen·syo·*nees*·ta
people *gente* ⓕ *khen*·te
pepper (vegetable) *pimiento* ⓜ
pee·*myen*·to
pepper (spice) *pimienta* ⓕ
pee·*myen*·ta
per (day) *por (dia)* por (*dee*·a)
percent *por ciento* por *thyen*·to
performance *actuación* ⓕ ak·twa·*thyon*
perfume *perfume* ⓜ per·*foo*·me
period pain *dolor* ⓜ *menstrual* do·*lor*
mens·*trwal*
permission *permiso* ⓜ per·*mee*·so
permit *permiso* ⓜ per·*mee*·so
permit *permitir* per·mee·*teer*
person *persona* ⓕ per·*so*·na
perspire *sudar* soo·*dar*
petition *petición* ⓕ pe·tee·*thyon*
petrol *gasolina* ⓕ ga·so·*lee*·na

pharmacy *farmacia* ① far·ma·thya

phone book *guía* ① *telefónica* gee·a te·le·fo·nee·ka

phone box *cabina* ① *telefónica* ka·bee·ka te·le·fo·nee·ka

phone card *tarjeta* ① *de teléfono* tar·khe·ta de te·le·fo·no

photo *foto* ① fo·to

photographer *fotógrafo/a* ⓜ/① fo·to·gra·fo/a

photography *fotografía* ① fo·to·gra·fee·a

phrasebook *libro* ⓜ *de frases* lee·bro de fra·ses

pick up *ligar* lee·gar

pickaxe *piqueta* ① pee·ke·ta

pickles *encurtidos* ⓜ pl en·koor·tee·dos

picnic *comida* ① *en el campo* ko·mee·da en el kam·po

pie *pastel* ⓜ pas·tel

piece *pedazo* ⓜ pe·da·tho

pig *cerdo* ⓜ ther·do

pill *pastilla* ① pas·tee·lya

pillow *almohada* ① al·mwa·da

pillowcase *funda* ① *de almohada* foon·da de al·mwa·da

pineapple *piña* ① pee·nya

pink *rosa* ro·sa

pistachio *pistacho* ⓜ pees·ta·cho

place *lugar* ⓜ loo·gar

place of birth *lugar* ⓜ *de nacimiento* loo·gar de na·thee·myen·to

plane *avión* ⓜ a·vyon

planet *planeta* ⓜ pla·ne·ta

plant *planta* ① plan·ta

plant *sembrar* sem·brar

plastic *plástico* ⓜ plas·tee·ko

plate *plato* ⓜ pla·to

plateau *meseta* ① me·se·ta

platform *plataforma* ① pla·ta·for·ma

play *obra* ① o·bra

play (musical instrument) *tocar* to·kar

play (sport/games) *jugar* khoo·gar

plug *tapar* ta·par

plum *ciruela* thee·rwe·la

pocket *bolsillo* ⓜ bol·see·lyo

poetry *poesía* ① po·e·see·a

point *apuntar* a·poon·tar

point (tip) *punto* ⓜ poon·to

poisonous *venenoso/a* ⓜ/① ve·ne·no·so/a

poker *póquer* ⓜ po·ker

police *policía* ① po·lee·thee·a

police station *comisaría* ① ko·mee·sa·ree·a

policy *política* ① po·lee·tee·ka

policy (insurance) *póliza* ① po·lee·tha

politician *político* ⓜ po·lee·tee·ko

politics *política* ① po·lee·tee·ka

pollen *polen* ⓜ po·len

polls *sondeos* ⓜ pl son·de·os

pollution *contaminación* ① kon·ta·mee·na·thyon

pool (swimming) *piscina* ① pees·thee·na

poor *pobre* po·bre

popular *popular* po·poo·lar

pork *cerdo* ⓜ ther·do

pork sausage *chorizo* ⓜ cho·ree·tho

port *puerto* ⓜ pwer·to

port (wine) *oporto* ⓜ o·por·to

possible *posible* po·see·ble

post code *código postal* ⓜ ko·dee·go pos·tal

post office *correos* ⓜ ko·re·os

postage *franqueo* ⓜ fran·ke·o

postcard *postal* ① pos·tal

poster *póster* ⓜ pos·ter

pot (kitchen) *cazuela* ① ka·thwe·la

pot (plant) *tiesto* ⓜ tyes·to

potato *patata* ① pa·ta·ta

pottery *alfarería* ① al·fa·re·ree·a

pound (money) *libra* ① lee·bra

poverty *pobreza* ① po·bre·tha

power *poder* ⓜ po·der

prawns *gambas* ① pl gam·bas

prayer *oración* ① o·ra·thyon

prayer book *devocionario* ⓜ de·vo·thyo·na·ryo

prefer *preferir* pre·fe·reer
pregnancy test *prueba* ① *del embarazo* prwe·ba del em·ba·ra·tho
pregnant *embarazada* ① em·ba·ra·tha·da
premenstrual tension *tensión* ① *premenstrual* ten·syon pre·mens·trwal
prepare *preparar* pre·pa·rar
president *presidente/a* ⓜ/① pre·see·den·te/a
pressure *presión* ① pre·syon
pretty *bonito/a* ⓜ/① bo·nee·to/a
prevent *prevenir* pre·ve·neer
price *precio* ⓜ pre·thyo
priest *sacerdote* ⓜ sa·ther·do·te
prime minister *primer ministro/ primera ministra* ⓜ/① pree·mer mee·nees·tro/pree·me·ra mee·nees·tra
prison *cárcel* ① kar·thel
prisoner *prisionero/a* ⓜ/① pree·syon·ne·ro/a
private *privado/a* ⓜ/① pree·va·do/a
private hospital *clínica* ① klee·nee·ka
produce *producir* pro·doo·theer
profit *beneficio* ⓜ be·ne·fee·thyo
programme *programa* ⓜ pro·gra·ma
projector *proyector* ⓜ pro·yek·tor
promise *promesa* ① pro·me·sa
protect *proteger* pro·te·kher
protected (species) *protegido/a* ⓜ/① pro·te·khee·do/a
protest *protesta* ① pro·tes·ta
protest *protestar* pro·tes·tar
provisions *provisiones* ① pl pro·bee·syo·nes
prune *ciruela* ① *pasa* thee·rwe·la pa·sa
pub *pub* ⓜ poob
public telephone *teléfono* ⓜ *público* te·le·fo·no poo·blee·ko
public toilet *servicios* ⓜ pl ser·vee·thyos
pull *tirar* tee·rar
pump *bomba* ① bom·ba

pumpkin *calabaza* ① ka·la·ba·tha
puncture *pinchar* peen·char
punish *castigar* kas·tee·gar
puppy *cachorro* ⓜ ka·cho·ro
pure *puro/a* ⓜ/① poo·ro/a
purple *lila* lee·la
push *empujar* em·poo·khar
put *poner* po·ner

Q

qualifications *cualificaciones* ① pl kwa·lee·fee·ka·thyo·nes
quality *calidad* ① ka·lee·da
quarantine *cuarentena* ① kwa·ren·te·na
quarrel *pelea* ① pe·le·a
quarter *cuarto* ⓜ kwar·to
queen *reina* ① rey·na
question *pregunta* ① pre·goon·ta
question *cuestionar* kwes·tyo·nar
queue *cola* ① ko·la
quick *rápido/a* ⓜ/① ra·pee·do/a
quiet *tranquilo/a* ⓜ/① tran·kee·lo/a
quiet *tranquilidad* ① tran·kee·lee·da
quit *dejar* de·khar

R

rabbit *conejo* ⓜ ko·ne·kho
race (people) *raza* ① ra·tha
race (sport) *carrera* ① ka·re·ra
racetrack (bicycles) *velódromo* ⓜ ve·lo·dro·mo
racetrack (cars) *circuito* ⓜ *de carreras* theer·kwee·to de ka·re·ras
racetrack (horses) *hipódromo* ⓜ ee·po·dro·mo
racetrack (runners) *pista* ① pees·ta
racing bike *bicicleta* ① *de carreras* bee·thee·kle·ta de ka·re·ras
racquet *raqueta* ① ra·ke·ta
radiator *radiador* ⓜ ra·dya·dor
radish *rábano* ⓜ ra·ba·no
railway station *estación* ① *de tren* es·ta·thyon de tren
rain *lluvia* ① lyoo·vya

raincoat *impermeable* ⓜ
eem·per·me·a·ble
raisin *uva* ⓕ *pasa* oo·va pa·sa
rally *concentración* ⓕ
kon·then·tra·thyon
rape *violar* vyo·lar
rare *raro/a* ⓜ/ⓕ ra·ro/a
rash *irritación* ⓕ ee·ree·ta·thyon
raspberry *frambuesa* ⓕ fram·bwe·sa
rat *rata* ⓕ ra·ta
rate of pay *salario* ⓜ sa·la·ryo
raw *crudo/a* ⓜ/ⓕ kroo·do/a
razor *afeitadora* ⓕ a·fey·ta·do·ra
razor blades *cuchillas* ⓕ pl *de afeitar*
koo·chee·lyas de a·fey·tar
read *leer* le·er
ready *listo/a* ⓜ/ⓕ lees·to/a
real estate agent *agente inmobiliario* ⓜ
a·khen·te een·mo·bee·lya·ryo
realise *darse cuenta de* dar·se kwen·ta de
realistic *realista* re·a·lees·ta
reason *razón* ⓕ ra·thon
receipt *recibo* ⓜ re·thee·bo
receive *recibir* re·thee·beer
recently *recientemente* re·thyen·te·men·te
recognise *reconocer* re·ko·no·ther
recommend *recomendar* re·ko·men·dar
recording *grabación* ⓕ gra·ba·thyon
recyclable *reciclable* re·thee·kla·ble
recycle *reciclar* re·thee·klar
red *rojo/a* ⓜ/ⓕ ro·kho/a
referee *árbitro* ⓜ ar·bee·tro
reference *referencias* ⓕ pl
re·fe·ren·thyas
refrigerator *nevera* ⓕ ne·ve·ra •
frigorífico ⓜ free·ge·ree·fee·ko
refugee *refugiado/a* ⓜ/ⓕ
re·foo·khya·do/a
refund *reembolso* ⓜ re·em·bol·so
refund *reembolsar* re·em·bol·sar
refuse *negar* ne·gar
registered mail *correo* ⓕ *certificado*
ko·re·o ther·tee·fee·ka·do
regret *lamentar* la·men·tar

relationship *relación* ⓕ re·la·thyon
relax *relajarse* re·la·khar·se
relic *reliquia* ⓕ re·lee·kya
religion *religión* ⓕ re·lee·khyon
religious *religioso/a* ⓜ/ⓕ
re·lee·khyo·so/a
remember *recordar* re·kor·dar
remote *remoto/a* ⓜ/ⓕ re·mo·to/a
remote control *mando* ⓜ *a distancia*
man·do a dees·tan·thya
rent *alquiler* ⓜ al·kee·ler
rent *alquilar* al·kee·lar
repair *reparar* re·pa·rar
repeat *repetir* re·pe·teer
republic *república* ⓕ re·poo·blee·ka
reservation *reserva* ⓕ re·ser·va
reserve *reservar* re·ser·var
rest *descansar* des·kan·sar
restaurant *restaurante* ⓜ res·tow·ran·te
resumé *currículum* ⓜ
koo·ree·koo·loom
retired *jubilado/a* ⓜ/ⓕ khoo·bee·la·do/a
return *volver* vol·ver
return ticket *billete* ⓜ *de ida y vuelta*
bee·lye·te de ee·da ee vwel·ta
review *crítica* ⓕ kree·tee·ka
rhythm *ritmo* ⓜ reet·mo
rice *arroz* ⓜ a·roth
rich *rico/a* ⓜ/ⓕ ree·ko/a
ride *paseo* ⓜ pa·se·o
ride *montar* mon·tar
right (correct) *correcto/a* ⓜ/ⓕ
ko·rek·to/a
right (not left) *derecha* de·re·cha
right-wing *derechista* de·re·chees·ta
ring *llamada* ⓕ lya·ma·da
ring *llamar por telefono* lya·mar por
te·le·fo·no
rip-off *estafa* ⓕ es·ta·fa
risk *riesgo* ⓜ ryes·go
river *río* ⓜ ree·o
road *carretera* ⓕ ka·re·te·ra
rob *robar* ro·bar
rock (stone) *roca* ⓕ ro·ka

rock (music) *rock* ⓜ rok

rock climbing *escalada* ⓕ es·ka·*la*·da

rock group *grupo* ⓜ *de rock* groo·po de rok

rollerblading *patinar* pa·tee·*nar*

romantic *romántico/a* ⓜ/ⓕ ro·*man*·tee·ko/a

room *habitación* ⓕ a·bee·ta·*thyon*

room number *número* ⓜ *de la habitación* noo·me·ro de la a·bee·ta·*thyon*

rope *cuerda* ⓕ *kwer*·da

round *redondo/a* ⓜ/ⓕ re·*don*·do/a

roundabout *glorieta* ⓕ glo·*rye*·ta

route *ruta* ⓕ *roo*·ta

rowing *remo* ⓜ *re*·mo

rubbish *basura* ⓕ ba·*soo*·ra

rug *alfombra* ⓕ al·*fom*·bra

rugby *rugby* ⓜ *roog*·bee

ruins *ruinas* ⓕ pl *rwee*·nas

rules *reglas* ⓕ pl *re*·glas

rum *ron* ron

run *correr* ko·*rer*

run out of *quedarse sin* ke·*dar*·se seen

S

sad *triste* *trees*·te

saddle *sillín* ⓜ see·*lyeen*

safe *seguro/a* ⓜ/ⓕ se·*goo*·ro/a

safe *caja* ⓕ *fuerte* ka·kha *fwer*·te

safe sex *sexo* ⓜ *seguro* *se*·kso se·*goo*·ro

saint *santo/a* ⓜ/ⓕ *san*·to/a

salad *ensalada* ⓕ en·sa·*la*·da

salami (Spanish sausage) *chorizo* cho·*ree*·tho

salary *salario* ⓜ sa·*la*·ryo

sales tax *IVA* ⓜ *ee*·va

salmon *salmón* ⓜ sal·*mon*

salt *sal* ⓕ sal

same *igual* ee·*gwal*

sand *arena* ⓕ a·*re*·na

sandals *sandalias* ⓕ pl san·*da*·lyas

sanitary napkins *compresas* ⓕ pl kom·*pre*·sas

sauna *sauna* ⓕ *sow*·na

sausage *salchicha* ⓕ sal·*chee*·cha

save *salvar* sal·*var*

save (money) *ahorrar* a·o·*rar*

say *decir* de·*theer*

scale/climb *trepar* tre·*par*

scarf *bufanda* ⓕ boo·*fan*·da

school *escuela* ⓕ es·*kwe*·la

science *ciencias* ⓕ pl *thyen*·thyas

scientist *científico/a* ⓜ/ⓕ thyen·*tee*·fee·ko/a

scissors *tijeras* ⓕ pl tee·*khe*·ras

score *marcar* mar·*kar*

scoreboard *marcador* ⓜ mar·ka·*dor*

Scotland *Escocia* ⓕ es·ko·thya

screen *pantalla* ⓕ pan·*ta*·lya

script *guión* ⓜ gee·*on*

sculpture *escultura* ⓕ es·kool·*too*·ra

sea *mar* ⓜ mar

seasick *mareado/a* ⓜ/ⓕ ma·re·a·do/a

seaside *costa* ⓕ *kos*·ta

season *estación* ⓕ es·ta·*thyon*

season (in sport) *temporada* ⓕ tem·po·*ra*·da

seat *asiento* ⓜ a·*syen*·to

seatbelt *cinturón* ⓜ *de seguridad* theen·too·*ron* de se·goo·ree·da

second *segundo/a* ⓜ/ⓕ se·*goon*·do/a

second *segundo* ⓜ se·*goon*·do

second-hand *de segunda mano* de se·*goon*·da *ma*·no

secretary *secretario/a* ⓜ/ⓕ se·kre·*ta*·ryo/a

see *ver* ver

selfish *egoísta* e·go·*ees*·ta

self-service *autoservicio* ⓜ ow·to·ser·*vee*·thyo

sell *vender* ven·*der*

send *enviar* en·vee·*ar*

sensible *prudente* proo·*den*·te

sensual *sensual* sen·*swal*

separate *separado/a* ⓜ/ⓕ se·pa·*ra*·do/a

separate *separar* se·pa·*rar*

series *serie* ⓕ *se*·rye

serious *serio/a* ⓜ/ⓕ se·ryo/a
service station *gasolinera* ⓕ
  ga·so·lee·*ne*·ra
service charge *carga* ⓕ *kar*·ga
several *varias/os* ⓜ/ⓕ *va*·ryas/os
sew *coser* ko·*ser*
sex *sexo* ⓜ *se*·kso
sexism *machismo* ⓜ ma·*chees*·mo
sexy *sexy* *se*·ksee
shadow *sombra* ⓕ *som*·bra
shampoo *champú* ⓜ cham·*poo*
shape *forma* ⓕ *for*·ma
share (a dorm) *compartir (un dormitorio)*
  kom·par·*teer* (oon dor·mee·*to*·ryo)
share (with) *compartir* kom·par·*teer*
shave *afeitarse* a·fey·*tar*·se
shaving cream *espuma* ⓕ *de afeitar*
  es·*poo*·ma de a·fey·*tar*
she *ella* ⓕ e·lya
sheep *oveja* ⓕ o·ve·kha
sheet (bed) *sábana* ⓕ sa·ba·na
sheet (of paper) *hoja* ⓕ o·kha
shelf *estante* ⓜ es·*tan*·te
ship *barco* ⓜ *bar*·ko
ship *enviar* en·vee·*ar*
shirt *camisa* ⓕ ka·*mee*·sa
shoe shop *zapatería* ⓕ tha·pa·te·*ree*·a
shoes *zapatos* ⓜ pl tha·*pa*·tos
shoot *disparar* dees·pa·*rar*
shop *tienda* ⓕ *tyen*·da
shoplifting *ratería* ⓕ ra·te·*ree*·a
shopping centre *centro* ⓜ *comercial*
  then·tro ko·mer·*thyal*
short (height) *bajo/a* ⓜ/ⓕ *ba*·kho/a
short (length) *corto/a* ⓜ/ⓕ *kor*·to/a
shortage *escasez* ⓕ es·ka·*seth*
shorts *pantalones* ⓜ pl *cortos*
  pan·ta·*lo*·nes
shoulders *hombros* ⓜ pl *om*·bros
shout *gritar* gree·*tar*
show *espectáculo* ⓜ es·pek·*ta*·koo·lo
show *mostrar* mos·*trar*
show *enseñar* en·se·*nyar*
shower *ducha* ⓕ *doo*·cha

shrine *capilla* ⓕ ka·*pee*·lya
shut *cerrado/a* ⓜ/ⓕ the·*ra*·do/a
shut *cerrar* the·*rar*
shy *tímido/a* ⓜ/ⓕ *tee*·mee·do/a
sick *enfermo/a* ⓜ/ⓕ en·*fer*·mo/a
side *lado* ⓜ *la*·do
sign *señal* ⓕ se·*nyal*
sign *firmar* feer·*mar*
signature *firma* ⓕ *feer*·ma
silk *seda* ⓕ *se*·da
silver *plateado/a* ⓜ/ⓕ pla·te·a·do/a
silver *plata* ⓕ *pla*·ta
similar *similar* see·mee·*lar*
simple *sencillo/a* ⓜ/ⓕ sen·*thee*·lyo/a
since *desde (mayo)* des·de (*ma*·yo)
sing *cantar* kan·*tar*
Singapore *Singapur* ⓜ seen·ga·*poor*
singer *cantante* ⓜ&ⓕ kan·*tan*·te
single *soltero/a* ⓜ/ⓕ sol·*te*·ro/a
single room *habitación* ⓕ *individual*
  a·bee·ta·*thyon* een·dee·vee·*dwal*
singlet *camiseta* ⓕ ka·mee·se·ta
sister *hermana* ⓕ er·*ma*·na
sit *sentarse* sen·*tar*·se
size (clothes) *talla* ⓕ *ta*·lya
skateboarding *monopatinaje* ⓜ
  mo·no·pa·tee·*na*·khe
ski *esquiar* es·kee·*ar*
skiing *esquí* ⓜ es·*kee*
skimmed milk *leche* ⓕ *desnatada*
  le·che des·na·*ta*·da
skin *piel* ⓕ pyel
skirt *falda* ⓕ *fal*·da
sky *cielo* ⓜ *thye*·lo
skydiving *paracaidismo* ⓜ
  pa·ra·kai·*dees*·mo
sleep *dormir* dor·*meer*
sleeping bag *saco* ⓜ *de dormir* sa·ko
  de dor·*meer*
sleeping car *coche cama* ⓜ ko·che
  ka·ma
sleeping pills *pastillas* ⓕ pl *para*
  dormir pas·*tee*·lyas *pa*·ra dor·*meer*
(to be) sleepy *tener sueño*
  te·*ner* swe·nyo

slide *diapositiva* ① dya·po·see·tee·va

slow *lento/a* ⓜ/① len·to/a

slowly *despacio* des·pa·thyo

small *pequeño/a* ⓜ/① pe·ke·nyo/a

smell *olor* ⓜ o·lor

smell *oler* o·ler

smile *sonreír* son·re·eer

smoke *fumar* foo·mar

snack *tentempié* ⓜ ten·tem·pye

snail *caracol* ① ka·ra·kol

snake *serpiente* ① ser·pyen·te

snorkel *tubos* ⓜ pl respiratorios

snorkel *buceo* ⓜ boo·the·o

snow *nieve* ① nye·ve

snowboarding *surf* ⓜ sobre la nieve
soorf so·bre la nye·ve

soap *jabón* ⓜ kha·bon

soap opera *telenovela* ① te·le·no·ve·la

soccer *fútbol* ⓜ foot·bol

social welfare *estado* ⓜ del bienestar
es·ta·do del byen·es·tar

socialist *socialista* ⓜ&① so·thya·lees·ta

socks *calcetines* ⓜ pl kal·the·tee·nes

soft drink *refresco* ⓜ re·fres·ko

soldier *soldado* ⓜ sol·da·do

some *alguno/a* ⓜ/① al·goon

someone *alguien* al·gyen

something *algo* al·go

sometimes *de vez en cuando* de veth
en kwan·do

son *hijo* ⓜ ee·kho

song *canción* ① kan·thyon

soon *pronto* pron·to

sore *dolorido/a* ⓜ/① do·lo·ree·do/a

soup *sopa* ① so·pa

sour cream *nata* ① agria na·ta a·grya

south *sur* ⓜ soor

souvenir *recuerdo* ⓜ re·kwer·do

souvenir shop *tienda* ① de recuerdos
tyen·da de re·kwer·dos

soy milk *leche* ① de soja le·che de
so·kha

soy sauce *salsa* ① de soja sal·sa de
so·kha

space *espacio* ⓜ es·pa·thyo

Spain *España* ① es·pa·nya

sparkling *espumoso/a* ⓜ/①
es·poo·mo·so

speak *hablar* a·blar

special *especial* es·pe·thyal

specialist *especialista* ⓜ&①
es·pe·thya·lees·ta

speed *velocidad* ① ve·lo·thee·da

speeding *exceso* ⓜ de velocidad
eks·the·so de ve·lo·thee·da

speedometer *velocímetro* ⓜ
ve·lo·thee·me·tro

spider *araña* ① a·ra·nya

spinach *espinacas* es·pee·na·kas

spoon *cuchara* ① koo·cha·ra

sport *deportes* ⓜ pl de·por·tes

sports store *tienda* ① deportiva
tyen·da de·por·tee·va

sportsperson *deportista* ⓜ&①
de·por·tees·ta

sprain *torcedura* ① tor·the·doo·ra

spring (wire) *muelle* ⓜ mwe·lye

spring (season) *primavera* ①
pree·ma·ve·ra

square (shape) *cuadrado* ⓜ kwa·dra·do

(main) square *plaza* ① (mayor) ①
pla·tha ma·yor

stadium *estadio* ⓜ es·ta·dyo

stage *escenario* ⓜ es·the·na·ryo

stairway *escalera* ① es·ka·le·ra

stamp *sello* ⓜ se·lyo

standby ticket *billete* ⓜ de lista de
espera bee·lye·te de lees·ta de
es·pe·ra

stars *estrellas* ① pl es·tre·lyas

start *comenzar* ko·men·thar

station *estación* ① es·ta·thyon

statue *estatua* ① es·ta·twa

stay (remain) *quedarse* ke·dar·se

stay (somewhere) *alojarse* a·lo·khar·se

steak (beef) *bistec* ⓜ bees·tek

steal *robar* ro·bar

steep *escarpado/a* ⓜ/① es·kar·pa·do/a

step *paso* ⓜ pa·so

stereo *equipo* ⓜ *de música* e·kee·po de moo·see·ka

stingy *tacaño/a* ⓜ/ⓕ ta·ka·nyo/a

stock *caldo* ⓜ kal·do

stockings *medias* ⓕ pl me·dyas

stomach *estómago* ⓜ es·to·ma·go

stomachache *dolor* ⓜ *de estómago* do·lor de es·to·ma·go

stone *piedra* ⓕ pye·dra

stoned *colocado/a* ⓜ/ⓕ ko·lo·ka·do/a

stop *parada* ⓕ pa·ra·da

stop *parar* pa·rar

storm *tormenta* ⓕ tor·men·ta

story *cuento* ⓜ kwen·to

stove *cocina* ⓕ ko·thee·na

straight *recto/a* ⓜ/ⓕ rek·to/a

strange *extraño/a* ⓜ/ⓕ eks·tra·nyo/a

stranger *desconocido/a* ⓜ/ⓕ des·ko·no·thee·do/a

strawberry *fresa* ⓕ fre·sa

stream *arroyo* ⓜ a·ro·yo

street *calle* ⓕ ka·lye

string *cuerda* ⓕ kwer·da

strong *fuerte* fwer·te

stubborn *testarudo/a* ⓜ/ⓕ tes·ta·roo·do/a

student *estudiante* ⓜ&ⓕ es·too·dyan·te

studio *estudio* ⓜ es·too·dyo

stupid *estúpido/a* ⓜ/ⓕ es·too·pee·do/a

style *estilo* ⓜ es·tee·lo

subtitles *subtítulos* ⓜ pl soob·tee·too·los

suburb *barrio* ⓜ ba·ryo

subway *parada* ⓕ *de metro* pa·ra·da de me·tro

suffer *sufrir* soo·freer

sugar *azúcar* ⓜ a·thoo·kar

suitcase *maleta* ⓕ ma·le·ta

summer *verano* ⓜ ve·ra·no

sun *sol* ⓜ sol

sunblock *crema* ⓕ *solar* kre·ma so·lar

sunburn *quemadura* ⓕ *de sol* ke·ma·doo·ra de sol

sun-dried tomato *tomate* ⓜ *secado al sol* to·ma·te se·ka·do al sol

sunflower oil *aceite* ⓜ *de girasol* a·they·te khee·ra·sol

sunglasses *gafas* ⓕ pl *de sol* ga·fas de sol

(to be) sunny *hace sol* a·the sol

sunrise *amanecer* ⓜ a·ma·ne·ther

sunset *puesta* ⓕ *del sol* pwes·ta del sol

supermarket *supermercado* ⓜ soo·per·mer·ka·do

superstition *superstición* ⓕ soo·pers·tee·thyon

supporters *hinchas* ⓜ&ⓕ pl een·chas

surf *hacer surf* a·ther soorf

surface mail *por vía terrestre* por vee·a te·res·tre

surfboard *tabla de surf* ⓕ ta·bla de soorf

surname *apellido* ⓜ a·pe·lyee·do

surprise *sorpresa* ⓕ sor·pre·sa

survive *sobrevivir* so·bre·vee·veer

sweater *jersey* ⓜ kher·sey

sweet *dulce* dool·the

sweets (candy) *dulces* ⓜ pl dool·thes

swim *nadar* na·dar

swimming pool *piscina* ⓕ pees·thee·na

swimsuit *bañador* ⓜ ba·nya·dor

synagogue *sinagoga* ⓕ see·na·go·ga

synthetic *sintético/a* ⓜ/ⓕ seen·te·tee·ko/a

syringe *jeringa* ⓕ khe·reen·ga

T

table *mesa* ⓕ me·sa

table tennis *ping pong* ⓜ peeng pong

tablecloth *mantel* ⓜ man·tel

tail *rabo* ⓜ ra·bo

tailor *sastre* ⓜ sas·tre

take (away) *llevar* lye·var

take (the train) *tomar* to·mar

take (photo) *sacar* sa·kar

take photographs *sacar fotos* sa·kar fo·tos

talk *hablar* a·blar
tall *alto/a* ⓜ/ⓕ al·to/a
tampons *tampones* ⓜ pl tam·po·nes
tanning lotion *bronceador* ⓜ
bron·the·a·dor
tap *grifo* ⓜ gree·fo
tasty *sabroso/a* ⓜ/ⓕ sa·bro·so/a
tax *impuestos* ⓜ pl eem·pwes·tos
taxi *taxi* ⓜ tak·see
taxi stand *parada* ⓕ *de taxis* pa·ra·da
de tak·sees
tea *té* ⓜ te
teacher *profesor/profesora* ⓜ/ⓕ
pro·fe·sor/pro·fe·so·ra
team *equipo* ⓜ e·kee·po
teaspoon *cucharita* ⓕ koo·cha·ree·ta
technique *técnica* ⓕ tek·nee·ka
teeth *dientes* ⓜ pl dyen·tes
telegram *telegrama* ⓜ te·le·gra·ma
telephone *teléfono* ⓜ te·le·fo·no
telephone *llamar (por teléfono)*
lya·mar (por te·le·fo·no)
telephone centre *central* ⓕ *telefónica*
then·tral te·le·fo·nee·ka
telescope *telescopio* ⓜ te·les·ko·pyo
television *televisión* ⓕ te·le·vee·syon
tell *decir* de·theer
temperature (fever) *fiebre* ⓕ fye·bre
temperature (weather) *temperatura* ⓕ
tem·pe·ra·too·ra
temple *templo* ⓜ tem·plo
tennis *tenis* ⓜ te·nees
tennis court *pista* ⓕ *de tenis* pees·ta
de te·nees
tent *tienda* ⓕ *(de campaña)* tyen·da
(de kam·pa·nya)
tent pegs *piquetas* ⓕ pl pee·ke·tas
terrible *terrible* te·ree·ble
test *prueba* ⓕ prwe·ba
thank *dar gracias* dar gra·thyas
the Pill *píldora* ⓕ peel·do·ra
theatre *teatro* ⓜ te·a·tro
their *su* soo
they *ellos/ellas* ⓜ/ⓕ e·lyos/e·lyas

thief *ladrón/ladrona* ⓜ/ⓕ la·dron/
la·dro·na
thin *delgado/a* ⓜ/ⓕ del·ga·do/a
think *pensar* pen·sar
third *tercio* ⓜ ter·thyo
thirst *sed* ⓕ se
this *éste/a* ⓜ/ⓕ es·te/a
this month *este mes* es·te mes
throat *garganta* ⓕ gar·gan·ta
ticket *billete* ⓜ bee·lye·te
ticket collector *revisor/revisora* ⓜ/ⓕ
re·vee·sor/re·vee·so·ra
ticket machine *máquina* ⓕ *de billetes*
ma·kee·na de bee·lye·tes
ticket office *taquilla* ⓕ ta·kee·lya
tide *marea* ⓕ ma·re·a
tight *apretado/a* ⓜ/ⓕ a·pre·ta·do/a
time *hora* ⓕ o·ra • *tiempo* ⓜ tyem·po
time difference *diferencia* ⓕ *de horas*
dee·fe·ren·thya de o·ras
timetable *horario* ⓜ o·ra·ryo
tin *hojalata* ⓕ o·kha·la·ta
tin opener *abrelatas* ⓜ a·bre·la·tas
tiny *pequeñito/a* ⓜ/ⓕ pe·ke·nyee·to/a
tip *propina* ⓕ pro·pee·na
tired *cansado/a* ⓜ/ⓕ kan·sa·do/a
tissues *pañuelos* ⓜ pl *de papel*
pa·nywe·los de pa·pel
toast *tostada* ⓕ tos·ta·da
toaster *tostadora* ⓕ tos·ta·do·ra
tobacco *tabaco* ⓜ ta·ba·ko
tobacconist *estanquero* ⓜ es·tan·ke·ro
tobogganing *ir en tobogán* eer en
to·bo·gan
today *hoy* oy
toe *dedo* ⓜ *del pie* de·do del pye
tofu *tofú* ⓜ to·foo
together *juntos/as* ⓜ/ⓕ khoon·tos/as
toilet *servicio* ⓜ ser·vee·thyo
toilet paper *papel* ⓜ *higiénico* pa·pel
ee·khye·nee·ko
tomato *tomate* ⓜ to·ma·te
tomato sauce *salsa* ⓕ *de tomate* sal·sa
de to·ma·te
tomorrow *mañana* ma·nya·na

tomorrow afternoon *mañana por la tarde* ma·nya·na por la *tar*·de

tomorrow evening *mañana por la noche* ma·nya·na por la *no*·che

tomorrow morning *mañana por la mañana* ma·nya·na por la ma·nya·na

tone *tono* ⓜ *to*·no

tonight *esta noche* es·ta *no*·che

too (expensive) *demasiado (caro/a)* ⓜ/ⓕ de·ma·sya·do (*ka*·ro/a)

tooth *diente* ⓜ *dyen*·te

tooth (back) *muela* ⓕ *mwe*·la

toothache *dolor* ⓜ *de muelas* do·lor de *mwe*·las

toothbrush *cepillo* ⓜ *de dientes* the·*pee*·lyo de *dyen*·tes

toothpaste *pasta* ⓕ *dentífrica* *pas*·ta den·*tee*·free·ka

toothpick *palillo* ⓜ pa·*lee*·lyo

torch *linterna* ⓕ leen·*ter*·na

touch *tocar* to·kar

tour *excursión* ⓕ eks·koor·*syon*

tourist *turista* ⓜ&ⓕ too·*rees*·ta

tourist (slang) *guiri* ⓜ *gee*·ree

tourist office *oficina* ⓕ *de turismo* o·fee·*thee*·na de too·*rees*·mo

towards *hacia* a·thya

towel *toalla* ⓕ to·a·lya

tower *torre* ⓕ *to*·re

toxic waste *residuos* ⓜ pl *tóxicos* re·*see*·dwos *tok*·see·kos

toyshop *juguetería* ⓕ khoo·ge·te·*ree*·a

track (car racing) *autódromo* ⓜ ow·*to*·dro·mo

track (footprints) *rastro* ⓜ *ras*·tro

trade *comercio* ⓜ ko·*mer*·thyo

traffic *tráfico* ⓜ *tra*·fee·ko

traffic lights *semáforos* ⓜ pl se·*ma*·fo·ros

trail *camino* ⓜ ka·*mee*·no

train *tren* ⓜ tren

train station *estación* ⓕ *de tren* es·ta·*thyon* de tren

tram *tranvía* ⓜ tran·*vee*·a

transit lounge *sala* ⓕ *de tránsito* *sa*·la de *tran*·see·to

translate *traducir* tra·doo·*theer*

transport *medios* ⓜ pl *de transporte* *me*·dyos de trans·*por*·te

travel *viajar* vya·*khar*

travel agency *agencia* ⓕ *de viajes* a·*khen*·thya de *vya*·khes

travel books *libros* ⓜ pl *de viajes* *lee*·bros de *vya*·khes

travel sickness *mareo* ⓜ ma·*re*·o

travellers cheque *cheques* ⓜ pl *de viajero* *che*·kes de vya·*khe*·ro

tree *árbol* ⓜ *ar*·bol

trip *viaje* ⓜ *vya*·khe

trousers *pantalones* ⓜ pl pan·ta·*lo*·nes

truck (car racing) *camión* ⓜ ka·*myon*

trust *confianza* ⓕ kon·fee·*an*·tha

trust *confiar* kon·fee·*ar*

try *probar* pro·*bar*

try (to do something) *intentar (hacer algo)* een·ten·*tar* (a·ther al·go)

T-shirt *camiseta* ⓕ ka·mee·*se*·ta

tube (tyre) *cámara* ⓕ *de aire* ka·ma·ra de *ai*·re

tuna *atún* ⓜ a·*toon*

tune *melodía* ⓕ me·lo·*dee*·a

turkey *pavo* ⓜ *pa*·vo

turn *doblar* do·*blar*

TV *tele* ⓕ *te*·le

TV series *serie* ⓕ *se*·rye

tweezers *pinzas* ⓕ pl *peen*·thas

twice *dos veces* dos *ve*·thes

twin beds *dos camas* ⓕ pl dos *ka*·mas

twins *gemelos* ⓜ pl khe·*me*·los

type *tipo* ⓜ *tee*·po

type *escribir a máquina* es·kree·*beer* a *ma*·kee·na

typical *típico/a* ⓜ/ⓕ *tee*·pee·ko/a

tyre *neumático* ⓜ ne·oo·ma·*tee*·ko

U

ultrasound *ecografía* ⓕ e·ko·gra·*fee*·a

umbrella *paraguas* ⓜ pa·*ra*·gwas

umpire *árbitro* ⓜ *ar*·bee·tro

uncomfortable *incómodo/a* ⓜ/ⓕ een·ko·mo·do/a

underpants (men) *calzoncillos* ⓜ pl
kal·thon·*thee*·lyos

underpants (women) *bragas* ⓕ pl
bra·gas

understand *comprender* kom·pren·*der*

underwear *ropa interior* ⓕ ro·pa
een·te·*ryor*

unemployed *en el paro* en el *pa*·ro

unfair *injusto* een·*khoos*·to

uniform *uniforme* ⓜ oo·nee·*for*·me

universe *universo* ⓜ oo·nee·*ver*·so

university *universidad* ⓕ
oo·nee·ver·see·*da*

unleaded *sin plomo* seen *plo*·mo

unsafe *inseguro/a* ⓜ/ⓕ een·se·goo·ro/a

until (June) *hasta (junio)* as·ta
(*khoo*·nyo)

unusual *extraño/a* ⓜ/ⓕ eks·*tra*·nyo/a

up *arriba* a·*ree*·ba

uphill *cuesta arriba* kwes·ta a·*ree*·ba

urgent *urgente* oor·*khen*·te

USA *Los Estados* ⓜ pl *Unidos*
los es·*ta*·dos oo·*nee*·dos

useful *útil* oo·teel

V

vacant *vacante* va·*kan*·te

vacation *vacaciones* ⓕ pl
va·ka·*thyo*·nes

vaccination *vacuna* ⓕ va·*koo*·na

vagina *vagina* ⓕ va·*khee*·na

validate *validar* va·lee·*dar*

valley *valle* ⓜ va·lye

valuable *valioso/a* ⓜ/ⓕ va·*lyo*·so/a

value *valor* ⓜ va·*lor*

van *caravana* ⓕ ka·ra·va·na

veal *ternera* ⓕ ter·ne·ra

vegetable *verdura* ⓕ ver·*doo*·ra

vegetables *verduras* ⓕ pl ver·*doo*·ras

vegetarian *vegetariano/a* ⓜ/ⓕ
ve·khe·ta·*rya*·no/a

vein *vena* ⓕ ve·na

venereal disease *enfermedad* ⓕ
venérea en·fer·me·*da* ve·ne·re·a

venue *local* ⓜ lo·*kal*

very *muy* mooy

video tape *cinta* ⓕ *de vídeo* theen·ta
de *vee*·de·o

view *vista* ⓕ *vees*·ta

village *pueblo* ⓜ *pwe*·blo

vine *vid* ⓕ veed

vinegar *vinagre* ⓜ vee·na·gre

vineyard *viñedo* ⓜ vee·*nye*·do

virus *virus* ⓜ *vee*·roos

visa *visado* ⓜ vee·*sa*·do

visit *visitar* vee·see·*tar*

vitamins *vitaminas* ⓕ pl
vee·ta·*mee*·nas

vodka *vodka* ⓕ *vod*·ka

voice *voz* ⓕ voth

volume *volumen* ⓜ vo·*loo*·men

vote *votar* vo·*tar*

wage *sueldo* ⓜ swel·do

W

wait *esperar* es·pe·*rar*

waiter *camarero/a* ⓜ/ⓕ ka·ma·re·ro/a

waiting room *sala* ⓕ *de espera* sa·la
de es·pe·ra

walk *caminar* ka·mee·*nar*

wall (inside) *pared* ⓕ pa·*re*

wallet *cartera* ⓕ kar·*te*·ra

want *querer* ke·rer

war *guerra* ⓕ ge·ra

wardrobe *vestuario* ⓜ ves·*twa*·ryo

warm *templado/a* ⓜ/ⓕ tem·*pla*·do/a

warn *advertir* ad·ver·*teer*

wash (oneself) *lavarse* la·*var*·se

wash (something) *lavar* la·*var*

wash cloth *toallita* ⓕ to·a·*lyee*·ta

washing machine *lavadora* ⓕ la·va·do·ra

watch *reloj* ⓜ *de pulsera* re·*lokh* de
pool·*se*·ra

watch *mirar* mee·*rar*

water *agua* ⓕ a·gwa
— **tap** *del grifo* del gree·fo
— **bottle** *cantimplora* ⓕ
kan·teem·*plo*·ra

waterfall *cascada* ⓕ kas·ka·da

watermelon ⓕ *sandía* san·dee·a

waterproof *impermeable* eem·per·me·a·ble

waterskiing *esquí* ⓜ *acuático* es·kee a·kwa·tee·ko

wave *ola* ⓕ o·la

way *camino* ⓜ ka·mee·no

we *nosotros/nosotras* ⓜ/ⓕ no·so·tros/ no·so·tras

weak *débil* de·beel

wealthy *rico/a* ⓜ/ⓕ ree·ko/a

wear *llevar* lye·var

weather *tiempo* ⓜ tyem·po

wedding *boda* ⓕ bo·da

wedding cake *tarta* ⓕ *nupcial* tar·ta noop·thyal

wedding present *regalo* ⓜ *de bodas* re·ga·lo de bo·das

weekend *fin de semana* ⓜ feen de se·ma·na

weigh *pesar* pe·sar

weight *peso* ⓜ pe·so

weights *pesas* ⓕ pl pe·sas

welcome *bienvenida* ⓕ byen·ve·nee·da

welcome *dar la bienvenida* dar la byen·ve·nee·da

welfare *bienestar* ⓜ byen·es·tar

well *bien* byen

well *pozo* ⓜ po·tho

west *oeste* ⓜ o·es·te

wet *mojado/a* ⓜ/ⓕ mo·kha·do/a

what *lo que* lo ke

wheel *rueda* ⓕ rwe·da

wheelchair *silla* ⓕ *de ruedas* see·lya de rwe·das

when *cuando* kwan·do

where *donde* don·de

whiskey *güisqui* ⓜ gwees·kee

white *blanco/a* ⓜ/ⓕ blan·ko/a

white-water rafting *rafting* ⓜ rahf·teen

who *quien* kyen

why *por qué* por ke

wide *ancho/a* ⓜ/ⓕ an·cho/a

wife *esposa* ⓕ es·po·sa

win *ganar* ga·nar

wind *viento* ⓜ vyen·to

window *ventana* ⓕ ven·ta·na

window-shopping *mirar los escaparates* mee·rar los es·ka·pa·ra·tes

windscreen *parabrisas* ⓜ pa·ra·bree·sas

windsurfing *hacer windsurf* a·ther ween·soorf

wine *vino* ⓜ vee·no

wineglass *copa* ⓕ *de vino* co·pa de vee·no

winery *bodega* ⓕ bo·de·ga

wings *alas* ⓕ pl a·las

winner *ganador/ganadora* ⓜ/ⓕ ga·na·dor/ga·na·do·ra

winter *invierno* ⓜ een·vyer·no

wire *alambre* ⓜ a·lam·bre

wish *desear* de·se·ar

with *con* kon

within (an hour) *dentro de (una hora)* den·tro de (oo·na o·ra)

without *sin* seen

woman *mujer* ⓕ moo·kher

wonderful *maravilloso/a* ⓜ/ⓕ ma·ra·vee·lyo·so/a

wood *madera* ⓕ ma·de·ra

wool *lana* ⓕ la·na

word *palabra* ⓕ pa·la·bra

work *trabajo* ⓜ tra·ba·kho

work *trabajar* tra·ba·khar

work experience *experiencia* ⓕ *laboral* eks·pe·ryen·thya la·bo·ral

work permit *permiso* ⓜ *de trabajo* per·mee·so de tra·ba·kho

workout *entreno* ⓜ en·tre·no

workshop *taller* ⓜ ta·lyer

world *mundo* ⓜ moon·do

World Cup *La Copa* ⓕ *Mundial* la ko·pa moon·dyal

worms *lombrices* ⓕ pl lom·bree·thes

worried *preocupado/a* ⓜ/ⓕ pre·o·koo·pa·do/a

worship *adoración* ① a·do·ra·*thyon*
wrist *muñeca* ① moo·*nye*·ka
write *escribir* es·kree·*beer*
writer *escritor/escritora* ⑩/①
  es·kree·*tor*/es·kree·*to*·ra
wrong *equivocado/a* ⑩/①
  e·kee·vo·ka·do/a

Y

yellow *amarillo/a* ⑩/① a·ma·ree·lyo/a
yes *sí* see
(not) yet *todavía (no)* to·da·*vee*·a (no)
yesterday *ayer* a·*yer*

yoga *yoga* ⑩ *yo*·ga
yogurt *yogur* ⑩ yo·*goor*
you pol sg *Usted* oos·*te*
you inf sg *tú* too
young *joven* kho·ven
your pol sg *su* soo
your inf sg *tu* too
youth hostel *albergue* ⑩ *juvenil*
  al·*ber*·ge khoo·ve·*neel*

Z

zodiac *zodíaco* ⑩ tho·*dee*·a·ko
zoo *zoológico* ⑩ zo·o·*lo*·khee·ko

A

Nouns in the dictionary have their gender indicated by ⓜ or ⓕ. If it's a plural noun, you'll also see pl. Where a word that could be either a noun or a verb has no gender indicated, it's a verb.

A

abajo a·ba·kho *below*
abanico ⓜ a·ba·*nee*·ko *fan (hand held)*
abarrotado a·ba·ro·ta·do *crowded*
abeja ⓕ a·*be*·kha *bee*
abierto/a ⓜ/ⓕ a·*byer*·to/a *open*
abogado/a ⓜ/ⓕ a·bo·*ga*·do/a *lawyer*
aborto ⓜ a·*bor*·to *abortion*
abrazo ⓜ a·*bra*·tho *hug*
abrebotellas ⓜ a·bre·bo·*te*·lyas *bottle opener*
abrelatas ⓜ a·bre·*la*·tas *can opener •
tin opener*
abrigo ⓜ a·*bree*·go *overcoat*
abrir a·*breer open*
abuela ⓕ a·*bwe*·la *grandmother*
abuelo ⓜ a·*bwe*·lo *grandfather*
aburrido/a ⓜ/ⓕ a·boo·*ree*·do/a
bored • boring
acabar a·ka·*bar end*
acampar a·kam·*par camp*
acantilado ⓜ a·kan·tee·*la*·do *cliff*
accidente ⓜ ak·thee·*den*·te *accident*
aceite ⓜ a·*they*·te *oil*
aceptar a·thep·*tar accept*
acera ⓕ a·*the*·ra *footpath*
acondicionador ⓜ
a·kon·dee·thyo·na·*dor conditioner*
acoso ⓜ a·*ko*·so *harassment*
activista ⓜ&ⓕ ak·tee·*vees*·ta *activist*
actuación ⓕ ak·twa·*thyon
performance*
acupuntura ⓕ a·koo·poon·*too*·ra
acupuncture
adaptador ⓜ a·dap·ta·*dor adaptor*
adentro a·*den*·tro *inside*
adivinar a·dee·vee·*nar guess*

administración ⓕ ad·mee·nees·tra·*thyon
administration*
admitir ad·mee·*teer admit*
adoración ⓕ a·do·ra·*thyon worship*
aduana ⓕ a·*dwa*·na *customs*
adulto/a ⓜ/ⓕ a·*dool*·to/a *adult*
aeróbic ⓜ ay·ro·beek *aerobics*
aerolínea ⓕ ay·ro·*lee*·nya *airline*
aeropuerto ⓜ ay·ro·*pwer*·to *airport*
afeitadora ⓕ a·fey·ta·*do*·ra *razor*
afeitarse a·fey·*tar*·se *shave*
afortunado/a ⓜ/ⓕ a·for·too·na·do/a
lucky
África ⓕ a·*free*·ka *Africa*
agencia ⓕ **de viajes** a·*khen*·thya de
vya·khes *travel agency*
agenda ⓕ a·*khen*·da *diary*
agente ⓜ **inmobiliario** a·*khen*·te
een·mo·bee·*lya*·ryo *real estate agent*
agresivo/a ⓜ/ⓕ a·gre·*see*·vo/a
aggressive
agricultor(a) ⓜ/ⓕ a·gree·kool·*tor*/
a·gree·kool·*to*·ra *farmer*
agricultura ⓕ a·gree·kool·*too*·ra
agriculture
agua ⓕ a·gwa *water*
  — caliente ka·*lyen*·te *hot water*
  — mineral mee·ne·*ral mineral water*
aguacate ⓜ a·gwa·*ka*·te *avocado*
aguja ⓕ a·goo·kha *needle (sewing)*
ahora a·o·ra *now*
ahorrar a·o·*rar save (money)*
aire ⓜ *ai*·re *air*
  — acondicionado
a·kon·dee·thyo·na·do *air-
conditioning*
ajedrez ⓜ a·khe·*dreth chess*
al lado de al *la*·do de *next to*

alambre ⓜ *a·lam·bre* wire
alba ① *al·ba* dawn
albaricoque ⓜ *al·ba·ree·ko·ke* apricot
albergue ⓜ **juvenil** *al·ber·ge khoo·ve·neel* youth hostel
alcachofa ① *al·ka·cho·fa* artichoke
alcohol ⓜ *al·col* alcohol
Alemania ① *a·le·ma·nya* Germany
alérgia ① *a·ler·khya* allergy
alérgia ① **al polen** *a·ler·khya al po·len* hay fever
alfarería ① *al·fa·re·ree·a* pottery
alfombra ① *al·fom·bra* rug
algo *al·go* something
algodón ⓜ *al·go·don* cotton
alguien *al·gyen* someone
algún *al·goon* some
alguno/a ⓜ/① *al·goo·no/a* any
almendras ① pl *al·men·dras* almonds
almohada ① *al·mwa·da* pillow
almuerzo ⓜ *al·mwer·tho* lunch
alojamiento ⓜ *a·lo·kha·myen·to* accommodation
alojarse *a·lo·khar·se* stay (somewhere)
alpinismo ⓜ *al·pee·nees·mo* mountaineering
alquilar *al·kee·lar* hire • rent
alquiler ⓜ *al·kee·ler* rent
— de coche *de ko·che* car hire
altar ⓜ *al·tar* altar
alto/a ⓜ/① *al·to/a* high • tall
altura ① *al·too·ra* altitude
ama ① **de casa** *a·ma de ka·sa* homemaker
amable *a·ma·ble* kind
amanecer ⓜ *a·ma·ne·ther* sunrise
amante ⓜ&① *a·man·te* lover
amarillo/a ⓜ/① *a·ma·ree·lyo/a* yellow
amigo/a ⓜ/① *a·mee·go/a* friend
ampolla ① *am·po·lya* blister
anacardo *a·na·kar·do* cashew nut
analgésicos ⓜ pl *a·nal·khe·see·kos* painkillers
análisis de sangre ⓜ *a·na·lee·sees de san·gre* blood test
anarquista ⓜ/① *a·nar·kees·ta* anarchist

ancho/a ⓜ/① *an·cho/a* wide
andar *an·dar* walk
animal ⓜ *a·nee·mal* animal
Año ⓜ **Nuevo** *a·nyo nwe·vo* New Year
antes *an·tes* before
antibióticos ⓜ pl *an·tee·byo·tee·kos* antibiotics
anticonceptivos ⓜ pl *an·tee·kon·thep·tee·vos* contraceptives
antigüedad ① *an·tee·gwe·da* antique
antiguo/a ⓜ/① *an·tee·gwo/a* ancient
antiséptico ⓜ *an·tee·sep·tee·ko* antiseptic
antología ① *an·to·lo·khee·a* anthology
anuncio ⓜ *a·noon·thyo* advertisement
aparcamiento ⓜ *a·par·ka·myen·to* carpark
apellido ⓜ *a·pe·lyee·do* surname
apéndice ⓜ *a·pen·dee·the* appendix
apodo ⓜ *a·po·do* nickname
aprender *a·pren·der* learn
apretado/a ⓜ/① *a·pre·ta·do/a* tight
apuesta ① *a·pwes·ta* bet
apuntar *a·poon·tar* point
aquí *a·kee* here
araña ① *a·ra·nya* spider
árbitro ⓜ *ar·bee·tro* referee
árbol ⓜ *ar·bol* tree
arena ① *a·re·na* sand
armario ⓜ *ar·ma·ryo* cupboard
arqueológico/a ⓜ/① *ar·ke·o·lo·khee·ko/a* archaeological
arquitecto/a ⓜ/① *ar·kee·tek·to/a* architect
arquitectura ① *ar·kee·tek·too·ra* architecture
arriba *a·ree·ba* above • up
arroyo ⓜ *a·ro·yo* stream
arroz ⓜ *a·roth* rice
arte ⓜ *ar·te* art
— gráfico *gra·fee·ko* graphic art
artes ⓜ pl **marciales** *ar·tes mar·thya·les* martial arts
artesanía ① *ar·te·sa·nee·a* crafts
artista ⓜ&① *ar·tees·ta* artist
ascensor ⓜ *as·then·sor* elevator
Asia ① *a·sya* Asia

asiento ⓜ *a·syen·to seat*
 — de seguridad para bebés *de se·goo·ree·da pa·ra be·bes child seat*
asma ⓜ *as·ma asthma*
aspirina ⓕ *as·pee·ree·na aspirin*
atascado/a ⓜ/ⓕ *a·tas·ka·do/a blocked*
atletismo ⓜ *at·le·tees·mo athletics*
atmósfera ⓕ *at·mos·fe·ra atmosphere*
atún ⓜ *a·toon tuna*
audífono ⓜ *ow·dee·fo·no hearing aid*
Australia ⓕ *ow·stra·lya Australia*
autobús ⓜ *ow·to·boos bus*
autocar ⓜ *ow·to·kar bus (intercity)*
autódromo ⓜ *ow·to·dro·mo track (car racing)*
autoservicio ⓜ *ow·to·ser·vee·thyo self-service*
autovía ⓕ *ow·to·vee·a motorway*
avenida ⓕ *a·ve·nee·da avenue*
avergonzado/a ⓜ/ⓕ *a·ver·gon·tha·do/a embarrassed*
avión ⓜ *a·vyon plane*
ayer *a·yer yesterday*
ayudar *a·yoo·dar help*
azúcar ⓜ *a·thoo·kar sugar*
azul *a·thool blue*

B

bailar *bai·lar dance*
bajo/a ⓜ/ⓕ *ba·kho/a short (height) • low*
balcón ⓜ *bal·kon balcony*
ballet ⓜ *ba·le ballet*
baloncesto ⓜ *ba·lon·thes·to basketball*
bálsamo de aftershave *bal·sa·mo de af·ter·sha·eev aftershave*
bálsamo de labios *bal·sa·mo de la·byos lip balm*
bañador ⓜ *ba·nya·dor bathing suit*
banco ⓜ *ban·ko bank*
bandera ⓕ *ban·de·ra flag*
bañera ⓕ *ba·nye·ra bath*
baño ⓜ *ba·nyo bathroom*
bar ⓜ *bar bar*
barato/a ⓜ/ⓕ *ba·ra·to/a cheap*

barco ⓜ *bar·ko boat*
barrio ⓜ *ba·ryo suburb*
basura ⓕ *ba·soo·ra rubbish*
batería ⓕ *ba·te·ree·a battery (car) • drums*
bebé ⓜ *be·be baby*
béisbol ⓜ *beys·bol baseball*
beneficio ⓜ *be·ne·fee·thyo profit*
berenjenas ⓕ pl *be·ren·khe·nas aubergine • eggplant*
besar *be·sar kiss*
beso ⓜ *be·so kiss*
biblia ⓕ *bee·blya bible*
biblioteca ⓕ *bee·blyo·te·ka library*
bicho ⓜ *bee·cho bug*
bici ⓕ *bee·thee bike*
bicicleta ⓕ *bee·thee·kle·ta bicycle*
 — de carreras *de ka·re·ras racing bike*
 — de montaña *de mon·ta·nya mountain bike*
bien *byen well*
bienestar ⓜ *byen·es·tar welfare*
bienvenida ⓕ *byen·ve·nee·da welcome*
billete ⓜ *bee·lye·te ticket*
 — de ida y vuelta *de ee·da ee vwel·ta return ticket*
 — de lista de espera *de lees·ta de es·pe·ra standby ticket*
billetes ⓜ pl **de banco** *bee·lye·tes de ban·ko banknotes*
biografía ⓕ *bee·o·gra·fee·a biography*
bistec ⓜ *bees·tek steak (beef)*
blanco y negro *blan·ko ee ne·gro B&W (film)*
blanco/a ⓜ/ⓕ *blan·ko/a white*
boca ⓕ *bo·ka mouth*
bocado ⓜ *bo·ka·do bite (food)*
boda ⓕ *bo·da wedding*
bodega ⓕ *bo·de·ga winery • liquor store*
bol ⓜ *bol bowl*
bolas ⓕ pl **de algodón** *bo·las de al·go·don cotton balls*
bolígrafo ⓜ *bo·lee·gra·fo pen*
bollos ⓜ pl *bo·lyos rolls (bread)*

bolo ⓜ *bo·lo gig*

bolsillo ⓜ *bol·see·lyo pocket*

bolso ⓜ *bol·so bag • handbag*

bomba ⓕ *bom·ba pump • bomb*

bombilla ⓕ *bom·bee·lya light bulb*

bondadoso/a ⓜ/ⓕ *bon·da·do·so/a caring*

bonito/a ⓜ/ⓕ *bo·nee·to/a pretty*

bordo ⓜ *bor·do edge*

a bordo *a bor·do aboard*

borracho/a ⓜ/ⓕ *bo·ra·cho/a drunk*

bosque ⓜ *bos·ke forest*

botas ⓕ pl *bo·tas boots*

— **de montaña** *de mon·ta·nya hiking boots*

botella ⓕ *bo·te·lya bottle*

botones ⓜ pl *bo·to·nes buttons*

boxeo ⓜ *bo·kse·o boxing*

bragas ⓕ pl *bra·gas underpants (women)*

brazo ⓜ *bra·tho arm*

broma ⓕ *bro·ma joke*

bronceador ⓜ *bron·the·a·dor tanning lotion*

bronquitis ⓕ *bron·kee·tees bronchitis*

brotes ⓜ pl **de soja** *bro·tes de so·kha bean sprouts*

brújula ⓕ *broo·khoo·la compass*

brumoso *broo·mo·so foggy*

buceo ⓜ *boo·the·o snorkelling*

budista ⓜ&ⓕ *boo·dees·ta Buddhist*

bueno/a ⓜ/ⓕ *bwe·no/a good*

bufanda ⓕ *boo·fan·da scarf*

buffet ⓜ *boo·fe buffet*

bulto ⓜ *bool·to lump*

burlarse de *boor·lar·se de make fun of*

burro ⓜ *boo·ro donkey*

buscar *boos·kar look for*

buzón ⓜ *boo·thon mailbox*

C

caballo ⓜ *ka·ba·lyo horse*

cabeza ⓕ *ka·be·tha head*

cabina ⓕ **telefónica** *ka·bee·na te·le·fo·nee·ka phone box*

cable ⓜ *ka·ble cable*

cables ⓜ pl **de arranque** *ka·bles de a·ran·ke jumper leads*

cabra ⓕ *ka·bra goat*

cacahuetes ⓜ pl *ka·ka·we·tes peanuts*

cacao ⓜ *ka·kow cocoa*

cachorro ⓜ *ka·cho·ro puppy*

cada *ka·da each*

cadena ⓕ **de bici** *ka·de·na de bee·thee bike chain*

café ⓜ *ka·fe coffee • cafe*

caída ⓕ *ka·ee·da fall*

caja ⓕ *ka·kha box • cashier*

— **fuerte** *fwer·te safe*

— **registradora** *re·khees·tra·do·ra cash register*

cajero ⓜ **automático** *ka·khe·ro ow·to·ma·tee·ko automatic teller machine*

calabacín ⓜ *ka·la·ba·theen zucchini • courgette*

calabaza ⓕ *ka·la·ba·tha pumpkin*

calcetines ⓜ pl *kal·the·tee·nes socks*

calculadora ⓕ *kal·koo·la·do·ra calculator*

caldo ⓜ *kal·do stock*

calefacción ⓕ **central** *ka·le·fak·thyon then·tral central heating*

calendario ⓜ *ka·len·da·ryo calendar*

calidad ⓕ *ka·lee·da quality*

caliente *ka·lyen·te hot*

calle ⓕ *ka·lye street*

calor ⓜ *ka·lor heat*

calzoncillos ⓜ pl *kal·thon·thee·lyos underpants (men)*

calzones ⓜ pl *kal·tho·nes boxer shorts*

cama ⓕ *ka·ma bed*

— **de matrimonio** *de ma·tree·mo·nyo double bed*

cámara ⓕ **(fotográfica)** *ka·ma·ra (fo·to·gra·fee·ka) camera*

cámara ⓕ **de aire** *ka·ma·ra de ai·re tube (tyre)*

camarero/a ⓜ/ⓕ *ka·ma·re·ro/a waiter*

cambiar *kam·byar change • exchange (money)*

cambio *kam·byo* ⓜ *loose change*

— **de dinero** *de dee·ne·ro currency exchange*

caminar *ka·mee·nar walk*

camino ⓜ ka-*mee*-no trail • way
caminos ⓜ pl **rurales** ka-*mee*-nos roo-*ra*-les hiking routes
camión ⓜ ka-*myon* truck
camisa ⓕ ka-*mee*-sa shirt
camiseta ⓕ ka-mee-*se*-ta singlet • T-shirt
cámping ⓜ *kam*-peen campsite
campo ⓜ *kam*-po countryside • field
Canadá ⓕ ka-na-*da* Canada
canasta ⓕ ka-*nas*-ta basket
cancelar kan-the-*lar* cancel
cáncer ⓜ *kan*-ther cancer
canción ⓕ kan-*thyon* song
candado ⓜ kan-*da*-do padlock
cangrejo ⓜ kan-*gre*-kho crab
cansado/a ⓜ/ⓕ kan-*sa*-do/a tired
cantalupo ⓜ kan-ta-*loo*-po cantaloupe
cantante ⓜ&ⓕ kan-*tan*-te singer
cantar kan-*tar* sing
cantimplora ⓕ kan-teem-*plo*-ra water bottle
capa ⓕ **de ozono** *ka*-pa de o-*tho*-no ozone layer
capilla ⓕ ka-*pee*-lya shrine
capote ⓜ ka-*po*-te cloak
cara ⓕ *ka*-ra face
caracol ⓜ ka-ra-*kol* snail
caramelos ⓜ pl ka-ra-*me*-los lollies
caravana ⓕ ka-ra-*va*-na caravan • van • traffic jam
cárcel ⓕ *kar*-thel prison
cardenal ⓜ kar-de-*nal* bruise
carne ⓕ *kar*-ne meat
  — **de vaca** de *va*-ka beef
  — **molida** mo-*lee*-da mince meat
carnet ⓜ kar-*ne* licence
  — **de identidad** de ee-den-tee-*da* identification card
  — **de conducir** de kon-doo-*theer* drivers licence
carnicería ⓕ kar-nee-the-*ree*-a butcher's shop
caro/a ⓜ/ⓕ *ka*-ro/a expensive
carpintero ⓜ kar-peen-*te*-ro carpenter
carrera ⓕ ka-*re*-ra race (sport)
carta ⓕ *kar*-ta letter

cartas ⓕ pl *kar*-tas cards
cartón ⓜ kar-*ton* carton • cardboard
casa ⓕ *ka*-sa house
(en) casa (en) *ka*-sa (at) home
casarse ka-*sar*-se marry
cascada ⓕ kas-*ka*-da waterfall
casco ⓜ *kas*-ko helmet
casete ⓜ ka-*se*-te cassette
casi *ka*-see almost
casino ⓜ ka-*see*-no casino
castigar kas-tee-*gar* punish
castillo ⓜ kas-*tee*-lyo castle
catedral ⓕ ka-te-*dral* cathedral
católico/a ⓜ/ⓕ ka-to-lee-ko/a Catholic
caza ⓕ *ka*-tha hunting
cazuela ⓕ ka-*thwe*-la pot (kitchen)
cebolla ⓕ the-*bo*-lya onion
celebración ⓕ the-le-bra-*thyon* celebration
celebrar the-le-*brar* celebrate (an event)
celoso/a ⓜ/ⓕ the-*lo*-so/a jealous
cementerio ⓜ the-men-*te*-ryo cemetery
cena ⓕ *the*-na dinner
cenicero ⓜ the-nee-*the*-ro ashtray
centavo ⓜ then-*ta*-vo cent
centímetro ⓜ then-*tee*-me-tro centimetre
central ⓕ **telefónica** then-*tral* te-le-fo-*nee*-ka telephone centre
centro ⓜ *then*-tro centre
  — **comercial** ko-mer-*thyal* shopping centre
  — **de la ciudad** de la theew-*da* city centre
cepillo ⓜ the-*pee*-lyo hairbrush
  — **de dientes** de *dyen*-tes toothbrush
cerámica ⓕ the-*ra*-mee-ka ceramic
cerca ⓕ *ther*-ka fence
cerca *ther*-ka near • nearby
cerdo ⓜ *ther*-do pork • pig
cereales ⓜ pl the-re-*a*-les cereal
cerillas ⓕ pl las the-*ree*-lyas matches
cerrado/a ⓜ/ⓕ the-*ra*-do/a closed
  — **con llave** kon *lya*-ve locked
cerradura ⓕ the-ra-*doo*-ra lock (padlock)
cerrar the-*rar* close • lock • shut

certificado ⓜ ther·tee·fee·ka·do *certificate*

cerveza ⓕ ther·ve·tha *beer*
— **rubia** roo·bya *lager*

cibercafé ⓜ thee·ber·ka·fe *Internet cafe*

ciclismo ⓜ thee·klees·mo *cycling*

ciclista ⓜ&ⓕ thee·klees·ta *cyclist*

ciego/a ⓜ/ⓕ thye·go/a *blind*

cielo ⓜ thye·lo *sky*

ciencias ⓕ pl thyen·thyas *science*

científico/a ⓜ/ⓕ thyen·tee·fee·ko/a *scientist*

cigarrillo ⓜ thee·ga·ree·lyo *cigarette*

cigarro ⓜ thee·ga·ro *cigarette*

cine ⓜ thee·ne *cinema*

cinta ⓕ **de vídeo** theen·ta de vee·de·o *video tape*

cinturón ⓜ **de seguridad** theen·too·ron de se·goo·ree·da *seatbelt*

circuito ⓜ **de carreras** theer·kwee·to de ka·re·ras *racetrack (cars)*

ciruela ⓕ thee·rwe·la *plum*
— **pasa** pa·sa *prune*

cistitis ⓕ thees·tee·tees *cystitis*

cita ⓕ thee·ta *appointment*

citarse thee·tar·se *date*

citología ⓕ thee·to·lo·khee·a *pap smear*

ciudad ⓕ theew·da *city*

ciudadanía ⓕ theew·da·da·nee·a *citizenship*

clase ⓕ **preferente** kla·se pre·fe·ren·te *business class*

clase ⓕ **turística** kla·se too·rees·tee·ka *economy class*

clásico/a ⓜ/ⓕ kla·see·ko/a *classical*

clienta/e ⓜ/ⓕ klee·en·ta/e *client*

clínica ⓕ klee·nee·ka *private hospital*

cobrar (un cheque) ko·brar (oon che·ke) *cash (a cheque)*

coca ⓕ ko·ka *cocaine*

cocaína ⓕ ko·ka·ee·na *cocaine*

coche ⓜ ko·che *car*
— **cama** ka·ma *sleeping car*

cocina ⓕ ko·thee·na *kitchen • stove*

cocinar ko·thee·nar *cook*

cocinero ⓜ ko·thee·ne·ro *chef • cook*

coco ⓜ ko·ko *coconut*

codeína ⓕ ko·de·ee·na *codeine*

código ⓜ **postal** ko·dee·go pos·tal *post code*

cojonudo/a ⓜ/ⓕ ko·kho·noo·do/a *fantastic*

col ⓜ kol *cabbage*

cola ⓕ ko·la *queue*

colchón ⓜ kol·chon *mattress*

colega ⓜ&ⓕ ko·le·ga *colleague • mate*

coles ⓜ pl **de Bruselas** ko·les de broo·se·las *brussels sprouts*

coliflor ⓕ ko·lee·flor *cauliflower*

colina ⓕ ko·lee·na *hill*

collar ⓜ ko·lyar *necklace*

color ⓜ ko·lor *colour*

comedia ⓕ ko·me·dya *comedy*

comenzar ko·men·thar *begin • start*

comer ko·mer *eat*

comerciante ⓜ&ⓕ ko·mer·thyan·te *business person*

comercio ⓜ ko·mer·thyo *trade*

comezón ⓜ ko·me·thon *itch*

comida ⓕ ko·mee·da *food*
— **de bebé** de be·be *baby food*
— **en el campo** en el kam·po *picnic*

comisaría ⓕ ko·mee·sa·ree·a *police station*

cómo ko·mo *how*

cómodo/a ⓜ/ⓕ ko·mo·do/a *comfortable*

cómpact ⓜ kom·pak *CD*

compañero/a ⓜ/ⓕ kom·pa·nye·ro/a *companion*

compañía ⓕ kom·pa·nyee·a *company*

compartir kom·par·teer *share (with)*

comprar kom·prar *buy*

comprender kom·pren·der *understand*

compresas ⓕ pl kom·pre·sas *sanitary napkins*

compromiso ⓜ kom·pro·mee·so *engagement*

comunión ⓕ ko·moo·nyon *communion*

comunista ⓜ&ⓕ ko·moo·nees·ta *communist*

con kon *with*

coñac ⓜ ko·nyak *brandy*

concentración ⓕ kon·then·tra·thyon *rally*

concierto ⓜ kon·*thyer*·to *concert*
condición ⓕ **cardíaca** kon·dee·*thyon* kar·*dee*·a·ka *heart condition*
condones ⓜ pl kon·*do*·nes *condoms*
conducir kon·doo·*theer* *drive*
conejo ⓜ ko·*ne*·kho *rabbit*
conexión ⓕ ko·ne·*ksyon* *connection*
confesión ⓕ kon·fe·*syon* *confession*
confianza ⓕ kon·fee·*an*·tha *trust*
confiar kon·fee·*ar* *trust*
confirmar kon·feer·*mar* *confirm*
conocer ko·no·*ther* *know (someone)*
conocido/a ⓜ/ⓕ ko·no·*thee*·do/a *famous*
consejo ⓜ kon·*se*·kho *advice*
conservador(a) ⓜ/ⓕ kon·ser·va·*dor*/kon·ser·va·*do*·ra *conservative*
consigna ⓕ kon·*seeg*·na *left luggage*
— **automática** ow·to·ma·*tee*·ka *luggage lockers*
construir kons·troo·*eer* *build*
consulado ⓜ kon·soo·*la*·do *consulate*
contaminación ⓕ kon·ta·mee·na·*thyon* *pollution*
contar kon·*tar* *count*
contestador ⓜ **automático** kon·tes·ta·*dor* ow·to·ma·*tee*·ko *answering machine*
contrato ⓜ kon·*tra*·to *contract*
control ⓜ kon·*trol* *checkpoint*
convento ⓜ kon·*ven*·to *convent*
copa ⓕ *ko*·pa *drink*
— **de vino** de *vee*·no *wineglass*
copos de maíz *ko*·pos de ma·*eeth* *corn flakes*
corazón ⓜ ko·ra·*thon* *heart*
cordero ⓜ kor·*de*·ro *lamb*
cordillera ⓕ kor·dee·*lye*·ra *mountain range*
correcto/a ⓜ/ⓕ ko·*rek*·to/a *right (correct)*
correo ⓜ ko·*re*·o *mail*
— **urgente** oor·*khen*·te *express mail*
correos ko·*re*·os *post office*
correr ko·*rer* *run*
corrida ⓕ **de toros** ko·*ree*·da de *to*·ros *bullfight*

corriente ⓕ ko·*ryen*·te *current (electricity)*
corriente ko·*ryen*·te *ordinary*
corrupto/a ⓜ/ⓕ ko·*roop*·to/a *corrupt*
cortar kor·*tar* *cut*
cortauñas ⓜ pl kor·ta·oo·nyas *nail clippers*
corto/a ⓜ/ⓕ *kor*·to/a *short (length)*
cosecha ⓕ ko·*se*·cha *crop*
coser ko·*ser* *sew*
costa ⓕ *kos*·ta *coast • seaside*
costar kos·*tar* *cost*
crecer kre·*ther* *grow*
crema ⓕ *kre*·ma *cream*
— **hidratante** ee·dra·*tan*·te *cream (moisturising)*
— **solar** so·*lar* *sunblock*
críquet ⓜ *kree*·ket *cricket*
cristiano/a ⓜ/ⓕ krees·*tya*·no/a *Christian*
crítica ⓕ *kree*·tee·ka *review*
cruce ⓜ *kroo*·the *intersection*
crudo/a ⓜ/ⓕ *kroo*·do/a *raw*
cuaderno ⓜ kwa·*der*·no *notebook • square*
cualificaciones ⓕ pl kwa·lee·fee·ka·*thyo*·nes *qualifications*
cuando *kwan*·do *when*
cuánto *kwan*·to *how much*
cuarentena ⓕ kwa·ren·*te*·na *quarantine*
Cuaresma ⓕ kwa·*res*·ma *Lent*
cuarto ⓜ *kwar*·to *quarter*
cubiertos ⓜ pl koo·*byer*·tos *cutlery*
cubo ⓜ *koo*·bo *bucket*
cucaracha ⓕ koo·ka·*ra*·cha *cockroach*
cuchara ⓕ koo·*cha*·ra *spoon*
cucharita ⓕ koo·cha·*ree*·ta *teaspoon*
cuchillas ⓕ pl **de afeitar** koo·*chee*·lyas de a·fey·*tar* *razor blades*
cuchillo ⓜ koo·*chee*·lyo *knife*
cuenta ⓕ *kwen*·ta *bill*
— **bancaria** ban·ka·*rya* *bank account*
cuento ⓜ *kwen*·to *story*
cuerda ⓕ *kwer*·da *rope • string*
— **para tender la ropa** *pa*·ra ten·*der* la *ro*·pa *clothes line*
cuero ⓜ *kwe*·ro *leather*
cuerpo ⓜ *kwer*·po *body*

cuesta abajo *kwes·*ta *a·ba·*kho *downhill*

cuesta arriba *kwes·*ta *a·ree·*ba *uphill*

cuestionar *kwes·tyo·nar* question

cuevas ① pl *kwe·*vas *caves*

cuidar *kwee·dar* care for • mind (an object)

cuidar de *kwee·dar* de care (for someone)

culo ⓜ *koo·*lo *bum (of body)*

culpable *kool·pa·*ble *guilty*

cumbre ① *koom·*bre *peak*

cumpleaños ⓜ *koom·ple·a·*nyos *birthday*

currículum ⓜ *koo·ree·koo·*loom *resumé*

curry ⓜ *koo·*ree *curry*

cus cus ⓜ *koos koos* cous cous

CH

chaleco ⓢ salvavidas *cha·le·*ko *sal·va·vee·*das *lifejacket*

champán ⓜ *cham·pan* Champagne

champiñón ⓜ *cham·pee·nyon* mushrooms

champú ⓜ *cham·poo* shampoo

chaqueta ① *cha·ke·*ta *jacket*

cheque ⓜ *che·*ke *check (bank)*

cheques ⓜ pl de viajero *che·*kes de *vya·khe·*ro *travellers cheque*

chica ① *chee·*ka *girl*

chicle ⓜ *chee·*kle *chewing gum*

chico ⓜ *chee·*ko *boy*

chocolate ⓜ *cho·ko·la·*te *chocolate*

choque ⓜ *cho·*ke *crash*

chorizo ⓜ *cho·ree·*tho *salami (Spanish sausage)*

chupete ⓜ *choo·pe·*te *dummy • pacifier*

D

dados ⓜ pl *da·*dos *dice (die)*

dañar *da·nyar* hurt

dar *dar* give

— de comer de *ko·mer* feed

— gracias *gra·*thyas *thank*

— la bienvenida la byen·ve·*nee·*da *welcome*

— una patada *oo·*na pa·*ta·*da *kick*

darse cuenta de *dar·*se *kwen·*ta de *realise*

de de *from*

— (cuatro) estrellas de *(kwa·*tro) es·*tre·*lyas *(four-)star*

— izquierda de eeth·*kyer·*da *left-wing*

— pena de *pe·*na *terrible*

— primera clase de pree·*me·*ra *kla·*se *first-class*

— segunda mano de se·*goon·*da *ma·*no *second-hand*

— vez en cuando de veth en *kwan·*do *sometimes*

deber de·*ver* owe

débil *de·*beel *weak*

decidir de·thee·*deer* decide

decir de·*theer* say • tell

dedo ⓜ *de·*do *finger*

— del pie de pye *toe*

defectuoso/a ⓜ/① de·fek·too·*o·*so/a *faulty*

deforestación ① de·fo·res·ta·*thyon* deforestation

dejar de·*khar* leave • quit

delgado/a ⓜ/① del·*ga·*do/a *thin*

delirante de·lee·*ran·*te *delirious*

demasiado caro/a ⓜ/① de·ma·*sya·*do *ka·*ro/a *too (expensive)*

democracia ① de·mo·*kra·*thya *democracy*

demora ① de·*mo·*ra *delay*

dentista ⓜ&① den·*tees·*ta *dentist*

dentro de (una hora) *den·*tro de *(oo·*na *o·*ra) *within (an hour)*

deportes ⓜ pl de·*por·*tes *sport*

deportista ⓜ&① de·por·*tees·*ta *sportsperson*

depósito ⓜ de·*po·*see·to *deposit*

derecha ① de·*re·*cha *right (not left)*

derechista de·re·*chees·*ta *right-wing*

derechos ⓜ pl civiles de·*re·*chos thee·*vee·*les *civil rights* derechos ⓜ pl **humanos** de·re·chos oo·ma·nos *human rights*

desayuno ⓜ des·a·yoo·no *breakfast*

descansar des·kan·sar *rest*

descanso ⓜ des·kan·so *intermission*

descendiente ⓜ des·then·dyen·te *descendant*

descomponerse des·kom·po·ner·se *decompose*

descubrir des·koo·breer *discover*

descuento ⓜ des·kwen·to *discount*

desde (mayo) *des·de (ma·yo) since (may)*

desear de·se·ar *wish*

desierto ⓜ de·syer·to *desert*

desodorante ⓜ de·so·do·ran·te *deodorant*

despacio des·pa·thyo *slowly*

desperdicios ⓜ pl **nucleares** des·per·dee·thyos noo·kle·a·res *nuclear waste*

despertador ⓜ des·per·ta·dor *alarm clock*

después de des·pwes de *after*

destino ⓜ des·tee·no *destination*

destruir des·troo·eer *destroy*

detallado/a ⓜ/ⓕ de·ta·lya·do/a *itemised*

detalle ⓜ de·ta·lye *detail*

detener de·te·ner *arrest*

detrás de de·tras de *behind*

devocionario ⓜ de·vo·thyo·na·ryo *prayer book*

día ⓜ dee·a *day*
— **festivo** fes·tee·vo *holiday*

diabetes ⓕ dee·a·be·tes *diabetes*

diafragma ⓕ dee·a·frag·ma *diaphragm*

diapositiva ⓕ dya·po·see·tee·va *slide*

diariamente dya·rya·men·te *daily*

diarrea ⓕ dee·a·re·a *diarrhoea*

dieta ⓕ dee·e·ta *diet*

dibujar dee·boo·khar *draw*

diccionario ⓜ deek·thyo·na·ryo *dictionary*

diente (de ajo) dyen·te (de a·kho) *clove (garlic)*

dientes ⓜ pl dyen·tes *teeth*

diferencia ⓕ **de horas** dee·fe·ren·thya de o·ras *time difference*

diferente dee·fe·ren·te *different*

dificil dee·fee·theel *difficult*

dinero ⓜ dee·ne·ro *money*
— **en efectivo** en e·fek·tee·vo *cash*

Dios dyos *god*

dirección ⓕ dee·rek·thyon *address*

directo/a ⓜ/ⓕ dee·rek·to/a *direct*

director(a) ⓜ/ⓕ dee·rek·tor/ dee·rek·to·ra *director*

disco ⓜ dees·ko *disk*

discoteca ⓕ dees·ko·te·ka *disco*

discriminación ⓕ dees·kree·mee·na·thyon *discrimination*

discutir dees·koo·teer *argue*

diseño ⓜ dee·se·nyo *design*

disparar dees·pa·rar *shoot*

DIU ⓜ de ee oo *IUD*

diversión ⓕ dee·ver·syon *fun*

divertirse dee·ver·teer·se *enjoy (oneself)*

doblar do·blar *turn* • *bend*

doble do·ble *double*

docena ⓕ do·the·na *dozen*

doctor(a) ⓜ/ⓕ dok·tor/dok·to·ra *doctor*

dólar ⓜ do·lar *dollar*

dolor ⓜ do·lor *pain*
— **de cabeza** de ka·be·tha *headache*
— **de estómago** de es·to·ma·go *stomachache*
— **de muelas** de mwe·las *toothache*
— **menstrual** mens·trwal *period pain*

dolorido/a ⓜ/ⓕ do·lo·ree·do/a *sore*

doloroso/a ⓜ/ⓕ do·lo·ro·so/a *painful*

donde don·de *where*

dormir dor·meer *sleep*

dos ⓜ/ⓕ pl dos *two*
— **camas** ka·mas *twin beds*
— **veces** ve·thes *twice*

drama ⓜ dra·ma *drama*

droga ⓕ dro·ga *drug* • *dope*

drogadicción ⓕ dro·ga·deek·thyon *drug addiction*

drogas ⓕ pl dro·gas *drugs*

ducha ⓕ doo·cha *shower*

dueño/a ⓜ/ⓕ dwe·nyo/a *owner*

dulce dool·the *sweet*

dulces ⓜ pl dool·thes *sweets*

duro/a ⓜ/ⓕ doo·ro/a *hard*

D

E

eczema ① ek·*the*·ma *eczema*
edad ① e·*da* *age*
edificio ⓜ e·dee·*fee*·thyo *building*
editor(a) ⓜ/① e·dee·*tor*/e·dee·*to*·ra *editor*
educación ① e·doo·ka·*thyon* *education*
egoista e·go·*ees*·ta *selfish*
ejemplo ⓜ e·*khem*·plo *example*
ejército ⓜ e·*kher*·thee·to *military*
él ⓜ el *he*
elecciones ① pl e·lek·*thyo*·nes *elections*
electricidad ① e·lek·tree·thee·*da* *electricity*
elegir e·le·*kheer* *pick • choose*
ella ① *e*·lya *she*
ellos/ellas ⓜ/① *e*·lyos/*e*·lyas *they*
embajada ① em·ba·*kha*·da *embassy*
embajador(a) ⓜ/① em·ba·kha·*dor*/em·ba·kha·*do*·ra *ambassador*
embarazada em·ba·ra·*tha*·da *pregnant*
embarcarse em·bar·*kar*·se *board (ship, etc)*
embrague ⓜ em·*bra*·ge *clutch*
emergencia ① e·mer·*khen*·thya *emergency*
emocional e·mo·thyo·*nal* *emotional*
empleado/a ⓜ/① em·ple·*a*·do/a *employee*
empujar em·poo·*khar* *push*
en en *on*
— **el extranjero** el eks·tran·*khe*·ro *abroad*
— **el paro** el *pa*·ro *unemployed*
encaje ⓜ en·*ka*·khe *lace*
encantador(a) ⓜ/① en·kan·ta·*dor*/en·kan·ta·*do*·ra *charming*
encendedor ⓜ en·then·de·*dor* *lighter*
encontrar en·kon·*trar* *find • meet*
encurtidos ⓜ pl en·koor·*tee*·dos *pickles*
energía ① **nuclear** e·ner·*khee*·a noo·kle·*ar* *nuclear energy*
enfadado/a ⓜ/① en·fa·*da*·do/a *angry*

enfermedad ① en·fer·me·*da* *disease*
— **venérea** ve·*ne*·re·a *venereal disease*
enfermero/a ⓜ/① en·fer·*me*·ro/a *nurse*
enfermo/a ⓜ/① en·*fer*·mo/a *sick*
enfrente de en·*fren*·te de *in front of*
enorme e·*nor*·me *huge*
ensalada en·sa·*la*·da *salad*
enseñar en·se·*nyar* *show • teach*
entrar en·*trar* *enter*
entre *en*·tre *among • between*
entregar en·tre·*gar* *deliver*
entrenador(a) ⓜ/① en·tre·na·*dor*/en·tre·na·*do*·ra *coach*
entreno ⓜ en·*tre*·no *workout*
entrevista ① en·tre·*vees*·ta *interview*
enviar en·vee·*ar* *send • ship off*
epilepsia ① e·pee·*lep*·sya *epilepsy*
equipaje ⓜ e·kee·*pa*·khe *luggage*
equipo ⓜ e·*kee*·po *equipment • team*
— **de inmersión** de een·mer·*syon* *diving equipment*
— **de música** de *moo*·see·ka *stereo*
equitación ① e·kee·ta·*thyon* *horse riding*
equivocado/a ⓜ/① e·kee·vo·*ka*·do/a *wrong*
error ⓜ e·*ror* *mistake*
escalada ① es·ka·*la*·da *rock climbing*
escalera ① es·ka·*le*·ra *stairway*
escaleras ① pl **mecánicas** es·ka·*le*·ras me·*kan*·icas *escalator*
escarcha ① es·*kar*·cha *frost*
escarpado/a ⓜ/① es·kar·*pa*·do/a *steep*
escasez ① es·ka·*seth* *shortage*
escenario ⓜ es·the·*na*·ryo *stage*
Escocia ① es·*ko*·thya *Scotland*
escoger es·ko·*kher* *choose*
escribir es·kree·*beer* *write*
— **a máquina** a *ma*·kee·na *type*
escritor(a) ⓜ/① es·kree·*tor*/es·kree·*to*·ra *writer*
escuchar es·koo·*char* *listen*
escuela ① es·*kwe*·la *school*
— **de párvulos** de *par*·voo·los *kindergarten*

escultura ① es·kool·too·ra *sculpture*

espacio ⓜ es·pa·thyo *space*

espalda ① es·pal·da *back (body)*

España ① es·pa·nya *Spain*

especial es·pe·thyal *special*

especialista ⓜ&① es·pe·thya·lees·ta *specialist*

especies ① pl **en peligro de extinción** es·pe·thyes en pe·lee·gro de eks·teen·thyon *endangered species*

espectáculo ⓜ es·pek·ta·koo·lo *show*

espejo ⓜ es·pe·kho *mirror*

esperar es·pe·rar *wait*

espinaca ① es·pee·na·ka *spinach*

esposa ① es·po·sa *wife*

espuma ① **de afeitar** es·poo·ma de a·fey·tar *shaving cream*

espumoso/a ⓜ/①es·poo·mo·so/a *sparkling • foamy*

esquí ⓜ es·kee *skiing*
— **acuático** a·kwa·tee·ko *waterskiing*

esquiar es·kee·ar *ski*

esquina ① es·kee·na *corner*

esta noche es·ta no·che *tonight*

éste/a ⓜ/① es·te/a *this*

estación ① es·ta·thyon *season • station*
— **de autobuses** de ow·to·boo·ses *bus station*
— **de metro** de me·tro *metro station*
— **de tren** de tren *railway station*

estacionar es·ta·thyo·nar *park (car)*

estadio ⓜ es·ta·dyo *stadium*

estado ⓜ **civil** es·ta·do thee·veel *marital status*

estado ⓜ **del bienestar** es·ta·do del byen·es·tar *social welfare • well being*

estafa ① es·ta·fa *rip-off*

estanquero ⓜ es·tan·ke·ro *tobacconist*

estante ⓜ es·tan·te *shelf*

estar es·tar *to be*
— **constipado/a** ⓜ/① kons·tee·pa·do/a *have a cold*
— **de acuerdo** de a·kwer·do *agree*

estatua ① es·ta·twa *statue*

este es·te *east*

esterilla ① es·te·ree·lya *mat*

estilo ⓜ es·tee·lo *style*

estómago ⓜ es·to·ma·go *stomach*

estrellas ① pl es·tre·lyas *stars*

estreñimiento ⓜ es·tre·nyee·myen·to *constipation*

estudiante ⓜ&① es·too·dyan·te *student*

estudio ⓜ es·too·dyo *studio*

estufa ① es·too·fa *heater*

estúpido/a ⓜ/① es·too·pee·do/a *stupid*

etiqueta ① **de equipaje** e·tee·ke·ta de e·kee·pa·khe *luggage tag*

euro ⓜ e·oo·ro *euro*

Europa ① e·oo·ro·pa *Europe*

eutanasia ① e·oo·ta·na·sya *euthanasia*

excelente eks·the·len·te *excellent*

excursión ① eks·koor·syon *tour*

excursionismo ⓜ eks·koor·syo·nees·mo *hiking*

experiencia ① eks·pe·ryen·thya *experience*
— **laboral** ① la·bo·ral *work experience*

exponer eks·po·ner *exhibit*

exposición ① eks·po·see·thyon *exhibition*

expreso eks·pre·so *express*

exterior ⓜ eks·te·ryor *outside*

extrañar eks·tra·nyar *miss (feel sad)*

extranjero/a ⓜ/① eks·tran·khe·ro/a *foreign*

F

fábrica ① fa·bree·ka *factory*

fácil fa·theel *easy*

facturación ① **de equipajes** fak·too·ra·thyon de e·kee·pa·khes *check-in*

falda ① fal·da *skirt*

falta ① fal·ta *fault*

familia ① fa·mee·lya *family*

fantástico/a ⓜ/① fan·tas·tee·ko/a *great*

farmacia ① far·ma·thya *chemist (shop) • pharmacy*

farmacéutico ⓜ far·ma·thee·oo·tee·ko *chemist (person)*

faros ⓜ pl fa·ros *headlights*

fecha ① fe·cha *date (time)*
— de nacimiento de na·thee·*myen*·to *date of birth*
feliz fe·*leeth* *happy*
ferretería ① fe·re·te·*ree*·a *hardware store*
festival ⓜ fes·tee·*val* *festival*
ficción ① feek·*thyon* *fiction*
fideos ⓜ pl fee·*de*·os *noodles*
fiebre ① *fye*·bre *fever*
— glandular glan·doo·*lar* *glandular fever*
fiesta ① *fyes*·ta *party*
filete ⓜ fee·*le*·te *fillet*
film ⓜ feelm *film*
fin ⓜ feen *end*
— de semana de se·*ma*·na *weekend*
final ⓜ fee·*nal* *end*
firma ① *feer*·ma *signature*
firmar feer·*mar* *sign*
flor ① flor *flower*
florista ⓜ&① flo·*rees*·ta *florist*
follar fo·*lyar* *fuck*
folleto ⓜ fo·*lye*·to *brochure*
footing ⓜ foo·teen *jogging*
forma ① *for*·ma *shape*
fotografía ① fo·to·gra·*fee*·a *photograph*
fotógrafo/a ⓜ/① fo·to·gra·fo/a *photographer*
fotómetro ⓜ fo·to·*me*·tro *light meter*
frágil fra·kheel *fragile*
frambuesa ① fram·*bwe*·sa *raspberry*
franela ① fra·*ne*·la *flannel*
franqueo ⓜ fran·*ke*·o *postage*
freír fre·*eer* *fry*
frenos ⓜ pl fre·nos *brakes*
frente a *fren*·te a *opposite*
fresa ① *fre*·sa *strawberry*
frío/a ⓜ/① *free*·o/a *a cold*
frontera ① fron·*te*·ra *border*
fruta ① *froo*·ta *fruit*
fruto ⓜ seco froo·to se·ko *dried fruit*
fuego ⓜ *fwe*·go *fire*
fuera de juego *fwe*·ra de *khwe*·go *offside*
fuerte *fwer*·te *strong*

fumar foo·*mar* *smoke*
funda ① de almohada *foon*·da de al·*mwa*·da *pillowcase*
funeral ⓜ foo·ne·*ral* *funeral*
fútbol ⓜ *foot*·bol *football • soccer*
— australiano ow·stra·*lya*·no *Australian Rules football*
futuro ⓜ foo·*too*·ro *future*

G

gafas ① pl *ga*·fas *glasses*
— de sol de sol *sunglasses*
— de submarinismo de soob·ma·ree·*nees*·mo *goggles*
galleta ① ga·*lye*·ta *biscuit • cookie*
galletas ① pl saladas ga·*lye*·tas sa·*la*·das *biscuits • crackers*
gambas ① pl gam·bas *prawns*
ganador(a) ⓜ/① ga·na·dor/ga·na·*do*·ra *winner*
ganar ga·*nar* *earn • win*
garbanzos ⓜ pl gar·ban·thos *chickpeas*
garganta ① gar·gan·ta *throat*
gasolina ① ga·so·*lee*·na *petrol*
gasolinera ① ga·so·lee·*ne*·ra *service station*
gatito/a ⓜ/① ga·*tee*·to/a *kitten*
gato/a ⓜ/① ga·to/a *cat*
gay gai *gay*
gemelos ⓜ pl khe·*me*·los *twins*
general khe·ne·*ral* *general*
gente ① *khen*·te *people*
gimnasia ① rítmica kheem·*na*·sya reet·mee·ka *gymnastics*
ginebra ① khee·*ne*·bra *gin*
ginecólogo ⓜ khee·ne·*ko*·lo·go *gynaecologist*
gobierno ⓜ go·*byer*·no *government*
gol ⓜ gol *goal*
goma ① go·ma *condom • rubber*
gordo/a ⓜ/① gor·do/a *fat*
grabación ① gra·ba·*thyon* *recording*
gracioso/a ⓜ/① gra·*thyo*·so/a *funny*
gramo ⓜ gra·mo *gram*
grande gran·de *big • large*

grande almacene m gran·de al·ma·*the*·ne department store
granja f gran·kha farm
gratis gra·tees free (of charge)
grifo m gree·fo tap
gripe f gree·pe influenza
gris grees grey
gritar gree·*tar* shout
grupo m groo·po group
— **de rock** de rok rock band
— **sanguíneo** san·gee·ne·o blood group
guantes m pl gwan·tes gloves
guardarropa m gwar·da·*ro*·pa cloakroom
guardería f gwar·de·ree·a childminding service • creche
guerra f ge·ra war
guía m&f gee·a guide (person)
guía f gee·a guidebook
— **audio** ow·dyo guide (audio)
— **del ocio** del o·thyo entertainment guide
— **telefónica** te·le·fo·nee·ka phone book
guindilla f geen·dee·lya chilli
guión m gee·on script
guiri m gee·ree tourist (slang)
guisantes gee·san·tes peas
güisqui gwees·kee whiskey
guitarra f gee·*ta*·ra guitar
gustar(le) goos·*tar*(·le) like

H

habitación f a·bee·ta·thyon bedroom • room
— **doble** do·ble double room
— **individual** een·dee·vee·dwal single room
hablar a·blar speak • talk
hace sol a·the sol sunny
hacer a·*ther* do • make
— **dedo** de·do hitchhike
— **surf** soorf surf
— **windsurf** ween·soorf windsurfing

hachís m a·*chees* hash
hacia a·thya towards
— **abajo** a·*ba*·kho down
halal a·*lal* Halal
hamaca f a·*ma*·ka hammock
hambriento/a m/f am·bryen·to/a hungry
harina f a·ree·na flour
hasta (junio) as·ta (khoo·nyo) until (June)
hecho/a m/f e·cho/a made
— **a mano** a *ma*·no handmade
— **de (algodón)** de (al·go·don) made of (cotton)
heladería f e·la·de·ree·a ice cream parlour
helado m e·*la*·do ice cream
helar e·lar freeze
hepatitis f e·pa·tee·tees hepatitis
herbolario m er·bo·*la*·ryo herbalist (shop)
herida f e·ree·da injury
hermana f er·ma·na sister
hermano m er·ma·no brother
hermoso/a m/f er·mo·so/a beautiful
heroína f e·ro·ee·na heroin
hielo m ye·lo ice
hierba f yer·ba grass
hierbas f pl yer·bas herbs
hígado m ee·ga·do liver
higos m pl ee·gos figs
hija f ee·kha daughter
hijo m ee·kho son
hijos m pl ee·khos children
hilo m **dental** ee·lo den·tal dental floss
hinchas m&f pl een·chas supporters
hindú een·doo Hindu
hipódromo m ee·po·dro·mo racetrack (horses)
historial m **profesional** ees·to·ryal pro·fe·syo·nal CV
histórico/a m/f ees·to·ree·ko/a historical
hockey m kho·kee hockey
— **sobre hielo** so·bre ye·lo ice hockey
hoja f o·kha leaf • sheet (of paper)

hojalata ⊕ o·kha·*la*·ta *tin*

Holanda ⊕ o·*lan*·da *Netherlands*

hombre ⓜ *om*·bre *man*

hombros ⓜ pl *om*·bros *shoulders*

homosexual ⓜ&⊕ o·mo·se·*kswal*
homosexual

hora ⊕ o·ra *time*

horario ⓜ o·ra·ryo *timetable*

horas ⊕ pl **de abrir** o·ras de a·*breer*
opening hours

hormiga ⊕ or·*mee*·ga *ant*

horno ⓜ *or*·no *oven*

horóscopo ⓜ o·*ros*·ko·po *horoscope*

hospital ⓜ os·pee·*tal* *hospital*

hostelería ⊕ os·te·le·*ree*·a *hospitality*

hotel ⓜ o·*tel* *hotel*

hoy oy *today*

hueso ⓜ *we*·so *bone*

huevo ⓜ *we*·vo *egg*

humanidades ⊕ pl oo·ma·nee·*da*·des
humanities

I

identificación ⊕ ee·den·tee·fee·ka·*thyon*
identification

idiomas ⓜ pl ee·*dyo*·mas *languages*

idiota ⓜ/⊕ ee·*dyo*·ta *idiot*

iglesia ⊕ ee·*gle*·sya *church*

igual ee·*gwal* *same*

igualdad ⊕ ee·gwal·*da* *equality*

impermeable ⓜ eem·per·me·*a*·ble
raincoat

impermeable eem·per·me·*a*·ble
waterproof

importante eem·por·*tan*·te *important*

impuesto ⓜ eem·*pwes*·to *tax*
— **sobre la renta** so·bre la *ren*·ta
income tax

incluido een·kloo·ee·do *included*

incómodo/a ⓜ/⊕ een·*ko*·mo·do/a
uncomfortable

India ⊕ een·dya *India*

indicador ⓜ een·dee·ka·*dor* *indicator*

indigestion ⊕ een·dee·khes·*tyon*
indigestion

industria ⊕ een·*doos*·trya *industry*

infección ⊕ een·fek·*thyon* *infection*

inflamación ⊕ een·fla·ma·*thyon*
inflammation

informática ⊕ een·for·*ma*·tee·ka *IT*

ingeniería ⊕ een·khe·nye·*ree*·a
engineering

ingeniero/a ⓜ/⊕ een·khe·*nye*·ro/a
engineer

Inglaterra ⊕ een·gla·*te*·ra *England*

inglés ⓜ een·*gles* *English*

ingrediente ⓜ een·gre·*dyen*·te
ingredient

injusto/a ⓜ/⊕ een·*khoos*·to/a *unfair*

inmigración ⊕ een·mee·gra·*thyon*
immigration

inocente ee·no·*then*·te *innocent*

inseguro/a ⓜ/⊕ een·se·*goo*·ro/a *unsafe*

instituto ⓜ eens·tee·*too*·to *high school*

intentar (hacer algo) een·ten·*tar* (a·*ther*
al·go) *try (to do something)*

interesante een·te·re·*san*·te *interesting*

internacional een·ter·na·thyo·*nal*
international

Internet ⓜ een·ter·net *Internet*

intérprete ⓜ&⊕ een·*ter*·pre·te
interpreter

inundación ⊕ ee·noon·da·*thyon*
flooding

invierno ⓜ een·*vyer*·no *winter*

invitar een·vee·*tar* *invite*

inyección ⊕ een·yek·*thyon* *injection*

inyectar(se) een·yek·*tar*(·se) *inject
(oneself)*

ir eer *go*
— **de compras** de *kom*·pras *go
shopping*
— **de excursión** de eks·koor·*syon* *hike*
— **en tobogán** en to·bo·*gan*
tobogganing

Irlanda ⊕ eer·*lan*·da *Ireland*

irritación ⊕ ee·ree·ta·*thyon* *rash*
— **de pañal** de pa·*nyal* *nappy rash*

isla ⊕ *ees*·la *island*

itinerario ⓜ ee·tee·ne·*ra*·ryo *itinerary*

IVA ⓜ *ee*·va *sales tax*

izquierda ⊕ eeth·*kyer*·da *left*

J

jabón ⓜ kha·*bon* soap
jamón ⓜ kha·*mon* ham
Japón ⓜ kha·*pon* Japan
jarabe ⓜ kha·ra·be *cough medicine*
jardín ⓜ **botánico** khar·*deen*
bo·ta·nee·ko *botanic garden*
jarra ⓕ *kha*·ra *jar*
jefe/a ⓜ/ⓕ *khe*·fe/a *boss • leader*
— **de sección** de sek·*thyon* manager
jengibre ⓜ khen·*khee*·bre ginger
jeringa ⓕ khe·*reen*·ga syringe
jersey ⓜ kher·*sey* jumper • sweater
jet lag ⓜ dyet lag *jet lag*
jockey ⓜ *dyo*·kee jockey
joven *kho*·ven young
joyería ⓕ kho·ye·*ree*·a jeweller (shop)
jubilado/a ⓜ/ⓕ khoo·bee·*la*·do/a
retired
judías ⓕ pl khoo·*dee*·as beans
judío/a ⓜ/ⓕ khoo·*dee*·o/a Jewish
juegos ⓜ pl **de ordenador** khwe·gos
de or·de·na·*dor* computer games
juegos ⓜ pl **olímpicos** *khwe*·gos
o·*leem*·pee·kos Olympic Games
juez ⓜ&ⓕ khweth judge
jugar khoo·*gar* play (sport • games)
jugo ⓜ *khoo*·go juice
juguetería ⓕ khoo·ge·te·*ree*·a toyshop
juntos/as ⓜ/ⓕ pl khoon·tos/as
together

K

kilo ⓜ *kee*·lo kilogram
kilómetro ⓜ kee·*lo*·me·tro
kilometre
kiwi ⓜ *kee*·wee kiwifruit
kosher ko·sher Kosher

L

La Copa ⓕ **Mundial** la *ko*·pa
moon·*dyal* World Cup
labios ⓜ pl *la*·byos lips
lado ⓜ *la*·do side

ladrón ⓜ la·*dron* thief
lagartija ⓕ la·gar·*tee*·kha lizard
lago ⓜ *la*·go lake
lamentar la·men·*tar* regret
lana ⓕ *la*·na wool
lápiz ⓜ *la*·peeth pencil
— **de labios** de *la*·byos lipstick
largo/a ⓜ/ⓕ *lar*·go/a long
lata ⓕ *la*·ta can
lavadero ⓜ la·va·*de*·ro laundry
lavadora ⓕ la·va·*do*·ra washing
machine
lavandería ⓕ la·van·de·*ree*·a
laundrette
lavar la·*var* wash (something)
lavarse la·*var*·se wash (oneself)
leche ⓕ *le*·che milk
— **de soja** de so·*kha* soy milk
— **desnatada** des·na·*ta*·da skimmed
milk
lechuga ⓕ le·*choo*·ga lettuce
leer le·*er* read
legal le·*gal* legal
legislación ⓕ le·khees·la·*thyon*
legislation
legumbre ⓕ le·*goom*·bre legume
lejos *le*·khos far
leña ⓕ *le*·nya firewood
lentejas ⓕ pl len·*te*·khas lentils
lentes ⓜ pl **de contacto** *len*·tes de
kon·*tak*·to contact lenses
lento/a ⓜ/ⓕ *len*·to/a slow
lesbiana ⓕ les·bee·*a*·na lesbian
leve *le*·ve light
ley ⓕ ley law
libra ⓕ *lee*·bra pound (money)
libre *lee*·bre free (not bound)
librería ⓕ lee·bre·*ree*·a bookshop
libro ⓜ *lee*·bro book
— **de frases** de *fra*·ses phrasebook
libros ⓜ pl **de viajes** *lee*·bros de
vya·khes travel books
líder ⓜ *lee*·der leader
ligar lee·*gar* pick up
lila *lee*·la purple
lima *lee*·ma lime

límite ⓜ **de equipaje** *lee*·mee·te de e·*kee*·pa·khe *baggage allowance*
limón ⓜ lee·*mon* *lemon*
limonada ⓕ lee·mo·*na*·da *lemonade*
limpio/a ⓜ/ⓕ *leem*·pyo/a *clean*
línea ⓕ *lee*·ne·a *line*
linterna ⓕ leen·*ter*·na *flashlight • torch*
listo/a ⓜ/ⓕ *lees*·to/a *ready*
lo que lo ke *what*
local ⓜ lo·*kal* *venue*
local lo·*kal* *local*
loco/a ⓜ/ⓕ *lo*·ko/a *crazy*
lodo ⓜ *lo*·do *mud*
lombrices ⓕ pl lom·*bree*·thes *earth worms*
los dos los dos *both*
Los Estados ⓜ pl **Unidos** los es·*ta*·dos oo·*nee*·dos *USA*
lubricante ⓜ loo·bree·*kan*·te *lubricant*
luces ⓕ pl *loo*·thes *lights*
luchar contra loo·*char* kon·tra *fight against*
lugar ⓜ loo·*gar* *place*
— **de nacimiento** de na·thee·*myen*·to *place of birth*
lujo ⓜ *loo*·kho *luxury*
luna ⓕ *loo*·na *moon*
— **llena** *lye*·na *full moon*
— **de miel** de myel *honeymoon*
luz ⓕ looth *light*

LL

llamada ⓕ lya·*ma*·da *phone call*
— **a cobro revertido** a *ko*·bro re·ver·*tee*·do *collect call*
llamar por telefono lya·*mar* por te·*le*·fo·no *to make a phone call*
llano/a ⓜ/ⓕ *lya*·no/a *flat*
llave ⓕ *lya*·ve *key*
llegadas ⓕ pl lye·*ga*·das *arrivals*
llegar lye·*gar* *arrive*
llenar lye·*nar* *fill*
lleno/a ⓜ/ⓕ *lye*·no/a *full*
llevar lye·*var* *carry • wear*
lluvia ⓕ *lyoo*·vya *rain*

M

machismo ⓜ ma·*chees*·mo *sexism*
madera ⓕ ma·*de*·ra *wood*
madre ⓕ *ma*·dre *mother*
madrugada ⓕ ma·droo·*ga*·da *early morning*
mago/a ⓜ/ⓕ *ma*·go/a *magician*
maíz ⓜ ma·*eeth* *corn*
maleta ⓕ ma·*le*·ta *suitcase*
maletín ⓜ ma·le·*teen* *briefcase*
— **de primeros auxilios** ⓜ de pree·*me*·ros ow·*ksee*·lyos *first-aid kit*
malo/a ⓜ/ⓕ *ma*·lo/a *bad*
mamá ⓕ ma·*ma* *mum*
mamograma ⓜ ma·mo·*gra*·ma *mammogram*
mañana ⓕ ma·*nya*·na *tomorrow • morning (6am - 1pm)*
— **por la mañana** por la ma·*nya*·na *tomorrow morning*
— **por la noche** por la *no*·che *tomorrow evening*
— **por la tarde** por la *tar*·de *tomorrow afternoon*
mandarina ⓕ man·da·*ree*·na *mandarin*
mandíbula ⓕ man·*dee*·boo·la *jaw*
mando ⓜ **a distancia** *man*·do a dees·*tan*·thya *remote control*
mango ⓜ *man*·go *mango*
manifestación ⓕ ma·nee·fes·ta·*thyon* *demonstration*
manillar ⓜ ma·nee·*lyar* *handlebar*
mano ⓕ *ma*·no *hand*
manta ⓕ *man*·ta *blanket*
manteca ⓕ man·*te*·ka *lard*
mantel ⓜ man·*tel* *tablecloth*
mantequilla ⓕ man·te·*kee*·lya *butter*
manzana ⓕ man·*tha*·na *apple*
mapa ⓜ *ma*·pa *map*
maquillaje ⓜ ma·kee·*lya*·khe *make-up*
máquina ⓕ *ma*·kee·na *machine*
— **de billetes** de bee·*lye*·tes *ticket machine*
— **de tabaco** de ta·*ba*·ko *cigarette machine*

mar ⓜ mar *sea*

marido ⓜ ma·*ree*·do *husband*

maravilloso/a ⓜ/ⓕ ma·ra·vee·*lyo*·so/a *wonderful*

marcador ⓜ mar·ka·*dor scoreboard*

marcapasos ⓜ mar·ka·*pa*·sos *pacemaker*

marcar mar·*kar score*

marea ⓕ ma·*re*·a *tide*

mareado/a ⓜ/ⓕ ma·re·a·do/a *dizzy • seasick*

mareo ⓜ ma·*re*·o *travel sickness*

margarina ⓕ mar·ga·*ree*·na *margarine*

marihuana ⓕ ma·ree·*wa*·na *marijuana*

mariposa ⓕ ma·ree·*po*·sa *butterfly*

marrón ma·*ron brown*

martillo ⓜ mar·*tee*·lyo *hammer*

más cercano/a ⓜ/ⓕ mas ther·*ka*·no/a *nearest*

masaje ⓜ ma·*sa*·khe *massage*

masajista ⓜ&ⓕ ma·sa·*khees*·ta *masseur*

matar ma·*tar kill*

matrícula ⓕ ma·*tree*·koo·la *license plate number*

matrimonio ⓜ ma·tree·*mo*·nyo *marriage*

mayonesa ⓕ ma·yo·*ne*·sa *mayonnaise*

mecánico ⓜ me·*ka*·nee·ko *mechanic*

mechero ⓜ me·*che*·ro *lighter*

medianoche ⓕ me·dya·*no*·che *midnight*

medias ⓜ pl *me*·dyas *stockings • pantyhose*

medicina ⓕ me·dee·*thee*·na *medicine*

medico/a ⓜ/ⓕ *me*·dee·co/a *doctor*

medio ⓜ ambiente *me*·dyo am·*byen*·te *environment*

medio/a ⓜ/ⓕ *me*·dyo/a *half*

mediodía ⓜ me·dyo·*dee*·a *noon*

medios ⓜ pl de comunicación *me*·dyos de ko·moo·nee·ka·*thyon media*

medios ⓜ pl de transporte *me*·dyos de trans·*por*·te *means of transport*

mejillones ⓜ pl me·khee·*lyo*·nes *mussels*

mejor me·*khor better • best*

melocotón ⓜ me·lo·ko·*ton peach*

melodía ⓕ me·lo·*dee*·a *tune*

melón ⓜ me·*lon melon*

mendigo/a ⓜ/ⓕ men·*dee*·go/a *beggar*

menos *me*·nos *less*

mensaje ⓜ men·*sa*·khe *message*

menstruación ⓕ mens·trwa·*thyon menstruation*

mentiroso/a ⓜ/ⓕ men·tee·ro·so/a *liar*

menú ⓜ me·*noo menu*

menudo/a ⓜ/ⓕ me·*noo*·do/a *little*

a menudo a me·*noo*·do *often*

mercado ⓜ mer·*ka*·do *market*

mermelada ⓕ mer·me·*la*·da *jam • marmalade*

mes ⓜ mes *month*

mesa ⓕ *me*·sa *table*

meseta ⓕ me·*se*·ta *plateau*

metal ⓜ me·*tal metal*

meter (un gol) me·*ter* (oon gol) *kick (a goal)*

metro ⓜ *me*·tro *metre*

mezclar meth·*klar mix*

mezquita ⓕ meth·*kee*·ta *mosque*

mi mee *my*

microondas ⓜ mee·kro·*on*·das *microwave*

miel ⓕ myel *honey*

miembro ⓜ *myem*·bro *member*

migraña ⓕ mee·*gra*·nya *migraine*

milímetro ⓜ mee·*lee*·me·tro *millimetre*

millón ⓜ mee·*lyon million*

minusválido/a ⓜ/ⓕ mee·noos·va·lee·do/a *disabled*

minuto ⓜ mee·*noo*·to *minute*

mirador ⓜ mee·ra·*dor lookout*

mirar mee·*rar look • watch*

— los escaparates los es·ka·pa·*ra*·tes *window-shopping*

misa ⓕ *mee*·sa *mass*

mochila ⓕ mo·*chee*·la *backpack*

módem ⓜ *mo*·dem *modem*

(carne) molida (*kar*·ne) mo·*lee*·da *mince (meat)*

mojado/a ⓜ/ⓕ mo·*kha*·do/a *wet*

monasterio ⓜ mo·nas·*te*·ryo *monastery*

monedas ① pl mo·*ne*·das *coins*

monja ① *mon*·kha *nun*

monopatinaje ⑩ mo·no·pa·tee·na·khe *skateboarding*

montaña ① mon·*ta*·nya *mountain*

montar mon·*tar* ride
— **en bicicleta** en bee·thee·*kle*·ta *cycle*

monumento ⑩ mo·noo·*men*·to *monument*

mordedura ① mor·de·*doo*·ra *bite (dog)*

morir mo·*reer* *die*

mosquitera ① mos·kee·*te*·ra *mosquito net*

mosquito ⑩ mos·*kee*·to *mosquito*

mostaza ① mos·*ta*·tha *mustard*

mostrador ⑩ mos·tra·*dor* *counter*

mostrar mos·*trar* *show*

motocicleta ① mo·to·thee·*kle*·ta *motorcycle*

motor ⑩ mo·*tor* *engine*

motora ① mo·*to*·ra *motorboat*

muchas/os ⑩/① pl *moo*·chas/os *many*

mudo/a ⑩/① *moo*·do/a *mute*

muebles ⑩ pl *mwe*·bles *furniture*

muela ① *mwe*·la *tooth (back)*

muelle ① *mwe*·lye *spring*

muerto/a ⑩/① *mwer*·to/a *dead*

muesli ⑩ *mwes*·lee *muesli*

mujer ① moo·*kher* *woman*

multa ① *mool*·ta *fine*

mundo ⑩ *moon*·do *world*

muñeca ① moo·*nye*·ka *doll* • *wrist*

murallas ① pl moo·*ra*·lyas *city walls*

músculo ⑩ *moos*·koo·lo *muscle*

museo ⑩ moo·*se*·o *museum*
— **de arte** de *ar*·te *art gallery*

música ① *moo*·see·ka *music*

músico/a ⑩/① *moo*·see·ko/a *musician*
— **ambulante** am·boo·*lan*·te *busker*

muslo ⑩ *moos*·lo *drumstick (chicken)*

musulmán(a) ⑩/① moo·sool·*man*/ moo·sool·*ma*·na *Muslim*

muy mooy *very*

nacionalidad ① na·thyo·na·lee·*da* *nationality*

nada *na*·da *none* • *nothing*

nadar na·*dar* *swim*

naranja ① na·*ran*·kha *orange*

nariz ① na·*reeth* *nose*

nata ① **agria** *na*·ta a·*grya* *sour cream*

naturaleza ① na·too·ra·*le*·tha *nature*

naturopatía ① na·too·ro·pa·*tee*·a *naturopathy*

náusea ① *now*·se·a *nausea*

náuseas ① pl **del embarazo** *now*·se·as del em·ba·*ra*·tho *morning sickness*

navaja ① na·va·kha *penknife*

Navidad ① na·vee·*da* *Christmas*

necesario/a ⑩/① ne·the·*sa*·ryo/a *necessary*

necesitar ne·the·see·*tar* *need*

negar ne·*gar* *deny*

negar ne·*gar* *refuse*

negocio ⑩ ne·*go*·thyo *business*
— **de artículos básicos** de ar·*tee*·koo·los ba·*see*·kos *convenience store*

negro/a ⑩/① ne·*gro*/a *black*

neumático ⑩ ne·oo·*ma*·tee·ko *tyre*

nevera ① ne·*ve*·ra *refrigerator*

nieto/a ⑩/① *nye*·to/a *grandchild*

nieve ① *nye*·ve *snow*

niño/a ⑩/① *nee*·nyo/a *child*

no no *no*
— **fumadores** foo·ma·*do*·res *non-smoking*
— **incluido** een·kloo·ee·*do* *excluded*

noche ① *no*·che *evening* • *night*

Nochebuena ① no·che·*bwe*·na *Christmas Eve*

Nochevieja ① no·che·*vye*·kha *New Year's Eve*

nombre ⑩ *nom*·bre *name*
— **de pila** de *pee*·la *Christian name*

norte ⑩ *nor*·te *north*

nosotros/as ⑩/① pl no·*so*·tros/ no·*so*·tras *we*

noticias ① pl no·tee·thyas *news*
— de actualidad de ak·twal·ee·da *current affairs*
novia ① no·vya *girlfriend*
novio ⑩ no·vyo *boyfriend*
nube ① noo·be *cloud*
nublado noo·*bla*·do *cloudy*
nueces nwe·thes *nuts*
— crudas kroo·das *raw nuts*
— tostadas tos·ta·das *roasted nuts*
nuestro/a ⑩/① nwes·tro/a *our*
Nueva Zelanda ① nwe·va the·*lan*·da *New Zealand*
nuevo/a ⑩/① nwe·vo/a *new*
número ⑩ noo·me·ro *number*
— de la habitación de la a·bee·ta·thyon *room number*
— de pasaporte de pa·sa·por·te *passport number*
nunca noon·ka *never*

O

o o *or*
obra ① o·bra *play* • *building site*
obrero/a ⑩/① o·bre·ro/a *factory worker* • *labourer*
océano ⑩ o·the·a·no *ocean*
ocupado/a ⑩/① o·koo·pa·do/a *busy*
ocupar o·koo·par *live (somewhere)*
oeste ⑩ o·es·te *west*
oficina ① o·fee·thee·na *office*
— de objetos perdidos de ob·khe·tos per·dee·dos *lost property office*
— de turismo de too·rees·mo *tourist office*
oír o·eer *hear*
ojo ⑩ o·kho *eye*
ola ① o·la *wave*
olor ⑩ o·lor *smell*
olvidar ol·vee·dar *forget*
ópera ① o·pe·ra *opera*
operación ① o·pe·ra·thyon *operation*
opinión ① o·pee·nyon *opinion*
oporto ⑩ o·por·to *port (wine)*
oportunidad ① o·por·too·nee·da *chance*

oración ① o·ra·thyon *prayer*
orden ⑩ or·den *order (placement)*
ordenador ⑩ or·de·na·dor *computer*
— portátil por·ta·teel *laptop*
ordenar or·de·nar *order*
oreja ① o·re·kha *ear*
orgasmo ⑩ or·gas·mo *orgasm*
original o·ree·khee·nal *original*
orquesta ① or·kes·ta *orchestra*
oscuro/a ⑩/① os·koo·ro/a *dark*
ostra ① os·tra *oyster*
otoño ⑩ o·to·nyo *autumn*
otra vez o·tra veth *again*
otro/a ⑩/① o·tro/a *other* • *another*
oveja ① o·ve·kha *sheep*
oxígeno ⑩ o·ksee·khe·no *oxygen*

P

padre ⑩ pa·dre *father*
padres ⑩ pl pa·dres *parents*
pagar pa·gar *pay*
página ① pa·khee·na *page*
pago ⑩ pa·go *payment*
país ⑩ pa·ees *country*
pájaro ⑩ pa·kha·ro *bird*
palabra ① pa·la·bra *word*
palacio ⑩ pa·la·thyo *palace*
palillo ⑩ pa·lee·lyo *toothpick*
pan ⑩ pan *bread*
— integral in·te·gral *wholemeal bread*
— moreno mo·re·no *brown bread*
panadería ① pa·na·de·ree·a *bakery*
pañal ⑩ pa·nyal *diaper* • *nappy*
pantalla ① pan·ta·lya *screen*
pantalones ⑩ pl pan·ta·lo·nes *pants* • *trousers*
— cortos kor·tos *shorts*
pañuelos ⑩ pl de papel pa·nywe·los de pa·pel *tissues*
papá ⑩ pa·pa *dad*
papel ⑩ pa·pel *paper*
— de fumar de foo·mar *cigarette papers*
— higiénico ee·khye·nee·ko *toilet paper*

paquete ⓜ pa·ke·te *packet • package • wear*

para llevar pa·ra lye·var *to take away*

parabrisas ⓜ pa·ra·bree·sas *windscreen*

paracaidismo ⓜ pa·ra·kai·dees·mo *skydiving*

parada ① pa·ra·da *stop*
— **de autobús** de ow·to·*boos* *bus stop*
— **de taxis** de ta·ksees *taxi stand*

paraguas ⓜ pa·ra·gwas *umbrella*

parapléjico/a ⓜ/① pa·ra·ple·khee·ko/a *paraplegic*

parar pa·rar *stop*

pared ① pa·red *wall (inside)*

pareja ① pa·re·kha *pair (couple)*

parlamento ⓜ par·la·men·to *parliament*

paro ⓜ pa·ro *dole*

parque ⓜ par·ke *park*
— **nacional** na·thyo·nal *national park*

parte ① par·te *part*

partida ① **de nacimiento** par·tee·da de na·thee·myen·to *birth certificate*

partido ⓜ par·tee·do *match (sport) • party (political)*

pasado ⓜ pa·sa·do *past*

pasado mañana pa·sa·do ma·nya·na *day after tomorrow*

pasado/a ⓜ/① pa·sa·do/a *off (food)*

pasajero ⓜ pa·sa·khe·ro *passenger*

pasaporte ⓜ pa·sa·por·te *passport*

Pascua ① pas·kwa *Easter*

pase ⓜ pa·se *pass*

paseo ⓜ pa·se·o *street*

paso ⓜ pa·so *step*
— **de cebra** de the·bra *pedestrian crossing*

pasta ① pas·ta *pasta*
— **dentífrica** den·tee·free·ka *toothpaste*

pastel ⓜ pas·tel *cake • pie*
— **de cumpleaños** de koom·ple·a·nyos *birthday cake*

pastelería ① pas·te·le·ree·a *cake shop*

pastilla ① pas·tee·lya *pill*

pastillas ① pl **de menta** pas·tee·lyas de men·ta *mints*

pastillas ① pl **para dormir** pas·tee·lyas pa·ra dor·meer *sleeping pills*

patata ① pa·ta·ta *potato*

paté ⓜ pa·te *pate (food)*

patinar pa·tee·nar *rollerblading • ice skating*

pato ⓜ pa·to *duck*

pavo ⓜ pa·vo *turkey*

paz ① path *peace*

peatón ⓜ&① pe·a·ton *pedestrian*

pecho ⓜ pe·cho *chest*

pechuga ① pe·choo·ga *breast (poultry)*

pedal ⓜ pe·dal *pedal*

pedazo ⓜ pe·da·tho *piece*

pedir pe·deer *ask (for something)*

peine ⓜ pey·ne *comb*

pelea ① pe·le·a *fight*

película ① pe·lee·koo·la *movie • film (camera)*
— **en color** en ko·lor *colour film*

peligroso/a ⓜ/① pe·lee·gro·so/a *dangerous*

pelo ⓜ pe·lo *hair*

pelota ① pe·lo·ta *ball*
— **de golf** de golf *golf ball*

peluquero/a ⓜ/① pe·loo·ke·ro/a *hairdresser*

pendientes ⓜ pl pen·dyen·tes *earrings*

pene ⓜ pe·ne *penis*

pensar pen·sar *think*

pensión ① pen·syon *boarding house*

pensionista ⓜ&① pen·syo·nees·ta *pensioner*

pepino ⓜ pe·pee·no *cucumber*

pequeñito/a ⓜ/① pe·ke·nyee·to/a *tiny*

pequeño/a ⓜ/① pe·ke·nyo/a *small*

pera ① pe·ra *pear*

perder per·der *lose*

perdido/a ⓜ/① per·dee·do/a *lost*

perdonar per·do·nar *forgive*

perejil ⓜ pe·re·kheel *parsley*

perfume ⓜ per·foo·me *perfume*

periódico ⓜ pe·ryo·dee·ko *newspaper*

periodista ⓜ&① pe·ryo·dees·ta *journalist*

permiso ⓜ per·mee·so permission •
permit
— de trabajo de tra·ba·kho work
permit
permitir per·mee·teer allow • permit
pero pe·ro but
perro/a ⓜ/ⓕ pe·ro/a dog
perro ⓜ lazarillo pe·ro la·tha·ree·lyo
guide dog
persona ⓕ per·so·na person
pesado/a ⓜ/ⓕ pe·sa·do/a heavy
pesar pe·sar weigh
pesas ⓕ pl pe·sas weights
pesca ⓕ pes·ka fishing
pescadería ⓕ pes·ka·de·ree·a fish shop
pescado ⓜ pes·ka·do fish (as food)
peso ⓜ pe·so weight
petición ⓕ pe·tee·thyon petition
pez ⓜ peth fish
picadura ⓕ pee·ka·doo·ra bite (insect)
picazón ⓕ pee·ka·thon itch
pie ⓜ pee·e foot
piedra ⓕ pye·dra stone
piel ⓕ pyel skin
pierna ⓕ pyer·na leg
pila ⓕ pee·la battery (small)
píldora ⓕ peel·do·ra the Pill
pimienta ⓕ pee·myen·ta pepper
pimiento ⓜ pee·myen·to capsicum •
bell pepper
— rojo ro·kho red capsicum
— verde ver·de green capsicum
piña ⓕ pee·nya pineapple
pinchar peen·char puncture
ping pong ⓜ peeng pong table tennis
pintar peen·tar paint
pintor(a) ⓜ/ⓕ peen·tor/peen·to·ra
painter
pintura ⓕ peen·too·ra painting
pinzas ⓕ pl peen·thas tweezers
piojos ⓜ pl pyo·khos lice
piqueta ⓕ pee·ke·ta pickaxe
piquetas ⓕ pl pee·ke·tas tent pegs
piscina ⓕ pees·thee·na swimming pool
pista ⓕ pees·ta court (tennis)
— de tenis de te·nees tennis court
pistacho ⓜ pees·ta·cho pistachio

plancha ⓕ plan·cha iron
planeta ⓜ pla·ne·ta planet
planta ⓕ plan·ta plant
plástico ⓜ plas·tee·ko plastic
plata ⓕ pla·ta silver
plataforma ⓕ pla·ta·for·ma platform
plátano ⓜ pla·ta·no banana
plateado/a ⓜ/ⓕ pla·te·a·do/a silver
plato ⓜ pla·to plate
playa ⓕ pla·ya beach
plaza ⓕ pla·tha square
— de toros de to·ros bullring
pobre po·bre poor
pobreza ⓕ po·bre·tha poverty
pocos po·kos few
poder po·der can (be able)
poder ⓜ po·der power
poesía ⓕ po·e·see·a poetry
polen ⓜ po·len pollen
policía ⓕ po·lee·thee·a police
política ⓕ po·lee·tee·ka policy •
politics
político ⓜ po·lee·tee·ko politician
póliza ⓕ po·lee·tha policy (insurance)
pollo ⓜ po·lyo chicken
pomelo ⓜ po·me·lo grapefruit
poner po·ner put
popular po·poo·lar popular
póquer ⓜ po·ker poker
por (día) por (dee·a) per (day)
por ciento por thyen·to percent
por qué por ke why
por vía aérea por vee·a a·e·re·a air mail
por vía terrestre por vee·a te·res·tre
surface mail
porque por·ke because
portero/a ⓜ/ⓕ por·te·ro/a goalkeeper
posible po·see·ble possible
postal ⓕ pos·tal postcard
póster ⓜ pos·ter poster
potro ⓜ po·tro foal
pozo ⓜ po·tho well
precio ⓜ pre·thyo price
— de entrada de en·tra·da admission
price
— del cubierto del koo·byer·to cover
charge

preferir pre·fe·*reer* prefer

pregunta ① pre·*goon*·ta question

preguntar pre·goon·*tar* ask (a question)

preocupado/a ⑩/① pre·o·koo·*pa*·do/a worried

preocuparse por pre·o·koo·*par*·se por care (about something)

preparar pre·pa·*rar* prepare

presidente/a ⑩/① pre·see·*den*·te/a president

presión ① pre·*syon* pressure
— arterial ar·te·*ryal* blood pressure

prevenir pre·ve·*neer* prevent

primavera ① pree·ma·ve·ra spring (season)

primer ministro ⑩ pree·*mer* mee·*nees*·tro prime minister

primera ministra ① pree·*me*·ra mee·*nees*·tra prime minister

primero/a ⑩/① pree·*me*·ro/a first

principal preen·thee·*pal* main

prisa ① *pree*·sa hurry

prisionero/a ⑩/① pree·syon·*ne*·ro/a prisoner

privado/a ⑩/① pree·va·do/a private

probar pro·*bar* try

producir pro·doo·*theer* produce

productos ⑩ pl congelados pro·*dook*·tos kon·khe·*la*·dos frozen foods

profesor(a) ⑩/① pro·fe·*sor*/ pro·fe·*so*·ra lecturer • instructor • teacher

profundo/a ⑩/① pro·*foon*·do/a deep

programa ⑩ pro·*gra*·ma programme

prolongación ① pro·lon·ga·*thyon* extension (visa)

promesa ① pro·*me*·sa promise

prometida ① pro·me·*tee*·da fiancee

prometido ① pro·me·*tee*·do fiance

pronto *pron*·to soon

propietaria ① pro·pye·*ta*·rya landlady

propietario ⑩ pro·pye·*ta*·ryo landlord

propina ① pro·*pee*·na tip

proteger pro·te·*kher* protect

protegido/a ⑩/① pro·te·*khee*·do/a protected

protesta ① pro·*tes*·ta protest

provisiones ① pl pro·bee·*syo*·nes provisions

proyector ⑩ pro·yek·*tor* projector

prudente proo·*den*·te sensible

prueba ① *prwe*·ba test
— del embarazo del em·ba·*ra*·tho pregnancy test kit

pruebas ① pl nucleares *prwe*·bas noo·kle·a·res nuclear testing

pub ⑩ poob bar (with music) • pub

pueblo ⑩ *pwe*·blo village

puente ⑩ *pwen*·te bridge

puerro ⑩ *pwe*·ro leek

puerta ① *pwer*·ta door

puerto ⑩ *pwer*·to port • harbour

puesta ① del sol *pwes*·ta del sol sunset

pulga ① *pool*·ga flea

pulmones ⑩ pl pool·*mo*·nes lungs

punto ⑩ *poon*·to point (tip) • point (score)

puro ⑩ *poo*·ro cigar

puro/a ⑩/① *poo*·ro/a pure

Q

(el mes) que viene (el mes) ke *vye*·ne next (month)

quedar ke·*dar* leave (behind)

quedarse ke·*dar*·se stay (remain)

quedarse sin ke·*dar*·se seen run out of

quejarse ke·*khar*·se complain

quemadura ① ke·ma·*doo*·ra burn
— de sol de sol sunburn

querer ke·*rer* love • want

queso ⑩ *ke*·so cheese
— crema *kre*·ma cream cheese
— de cabra de *ka*·bra goat's cheese

quien kyen who

quincena ① keen·*the*·na fortnight

quiosco ⑩ *kyos*·ko news stand • newsagency

quiste ⑩ ovárico *kees*·te o·va·ree·ko ovarian cyst

quizás kee·*thas* maybe

R

rábano @ ra·ba·no *radish*
— **picante** pee·kan·te *horseradish*
rápido/a @/① ra·pee·do/a *fast*
raqueta ① ra·ke·ta *racquet*
raro/a @/① ra·ro/a *rare (item)*
rastro @ ras·tro *track (footprints)*
rata ① ra·ta *rat*
ratón @ ra·ton *mouse*
raza ① ra·tha *race (people)*
razón ① ra·thon *reason*
realista re·a·lees·ta *realistic*
recibir re·thee·beer *receive*
recibo @ re·thee·bo *receipt*
reciclable re·thee·kla·ble *recyclable*
reciclar re·thee·klar *recycle*
recientemente re·thyen·te·men·te
recently
recogida ① **de equipajes** re·ko·khee·da
de e·kee·pa·khes *baggage claim*
recolección ① **de fruta** re·ko·lek·thyon
de froo·ta *fruit picking*
recomendar re·ko·men·dar *recommend*
reconocer re·ko·no·ther *recognise*
recordar re·kor·dar *remember*
recorrido @ **guiado** re·ko·ree·do
gee·a·do *guided tour*
recto/a @/① rek·to/a *straight*
recuerdo @ re·kwer·do *souvenir*
red ① red *net*
redondo/a @/① re·don·do/a *round*
reembolsar re·em·bol·sar *refund*
reembolso @ re·em·bol·so *refund*
referencias ① pl re·fe·ren·thyas
references
refresco @ re·fres·ko *soft drink*
refugiado/a @/① re·foo·khya·do/a
refugee
regalar re·ga·lar *exchange (gifts)*
regalo @ re·ga·lo *gift*
— **de bodas** de bo·das *wedding
present*
régimen @ re·khee·men *diet*
reglas ① pl re·glas *rules*
reina ① rey·na *queen*

reírse re·eer·se *laugh*
relación ① re·la·thyon *relationship*
relajarse re·la·khar·se *relax*
religión ① re·lee·khyon *religion*
religioso/a @/① re·lee·khyo·so/a
religious
reliquia ① re·lee·kya *relic*
reloj @ re·lokh *clock*
— **de pulsera** de pool·se·ra *watch*
remo @ re·mo *rowing*
remolacha ① re·mo·la·cha *beetroot*
remoto/a @/① re·mo·to/a *remote*
reparar re·pa·rar *repair*
repartir re·par·teer *divide up (share)*
repetir re·pe·teer *repeat*
república ① re·poo·blee·ka *republic*
requesón @ re·ke·son *cottage cheese*
reserva ① re·ser·va *reservation*
reservar re·ser·var *book (make a
reservation)*
resfriado @ res·free·a·do *cold*
residencia ① **de estudiantes**
re·see·den·thya de es·too·dyan·tes
college
residuos @ pl **tóxicos** re·see·dwos
to·ksee·kos *toxic waste*
respirar res·pee·rar *breathe*
respuesta ① res·pwes·ta *answer*
restaurante @ res·tow·ran·te *restaurant*
revisar re·vee·sar *check*
revisor(a) @/① re·vee·sor/re·vee·so·ra
ticket collector
revista ① re·vees·ta *magazine*
rey @ rey *king*
rico/a @/① ree·ko/a *rich*
riesgo @ ryes·go *risk*
río @ ree·o *river*
ritmo @ reet·mo *rhythm*
robar ro·bar *rob • steal*
roca ① ro·ka *rock*
rock @ rok *rock (music)*
rodilla ① ro·dee·lya *knee*
rojo/a @/① ro·kho/a *red*
rollo @ **repelente contra mosquitos**
ro·lyo re·pe·len·te kon·tra
mos·kee·tos *mosquito coil*

romántico/a ⓜ/ⓕ ro·man·tee·ko/a
romantic
romper rom·per break
ron ⓜ ron rum
ropa ⓕ ro·pa clothing
— **de cama** de ka·ma bedding
— **interior** een·te·ryor underwear
rosa ro·sa pink
roto/a ⓜ/ⓕ ro·to/a broken
rueda ⓕ rwe·da wheel
rugby ⓜ roog·bee rugby
ruidoso/a ⓜ/ⓕ rwee·do·so/a loud
ruinas ⓕ pl rwee·nas ruins
ruta ⓕ roo·ta route

S

sábado ⓜ sa·ba·do Saturday
sábana ⓕ sa·ba·na sheet (bed)
saber sa·ber know (something)
sabroso/a ⓜ/ⓕ sa·bro·so/a tasty
sacar sa·kar take out • take (photo)
sacerdote ⓜ sa·ther·do·te priest
saco de dormir sa·ko de dor·meer
sleeping bag
sal ⓕ sal salt
sala de espera sa·la de es·pe·ra
waiting room
sala de tránsito sa·la de tran·see·to
transit lounge
salario ⓜ sa·la·ryo rate of pay • salary
salchicha ⓕ sal·chee·cha sausage
saldo ⓜ sal·do balance (account)
salida ⓕ sa·lee·da departure • exit
saliente ⓜ sa·lyen·te ledge
salir con sa·leer kon go out with
salir de sa·leer de depart
salmón ⓜ sal·mon salmon
salón de belleza ⓜ sa·lon de be·lye·tha
beauty salon
salsa ⓕ sal·sa sauce
— **de guindilla** de geen·dee·lya chilli
sauce
— **de soja** de so·kha soy sauce
— **de tomate** de to·ma·te tomato
sauce • ketchup
saltar sal·tar jump

salud ⓕ sa·loo health
salvaeslips ⓜ pl sal·va·e·sleeps panty
liners
salvar sal·var save
sandalias ⓕ pl san·da·lyas sandals
sandía ⓕ san·dee·a watermelon
sangrar san·grar bleed
sangre ⓕ san·gre blood
santo/a ⓜ/ⓕ san·to/a saint
sarampión ⓜ sa·ram·pyon measles
sartén ⓕ sar·ten frying pan
sauna ⓕ sow·na sauna
secar se·kar dry
secretario/a ⓜ/ⓕ se·kre·ta·ryo/a
secretary
sed ⓕ se thirst
seda ⓕ se·da silk
seguir se·geer follow
segundo/a ⓜ/ⓕ se·goon·do/a second
seguro ⓜ se·goo·ro insurance
seguro/a ⓜ/ⓕ se·goo·ro/a safe
sello ⓜ se·lyo stamp
semáforos ⓜ pl se·ma·fo·ros traffic lights
Semana Santa se·ma·na san·ta Holy
Week
sembrar sem·brar plant
semidirecto/a ⓜ/ⓕ se·mee·dee·rek·to/
a non-direct
señal ⓕ se·nyal sign
sencillo/a ⓜ/ⓕ sen·thee·lyo/a simple
(un billete) sencillo ⓜ (oon bee·lye·te)
sen·thee·lyo one-way (ticket)
sendero ⓜ sen·de·ro mountain path •
path
senos ⓜ pl se·nos breasts
sensibilidad ⓕ sen·see·bee·lee·da
sensitivity • film speed
sensual sen·swal sensual
sentarse sen·tar·se sit
sentimientos ⓜ pl sen·tee·myen·tos
feelings
sentir sen·teer feel
separado/a ⓜ/ⓕ se·pa·ra·do/a separate
separar se·pa·rar separate
ser ser be

serie ① se·rye *series*
serio/a ⑨/① se·ryo/a *serious*
seropositivo/a ⑨/①
se·ro·po·see·tee·vo/a *HIV positive*
serpiente ① ser·pyen·te *snake*
servicio ⑨ ser·vee·thyo *service charge*
— militar mee·lee·tar *military service*
— telefónico automático
te·le·fo·nee·ko ow·to·ma·tee·ko
direct-dial
servicios ⑨ pl ser·vee·thyos *toilets*
servilleta ① ser·vee·lye·ta *napkin*
sexo ⑨ se·kso *sex*
— seguro se·goo·ro *safe sex*
sexy se·ksee *sexy*
si see *if • yes*
SIDA ⑨ see·da *AIDS*
sidra ① see·dra *cider*
siempre syem·pre *always*
silla ① see·lya *chair*
— de ruedas de rwe·das *wheelchair*
sillín ⑨ see·lyeen *saddle*
similar see·mee·lar *similar*
simpático/a ⑨/① seem·pa·tee·ko/a *nice*
sin seen *without*
— hogar o·gar *homeless*
— plomo plo·mo *unleaded*
sinagoga ① see·na·go·ga *synagogue*
Singapur ⑨ seen·ga·poor *Singapore*
sintético/a ⑨/① seen·te·tee·ko/a
synthetic
soborno ⑨ so·bor·no *bribe*
sobre so·bre *about • on top of*
sobre ⑨ so·bre *envelope*
sobredosis ① so·bre·do·sees *overdose*
sobrevivir so·bre·vee·veer *survive*
socialista ⑨&① so·thya·lees·ta *socialist*
sol ⑨ sol *sun*
soldado ⑨ sol·da·do *soldier*
sólo so·lo *only*
solo/a ⑨/① so·lo/a *alone*
soltero/a ⑨/① sol·te·ro/a *single*
sombra ① som·bra *shadow*
sombrero ⑨ som·bre·ro *hat*
soñar so·nyar *dream*
sondeos ⑨ pl son·de·os *polls*

sonreír son·re·eer *smile*
sopa ① so·pa *soup*
sordo/a ⑨/① sor·do/a *deaf*
sorpresa ① sor·pre·sa *surprise*
su soo *her • his • their*
subir soo·beer *climb*
submarinismo ⑨ soob·ma·ree·nees·mo
diving
subtítulos ⑨ pl soob·tee·too·los *subtitles*
sucio/a ⑨/① soo·thyo/a *dirty*
sucursal ① soo·koor·sal *branch office*
sudar soo·dar *perspire*
suegra ① swe·gra *mother-in-law*
suegro ⑨ swe·gro *father-in-law*
sueldo ⑨ swel·do *wage*
suelo ⑨ swe·lo *floor*
suerte ① swer·te *luck*
suficiente soo·fee·thyen·te *enough*
sufrir soo·freer *suffer*
sujetador ⑨ soo·khe·ta·dor *bra*
supermercado ⑨ soo·per·mer·ka·do
supermarket
superstición ① soo·pers·tee·thyon
superstition
sur ⑨ soor *south*
surf ⑨ sobre la nieve soorf so·bre la
nye·ve *snowboarding*

T

tabaco ⑨ ta·ba·ko *tobacco*
tabla ① de surf ta·bla de soorf *surfboard*
tablero ⑨ de ajedrez ta·ble·ro de
a·khe·dreth *chess board*
tacaño/a ⑨/① ta·ka·nyo/a *stingy*
talco ⑨ tal·ko *baby powder*
talla ① ta·lya *size (clothes)*
taller ⑨ ta·lyer *workshop*
también tam·byen *also*
tampoco tam·po·ko *neither*
tampones ⑨ pl tam·po·nes *tampons*
tanga ① tan·ga *g-string*
tapones ⑨ pl para los oídos ta·po·nes
pa·ra los o·ee·dos *earplugs*
taquilla ① ta·kee·lya *ticket office*
tarde tar·de *late*

tarjeta tar·khe·ta *card*
— **de crédito** de kre·dee·to *credit card*
— **de embarque** de em·bar·ke *boarding pass*
— **de teléfono** de te·le·fo·no *phone card*

tarta ① *nupcial* tar·ta noop·thyal *wedding cake*

tasa ① **del aeropuerto** ta·sa del ay·ro·pwer·to *airport tax*

taxi ⑩ ta·ksee *taxi*

taza ① ta·tha *cup*

té ⑩ te *tea*

teatro ⑩ te·a·tro *theatre*

teclado ⑩ te·kla·do *keyboard*

técnica ① tek·nee·ka *technique*

tela ① te·la *fabric*

tele ① te·le *TV*

teleférico ⑩ te·le·fe·ree·ko *cable car*

teléfono ⑩ te·le·fo·no *telephone*
— **móvil** mo·veel *mobile phone*
— **público** poo·blee·ko *public telephone*

telegrama ⑩ te·le·gra·ma *telegram*

telenovela ① te·le·no·ve·la *soap opera*

telescopio ⑩ te·les·ko·pyo *telescope*

televisión ① te·le·vee·syon *television*

temperatura ① tem·pe·ra·too·ra *temperature (weather)*

templado/a ⑩/① tem·pla·do/a *warm*

templo ⑩ tem·plo *temple*

temporada ① tem·po·ra·da *season (in sport)*

temprano tem·pra·no *early*

tenedor ⑩ te·ne·dor *fork*

tener te·ner *have*
— **hambre** am·bre *to be hungry*
— **prisa** pree·sa *to be in a hurry*
— **sed** seth *to be thirsty*
— **sueño** swe·nyo *to be sleepy*

tenis ⑩ te·nees *tennis*

tensión ① *premenstrual* ten·syon pre·mens·trwal *premenstrual tension*

tentempié ⑩ ten·tem·pye *snack*

tercio ⑩ ter·thyo *third*

terminar ter·mee·nar *finish*

ternera ① ter·ne·ra *veal*

ternero ⑩ ter·ne·ro *calf*

terremoto ⑩ te·re·mo·to *earthquake*

testarudo/a ⑩/① tes·ta·roo·do/a *stubborn*

tía ① tee·a *aunt*

tiempo ⑩ tyem·po *time • weather*
— **a** — a tyem·po *on time*
— **a** — **completo/parcial** a tyem·po kom·ple·to/par·thyal *full-time/part-time*

tienda ① **(de campaña)** tyen·da (de kam·pa·nya) *tent*

tienda ① tyen·da *shop*
— **de comestibles** de ko·mes·tee·bles *grocery*
— **de fotografía** de fo·to·gra·fee·a *camera shop*
— **de eléctrodomésticos** de e·lek·tro·do·mes·tee·kos *electrical store*
— **de provisiones de cámping** de pro·vee·syo·nes de kam·peen *camping store*
— **de recuerdos** de re·kwer·dos *souvenir shop*
— **de ropa** de ro·pa *clothing store*
— **deportiva** de·por·tee·va *sports store*

Tierra ① tye·ra *Earth*

tierra ① tye·ra *land*

tiesto ⑩ tyes·to *pot (plant)*

tijeras ① pl tee·khe·ras *scissors*

tímido/a ⑩/① tee·mee·do/a *shy*

típico/a ⑩/① tee·pee·ko/a *typical*

tipo ⑩ tee·po *type*
— **de cambio** de kam·byo *exchange rate*

tirar tee·rar *pull*

tiritas ① pl tee·ree·tas *band-aids*

título ⑩ tee·too·lo *degree*

toalla ① to·a·lya *towel*

toallita ① to·a·lyee·ta *face cloth*

tobillo ⑩ to·bee·lyo *ankle*

tocar to·kar *touch*
— **la guitarra** la gee·ta·ra *play (guitar)*

tocino ⓜ to·*thee*·no *bacon*
todavía (no) to·da·*vee*·a (no) *(not) yet*
todo *to·*do *all • everything*
tofú ⓜ to·*foo tofu*
tomar to·*mar take • drink (something)*
tomate ⓜ to·*ma*·te *tomato*
— **secado al sol** se·*ka*·do al sol *sun-dried tomato*
tono ⓜ *to*·no *tone*
torcedura ⓕ tor·the·*doo*·ra *sprain*
tormenta ⓕ tor·*men*·ta *storm*
toro ⓜ *to*·ro *bull*
torre ⓕ *to*·re *tower*
tos ⓕ tos *cough*
tostada ⓕ tos·*ta*·da *toast*
tostadora ⓕ tos·ta·*do*·ra *toaster*
trabajar tra·ba·*khar work*
trabajo ⓜ tra·*ba*·kho *job • work*
— **administrativo**
ad·mee·nees·tra·*tee*·vo *paperwork*
— **de camarero/a** ⓜ/ⓕ de
ka·ma·*re*·ro/a *bar work*
— **de casa** de *ka*·sa *housework*
— **de limpieza** de leem·*pye*·tha
cleaning
— **eventual** e·ven·*twal casual work*
traducir tra·doo·*theer translate*
traer tra·*er bring*
traficante ⓜ&ⓕ **de drogas**
tra·fee·*kan*·te de *dro*·gas *drug dealer*
tráfico ⓜ *tra*·fee·ko *traffic*
tramposo/a ⓜ/ⓕ tram·*po*·so/a *cheat*
tranquilo/a ⓜ/ⓕ tran·*kee*·lo/a *quiet*
tranvía ⓜ tran·*vee*·a *tram*
a través a tra·*ves across*
tren ⓜ tren *train*
— **de cercanías** de ther·ka·*nee*·as
local train
trepar tre·*par scale • climb*
tres en raya tres en *ra*·ya *noughts & crosses*
triste *trees*·te *sad*
tú too *you (informal)*
tu too *your*
tubo ⓜ **de escape** *too*·bo de es·*ka*·pe
exhaust

tumba ⓕ *toom*·ba *grave*
tumbarse toom·*bar*·se *lie (not stand)*
turista ⓜ&ⓕ too·*rees*·ta *tourist*
— **operador(a)** ⓜ/ⓕ o·pe·ra·*dor*/
o·pe·ra·*do*·ra *tourist operator*

U

uniforme ⓜ oo·nee·*for*·me *uniform*
universidad ⓕ oo·nee·ver·see·*da*
university
universo ⓜ oo·nee·*ver*·so *universe*
urgente oor·*khen*·te *urgent*
usted oos·*te you (pol)*
útil *oo*·teel *useful*
uvas ⓕ pl *oo*·vas *grapes*
— **pasas** *pa*·sas *raisins*

V

vaca ⓕ *va*·ka *cow*
vacaciones ⓕ pl va·ka·*thyo*·nes *holidays • vacation*
vacante va·*kan*·te *vacant*
vacío/a ⓜ/ⓕ va·*thee*·o/a *empty*
vacuna ⓕ va·*koo*·na *vaccination*
vagina ⓕ va·*khee*·na *vagina*
vagón ⓜ **restaurante** va·*gon*
res·tow·*ran*·te *dining car*
validar va·lee·*dar validate*
valiente va·*lyen*·te *brave*
valioso/a ⓜ/ⓕ va·*lyo*·so/a *valuable*
valle ⓜ *va*·lye *valley*
valor ⓜ va·*lor value*
vaqueros ⓜ pl va·*ke*·ros *jeans*
varios/as ⓜ/ⓕ pl *va*·ryos/as *several*
vaso ⓜ *va*·so *(drinking) glass*
vegetariano/a ⓜ/ⓕ ve·khe·ta·*rya*·no/a
vegetarian
vela ⓕ *ve*·la *candle*
velocidad ⓕ ve·lo·thee·*da speed*
velocímetro ⓜ ve·lo·*thee*·me·tro
speedometer
velódromo ⓜ ve·*lo*·dro·mo *racetrack (bicycles)*
vena ⓕ *ve*·na *vein*

vendaje ⓜ ven·*da*·khe *bandage*
vendedor(a) ⓜ/ⓕ **de flores**
 ven·de·*dor*/ven·de·*do*·ra de *flo*·res
 florist
vender ven·*der* *sell*
venenoso/a ⓜ/ⓕ ve·ne·*no*·so/a
 poisonous
venir ve·*neer* *come*
ventana ⓕ ven·*ta*·na *window*
ventilador ⓜ ven·tee·la·*dor* *fan (machine)*
ver ver *see*
verano ⓜ ve·*ra*·no *summer*
verde ver·de *green*
verdulería ⓕ ver·doo·le·*ree*·a
 greengrocery (shop)
verdulero/a ⓜ/ⓕ ver·doo·*le*·ro/a
 grocer (shopkeeper)
verduras ⓕ pl ver·*doo*·ras *vegetables*
vestíbulo ⓜ ves·*tee*·boo·lo *foyer*
vestido ⓜ ves·*tee*·do *dress*
vestuario ⓜ ves·*twa*·ryo *wardrobe*
vestuarios ⓜ pl ves·*twa*·ryos
 changing room
vez ⓕ veth *once*
viajar vya·*khar* *travel*
viaje ⓜ *vya*·khe *trip*
vid ⓕ veed *vine*
vida ⓕ *vee*·da *life*
vidrio ⓜ *vee*·dryo *glass*
viejo/a ⓜ/ⓕ *vye*·kho/a *old*
viento ⓜ *vyen*·to *wind*
vinagre ⓜ vee·*na*·gre *vinegar*
viñedo ⓜ vee·*nye*·do *vineyard*
vino ⓜ *vee*·no *wine*
violar vyo·*lar* *rape*

virus ⓜ *vee*·roos *virus*
visado ⓜ vee·*sa*·do *visa*
visitar vee·see·*tar* *visit*
vista ⓕ *vees*·ta *view*
vitaminas ⓕ pl vee·ta·*mee*·nas
 vitamins
víveres ⓜ pl *vee*·ve·res *food supplies*
vivir vee·*veer* *live (life)*
vodka ⓕ *vod*·ka *vodka*
volar vo·*lar* *fly*
volumen ⓜ vo·*loo*·men *volume*
volver vol·*ver* *return*
votar vo·*tar* *vote*
voz ⓕ voth *voice*
vuelo ⓜ **doméstico** *vwe*·lo
 do·mes·*tee*·ko *domestic flight*

y ee *and*
ya ya *already*
yip ⓜ yeep *jeep*
yo yo *I*
yoga ⓜ *yo*·ga *yoga*
yogur ⓜ yo·*goor* *yogurt*

zanahoria ⓕ tha·na·o·rya *carrot*
zapatería ⓕ tha·pa·te·*ree*·a *shoe shop*
zapatos ⓜ pl tha·*pa*·tos *shoes*
zodíaco ⓜ tho·*dee*·a·ko *zodiac*
zoológico ⓜ zo·o·*lo*·khee·ko *zoo*
zumo ⓜ *thoo*·mo *juice*
 — de naranja de na·*ran*·kha
 orange juice